SEVEN STEPS TOWARD DETERMINING
WHETHER BECOMING A STEPPARENT IS
IN THE BEST INTEREST OF THE *STEPPARENT*

DO YOU *REALLY* WANT TO BE A STEPPARENT?

ARLINE S. KERMAN, J.D., Ph.D. (Psychology)

SugarPress, Ltd., Publishers
Atlanta

DO YOU *REALLY* WANT TO BE A STEPPARENT?

By: ARLINE S. KERMAN, J.D., Ph.D. (Psychology)

Published by:
    SugarPress, Ltd., Publishers
    Post Office Box 502649
    Atlanta, Georgia 31150-2649

All rights in this book are reserved. No part of this book may be reproduced or transmitted in any form or by any means, electronic or mechanical, including photocopying, recording, or by any information storage and retrieval system without written permission from the author, except for the inclusion of brief quotations in a review.

Copyright © 2001, by Arline S. Kerman, J.D., Ph.D.
First Printing 2001

ISBN 0-9679306-1-8

Library of Congress Control Number: 2001 126661

Printed in the United States of America

SugarPress, Ltd., Publishers
Atlanta

ABOUT THE AUTHOR

Following the acquiring of her law degree and doctorate in psychology, Arline S. Kerman established her divorce and custody practice in Georgia in 1976. She has represented many mothers, fathers, children, and grandparents. Since that time, she has tried cases in Florida, Ohio, Texas, New York, and Massachusetts as well as Georgia. She has also completed classes in marriage and family therapy.

She has taught courses in domestic relations and psychology.

She became registered with the State Bar of Georgia as a domestic relations mediator, general mediator, arbitrator, and case evaluator/domestic relations.

Her exposure and experience has made her a sought-after presenter at seminars and on various radio and television programs.

She is a member of various professional organizations, including the American Psychological Association, Georgia Psychological Association, Association for Conflict Resolution, Family Mediation Association of Georgia, Georgia Bar Association, Georgia Bar Foundation, Atlanta Press Club, and the San Diego Psych-Law Society, which she founded over twenty-five years ago.

Her publications have also focused on the issue of child custody. She wrote an article for a feature entitled "Who Should Get The Kids After A Divorce?" that was published in the Atlanta Journal and Constitution on April 29, 1978. In 1989, she wrote an article entitled "Georgia Needs A Family Court Now." that was published in the Verdict, the Georgia Trial Lawyers Association publication. In 2000, she wrote and published her book entitled *Should You Really Seek Custody Of Your Child?*

HOW TO CONTACT THE AUTHOR

Dr. Arline S. Kerman is available for professional consultations to parents, stepparents, people who are considering becoming stepparents, and professionals, including attorneys, psychologists, psychiatrists, and counselors. The professionals may bring their clients with them for the consultations.

The workshops for parents, stepparents, people who are considering becoming stepparents, and professionals are scheduled throughout the year.

Requests for detailed information concerning speaking engagements, workshops, and professional consultations will be received by her at the address shown below. Readers of this book are invited to submit comments and suggestions for inclusion in future editions.

SugarPress, Ltd., Publishers
Post Office Box 502649
Atlanta, Georgia 31150-2649

ACKNOWLEDGMENT

I would like to acknowledge the many people, including parents, stepparents, stepchildren, mediators, judges, attorneys, psychiatrists, psychologists, and friends who offered their input and advice on this subject.

Additionally, I want to express my special thanks to those who assisted me, including Carol Haas, Esq., Janet Dennison, Betty Climer, Stuart Myers, Esq., William K. Travis, Esq., David Lipscomb, Esq., and Sarah Mallas Wayman, Esq. These very special friends and professionals not only offered their encouragement, but contributed their valuable talents and ideas to this project.

Finally, I wish to recognize my son, Mark, whose constructive criticisms improved the book, my brother, Eugene Sugar, who made some very valuable suggestions, and my toy poodle and constant companion, Sugar, who gave up so much of her play time so that I could finish this book.

Arline S. Kerman, J.D., Ph.D.
Atlanta, Georgia

WARNING-DISCLAIMER

This book is designed to provide information regarding the subject matter covered. It is sold with the express understanding that the publisher and the author are not engaged in rendering legal or other professional services. Readers are specifically advised to seek the advice and representation of attorneys licensed in their state.

It is not the purpose of this book to reprint all of the statutory laws, case laws, and other information that is otherwise available to the author and/or publisher, but to supplement the information that is received from other sources, including legal counsel.

Every effort has been made to make this book as accurate and complete as possible. However, readers should be aware that there may be errors both typographical and in content. Therefore, readers are advised that they should use this book only as a general guide and not as the ultimate source of the law and information that is printed in the book. Moreover, this book contains the statutory law, case law, and other information only up to the date of the printing.

The object of this book is to assist readers who want to make intelligent and informed decisions about whether or not they really want to be stepparents. Readers should not use this book alone in making those decisions, but should consult with their attorneys and other professionals before arriving at their final decisions.

The author and publisher specifically disclaim any responsibility for any liability, loss, or risk, personal or otherwise, which is incurred as a consequence, directly or indirectly, of the use and application of any of the contents of this book.

If you do not agree to be bound by the above provisions, please return this book to the publisher for a refund within five days from the date of the purchase and include the original receipt indicating the date of the purchase.

TABLE OF CONTENTS

CHAPTER ONE
IN THE BEST INTEREST OF THE STEPPARENT 1

Why You Should First Consider Whether You Really
Want To Be A Stepparent 1

Why This Book Is Necessary 6

Why It Is Important That Your Significant Other Be
Involved In His Or Her Child's Life After The Divorce,
Especially When The Child Is Under The Age Of Six 12

Opinions Of Experts 14

How Do You Feel About These Issues? 17

Questions 18

Summary 19

Citations 20

CHAPTER TWO
**THE FIRST STEP TOWARD DETERMINING
WHETHER YOU REALLY WANT TO BE
A STEPPARENT** 21

Ascertaining How You Really Feel 21

What The Stepparent Should Expect 23

    Your Relationship With Your Significant Other
    May Be Strained 23

    Your Personal Life May Be Exposed 26

    There May Be Personal Attacks From All Sides 29

Contents

You May Feel Like An Outsider	31
Your Financial Resources May Be Depleted	32
Your Employment Or Activities May Be Disrupted	33
Your Housekeeping Duties May Be Increased	34
Your Furniture May Be Damaged	34
Your Relationship With Your Stepchild May Be Difficult	35
You May Have To Perform Child Care Duties	37
Your Relationship With Your Child And Your Stepchild Will Be Monitored And Compared	39
You Have To Know How To Discipline Your Stepchild	40
Your Stepchild May Not Want A Relationship With Your Parents	42
What The Stepparent Should Not Expect	43
The Stepparent Has Rights	44
Reviewing The Stepparent Issue	45
Questions	46
Summary	50

CHAPTER THREE
THE SECOND STEP TOWARD DETERMINING WHETHER YOU REALLY WANT TO BE A STEPPARENT — 51

Why You Should Examine Your Motives For Wanting And Not Wanting To Be A Stepparent — 51

Defining The Term Motivation — 52

Why Some People Want To Be Stepparents — 54

- People Who Fear That Their Lives Will Be Empty — 54
- People Who Want To Fit In — 55
- People Who Are In Love With A Person Who Has A Child — 56
- People Who Are Parents And Believe That It Is Easy To Have A Blended Family — 57
- People Who Never Consider What They Are Getting Themselves Into — 57
- People Who Think That They Will Live Like The "Brady Bunch" — 58
- People Who Believe That Their Significant Other Will Never Seek Custody Of His Or Her Child — 58
- People Who Want To Show Their Significant Other That They Can Be Better Parents Than Their Stepchild's Other Parent — 59
- People Who Need To Rescue Their Significant Other — 60

Why Some People Do Not Want To Be Stepparents	61
People Who Know That Some Marriages Fail When Their Stepchild Lives Full-Time In The Home	61
People Who Do Not Want To Financially Support Their Stepchild	62
People Who Do Not Want To Have Their Lives Interfered With	63
People Who Are Afraid To Discipline Their Stepchild	65
People Who Fear That They Will Be Accused Of Child Abuse	66
People Who Do Not Want To Be In Line Behind Their Stepchild	66
Examining Your Motives For Wanting To Be A Stepparent And Not Wanting To Be A Stepparent	67
Questions	68
Summary	77
Citations	78

CHAPTER FOUR
THE THIRD STEP TOWARD DETERMINING
WHETHER YOU REALLY WANT TO BE
A STEPPARENT   79

The Kerman Stepparent Questionnaire   79

    Issue One: Your Stepchild's Development As An
    Individual   83

    Issue Two: Your Stepchild's Need For A Stable
    Home   85

    Issue Three: Cooperation With Both Parents   87

    Issue Four: Creating A Positive Relationship
    Between Your Stepchild And Extended Family
    Members   89

    Issue Five: The Need To Refrain From Maligning
    Your Stepchild's Other Parent   91

    Issue Six: Dealing With Your Stepchild's Other
    Parent On An Equal Basis   93

    Issue Seven: Your Stepchild's Need For A Daily
    Caretaker   95

    Issue Eight: Viewing Your Life As Separate From
    Your Stepchild's   97

    Issue Nine: The Need For Organization   99

    Issue Ten: Maintaining Good Physical And Mental
    Health   101

Summary   103

CHAPTER FIVE
THE FOURTH STEP TOWARD DETERMINING
WHETHER YOU REALLY WANT TO BE
A STEPPARENT   107

The Stepparent Data Record   107

    The Stepparent's Information   108

        General Data   108

        Educational Data   108

        Occupational Data   109

        Military Data   109

        Arrest And Citation Record Data   110

        Tobacco, Alcohol, And Drug Use Data   111

        Prescription Medication Use Data   112

        Physical Health Data   112

        Mental Health Data   113

        Parenting Skills Data   113

        Relationship With Parents, Siblings,
        Extended Family Members, And In-Laws
        Data   114

        Marriage Data   115

        Custodial Arrangement Data   115

The Stepchild's Information	116
General Data	116
Educational Data	117
Occupational Data	117
Arrest And Citation Record Data	117
Physical Health Data	118
Mental Health Data	118
Extracurricular Activities Data	119
Where The Stepchild Wants To Live	120
The Stepparent Data Record Instructions	121
The Stepparent Data Record	122
The Stepparent's Information	122
The Stepchild's Information	129
Summary	139

CHAPTER SIX
THE FIFTH STEP TOWARD DETERMINING WHETHER YOU REALLY WANT TO BE A STEPPARENT — 141

Reviewing Some Georgia Cases And Statutes Relating To Custody Issues — 141

Before The Trial Issues — 147

    State's Policy Regarding Child Custody — 147

    The Parents May Enter Into Custody Agreements — 149

    Mediation Is Best For Resolving Custody Disputes — 150

    The Child Who Is Age 14 May Make An Election — 152

    The Child Who Is Age 11 May Tell The Judge Where The Child Wants To Live — 154

    The Child Who Is Age 14 May Affect The Custody Of The Younger Sibling — 157

During The Trial Issues — 159

    The Judge Decides The Custody Issue Unless The Parents Decide — 159

    The Judge May Order An Evaluation And Investigation — 160

    The Judge May Appoint A Guardian Ad Litem — 162

    Factors The Judge May Consider Before Awarding Custody — 164

    The Child Shall Be Available For Consultation — 167

The Judge May Award Temporary Custody	168
The Judge May Change Temporary Custody	169
The Judge Must Consider Awarding Joint Custody If Both Parents Are Fit And Proper	170
Various Types Of Custody That May Be Awarded	171
In Joint Legal Custody, One Parent Is Usually Designated To Make The Final Decision	175
The Judge May Order Joint Legal Custody Without Ordering Joint Physical Custody	176
Custody May Be Awarded To A Third Party	176
Modification Of Custody	177
The Parent Who Has Been Awarded Custody Is Favored	177
Power And Duty Of The Court In Modification Cases	177
What The Court Must Find In Order To Change Custody	178
No Legal Definition Of "Changed Condition"	180
New Evidence After The Filing Of The Petition Is Admissible	180
Examples Of Evidence That Will Not Warrant Changing Custody	181
No New And Material Conditions That Affect The Welfare Of The Child	181

Moving And Remarriage		182
Best Interest And Welfare Alone		182
Examples Of Evidence That Will Warrant Changing Custody		183
New And Material Conditions That Affect The Welfare Of The Child		183
Award Of Custody Of The 14-Year-Old Child		183
Stress Due To Joint Physical Custody		184
Smoking May Be A Relevant Factor		186
Living With A Person Who Is Not A Spouse		187
Repeated Denial Of Visitation Rights		188
Miscellaneous Provisions		191
The Judge May Not Change Custody By Modifying Visitation		191
The Judge May Not Change Custody In A Contempt Proceeding		191
Self-Executing Provision In The Agreement Is Permissible		192
Attorney's Fees Are Not Awarded		192
After The Trial Issues		193
The Custodial Parent Must Notify The Noncustodial Parent Of A Change In The Child's Address		193

Civil And Criminal Remedies For Violating Custodial Rights	194
The Surviving Parent, Not The Stepparent, Has Custody	195
The Grandparent's Custody Rights	196
Reviewing The Custody Options	197
Questions	198
Summary	215
Key To The Citations	217
Citations	218

CHAPTER SEVEN
THE SIXTH STEP TOWARD DETERMINING WHETHER YOU REALLY WANT TO BE A STEPPARENT — 221

Reviewing Some Georgia Cases And Statutes Relating To Visitation Issues	221
Two Basic Principles	225
Before The Trial Issues	225
Visitation Rights Differ From Custodial Rights	225
State's Policy Regarding Visitation Rights	226
During The Trial Issues	227
The Judge Decides Visitation Rights	227

Standard Provisions For Visitation	227
The Divorced Parent's Visitation Rights	230
The Parent's Immoral Conduct Might Warrant Limitations	232
The Parent Who Is Guilty Of Family Violence May Have Visitation With Certain Stipulations	233
The Judge May Order The Noncustodial Parent To Post A Bond	235
The Judge May Not Overburden The Parent Who Moves	236
Visitation Provision In A Settlement Agreement Must Not Be Contrary To Public Policy	237
The Noncustodial Parent Usually Provides The Transportation	238
Modification Of Visitation	**239**
Visitation May Be Modified	239
Test For Modification Of Visitation	239
The Therapist Does Not Have The Authority To Modify Visitation	240
The Child Who Is Age 14 May Cease Visitation With A Court Order	240
The Judge May Not Change Custody By Modifying Visitation	242

The Judge May Modify Visitation Rights In A Contempt Proceeding	242
After The Trial Issues	243
Remedies For Enforcing A Visitation Order	243
The Noncustodial Parent May Not Withhold Child Support As A Method Of Enforcing Visitation Rights	243
The Custodial Parent May Not Unilaterally Decide Visitation Rights	244
The Custodial Parent Who Moved To Another State Was Not In Contempt Of The Court's Order	245
The Custodial Parent May Or May Not Be Found In Contempt For Denying Visitation Rights	245
Instances Where Attorney's Fees May Be Awarded	246
Reviewing The Visitation Issue	247
Questions	248
Summary	251
Key To The Citations And Citations	253

CHAPTER EIGHT
THE SEVENTH STEP TOWARD DETERMINING WHETHER YOU REALLY WANT TO BE A STEPPARENT — 255

Reviewing Some Georgia Cases And Statutes Relating To Child Support Issues — 255

Before The Trial Issues — 261

    Definition Of Some Terms — 261

        Age Of Majority — 261

        Child Support Obligee — 261

        Child Support Obligor — 261

        Child Support Order — 261

        Emancipation — 262

        Modification Of A Child Support Order — 262

    State's Policy Regarding Child Support — 262

    The Parent's Obligation To Support The Child — 262

    Child Support Belongs To The Child — 263

    Controlling Factors To Be Applied — 264

    The Judge Has The Authority To Approve Or Not Approve The Parents' Agreement As To The Amount Of Child Support — 265

During The Trial Issues	269
Child Support Guidelines Statute	269
Guidelines Statute Offers A Computational Reference	276
Initial Percentage Is Based On Number Of Children For Whom The Trier Of Fact Is Determining Support	277
The Parties, Judge, Or Jury May Vary The Amount Of Child Support	278
Calculating The Amount Of Child Support	279
Payment Of Medical Premiums	279
The Obligor's Other Child Support Obligations	280
Gross Income Of The Recipient	280
Joint Legal Custody	281
Social Security Benefits	281
The Judge Or Jury May Not Ignore The Evidence Regarding The Obligor's Gross Income	282
The Obligor May Be Ordered To Obtain Health Insurance	283
The Parent May Be Ordered To Pay Medical And Dental Expenses	284
The Parent May Be Ordered To Obtain Life Insurance	285

Contents

Child Support May Be Increased As The Obligor's Gross Income Increases	286
How Child Support Is Paid	287
The Judge Or Jury May Award The Use Of Property As Part Of Child Support	287
The Obligor's Voluntary Expenditures May Not Be Taken As A Credit Toward Child Support	288
Payment Of Child Support Is Not Contingent On Visitation	289
The Parent's Obligation To Pay The College Expenses	289
The Judge May Not Award The Dependency Exemption	291
Duration Of The Child Support Obligation	292
Death Of The Obligor Terminates The Child Support Obligation	292
Provisions In Child Support Orders	293
Modification Of Child Support	**296**
Child Support May Be Modified Under Certain Circumstances	296
The Petitioner Has The Burden Of Proof	297
Income And Financial Status Of The Defendant Is Admissible	297
Definition Of "Substantial Change"	297

Child Support Guidelines Do Not Constitute Substantial Change	298
Child Support Guidelines Apply To Modification Actions	298
The Judge May Grant A Temporary Modification Of Child Support	299
There Is No Absolute Right To A Modification	299
The Judge May Not Modify Post-Majority Child Support Unless The Parties Authorize The Judge To Do So	300
The Obligee May Never Waive The Right To Seek A Modification	301
The Obligor May Waive The Right To Seek A Modification	301
Modification Agreement Entered Into By The Parties Is Not Enforceable If It Is Not Approved By The Judge	302
The Obligor May File A Modification Action, Even If The Obligor's Gross Income Has Increased	303
Child Support May Not Be Modified Retroactively	304
The Obligor May Seek A Modification Without Complying With The Divorce Decree	304
Financial Contribution Of A New Spouse May Be Considered In A Modification Action	305
Attorney's Fees May Be Awarded	307

The Judge May Not Modify Child Support In A Contempt Proceeding	307
Self-Executing Provision In The Agreement Is Permissible	308
Obtaining Custody Of One Child May Not Reduce Child Support	310
After The Trial Issues	311
Child Support Accrues Interest From The Date The Payment Is Due	311
Child Support Order Is Enforced In Georgia	311
Child Support Order May Be Enforced By Attachment For Contempt And By Writ of Fieri Facias	311
The Child May Enforce The Payment Of Child Support	312
The Obligee Is Regarded As A Creditor	313
A License May Be Suspended For Failure To Pay Child Support	313
The Employed Parent May Be Confined For Not Paying Child Support	314
Reviewing The Child Support Issue	315
Questions	316
Summary	323
Key To The Citations And Citations	327

CHAPTER NINE
ALTERNATIVES TO LITIGATION — 331

Alternative Dispute Resolution (ADR)	331
Definition Of The Term- Alternative Dispute Resolution	335
Definition Of The Term- Neutral	335
Definition Of The Term- Mediation	335
Definition Of The Term- Arbitration	336
Definition Of The Term- Case Evaluation Or Early Neutral Evaluation	336
Definition Of The Term- Summary Jury Trial	337
Definition Of The Term- Mini Trial	337
Definition Of The Term- Confidentiality	337
Definition Of The Term- Immunity	340
Arbitration- The Process And The Benefits	341
Case Evaluation Or Early Neutral Evaluation- The Process And The Benefits	345
Mediation- The Process And The Benefits	349
Reviewing The Domestic Guidelines For Mediation	355
Domestic Guidelines For Mediation	356
Reviewing The Domestic Relations Financial Affidavit	361
Domestic Relations Financial Affidavit	367
Summary	373

CHAPTER TEN
LITIGATION: THE WORST CHOICE — 377

Choosing The Attorney And Planning The First Meeting — 379
- Find The Family Law Attorney — 379
- Determine The Attorney's Expertise, Attitude, And Biases — 379
- Understand The Law Office Procedures — 382
- Avoid Possible Conflicts — 383
- Review The Contract Of Employment — 384
- Meet The Office Staff — 385
- Provide The Attorney With Relevant Documents — 387

Some Of The Legal Issues — 391
- Approximate Cost Of The Litigation — 391
- Alternatives To Litigation — 392
- Types Of Custody That May Be Awarded — 393
- Chances Of Being Awarded Permanent Custody — 396
- The Custodial Parent's Rights And Obligations — 397
- Legal Consequences For Failing To Comply With A Court Order — 399
- The 14-Year-Old Child's Right To Make An Election — 399
- Modification Of Custody — 400

Visitation Arrangement In The Event The Custodial Parent Moves	400
Importance Of A Definite Visitation Schedule	400
The Noncustodial Parent's Visitation Rights	401
Modification Of Visitation Rights	402
Amount Of Child Support That May Be Awarded	402
Duration Of The Child Support Obligation	403
The Parent's Obligation To Provide Insurance	403
The Parent's Obligation To Pay The College Expenses	404
The Judge's Power To Award The Tax Exemption	404
Tax Consequences Of Paying And Receiving Child Support	405
Documents That May Be Required At A Deposition, Mediation Session, And In Court	405
Specific Laws That Relate To The Issues In The Case	408
Specific Problems In The Case	409
Some Of The Legal Procedures	409
Discovery Process	413
Importance Of The Psychological Evaluation	416
The Witnesses	420
The Guardian Ad Litem	424

xxii Contents

Courtroom Proceedings	425
A Visit To An Actual Trial	425
Transferring The Case To The Juvenile Court	425
Pretrial Conference And Pretrial Order	426
Temporary Hearing	427
Final Trial	429
Courtroom Procedures	429
Courtroom Tips For Litigants And Other Witnesses	433
Summary	435

CHAPTER ELEVEN
LIVING WITH YOUR FINAL DECISION — 437

The Bill Of Rights For Stepparents	441
Summary	443
Golden Rules	444
GLOSSARY	445
INDEX	467

CHAPTER ONE

IN THE BEST INTEREST OF THE STEPPARENT

Why You Should First Consider Whether You Really Want To Be A Stepparent

This book is for the person who wants to make an informed and intelligent decision about whether or not he or she really wants to be a stepparent. If you are such a person, this book may help you make a decision that is right for you.

Obviously, you are reading this book because your significant other already has custody of his or her child, or your significant other is a party in a divorce and custody action in which he or she is seeking custody, or he or she is a party in a modification of custody action in which he or she is seeking custody. Even if these situations do not exist now, you need to be aware that at some future date your significant other may be required to assume custody of his or her child because of certain circumstances that may arise. For example, the custodial parent may die, or may become unable to care for the child, or may decide that the child is too much of a handful, or the child may elect to live with your significant other. Therefore, if it becomes necessary, you should be prepared to accept your significant other's child in your home, regardless of how you feel.

2   DO YOU REALLY WANT TO BE A STEPPARENT?

If you do not want to have your stepchild live full-time in your home, you may be tempted to make your significant other choose between his or her child and you. This is not a good idea because you will usually lose. Your significant other may be subjected to many pressures from society and relatives, or he or she may have feelings of guilt that may compel him or her to seek custody of his or her child. Therefore, the real issue is whether or not you are prepared and willing to be responsible for the welfare of a child who is not your biological child. If you cannot do so, do not agree to become a stepparent. Even if the possibility of having your stepchild live with you is remote, it can and does happen.

Be honest enough with yourself to state how you truly feel. This is really in everyone's best interest, including your significant other, your stepchild, and your child, if you have a child. As an experienced divorce and custody attorney and mediator, with a Ph.D. in psychology, I understand many of the complexities involved in this issue. All of my professional experience has convinced me that a person should make an informed decision about whether or not he or she really wants to be a stepparent. Otherwise, everyone suffers the consequences.

As you begin your analysis, you will want to consider the many pros and cons of becoming a stepparent. I know that you may be tempted to become a stepparent because you believe that it is the right thing to do for your significant other and your stepchild. But is it right for you?

To begin on a positive note, you may discover that becoming a stepparent compliments your lifestyle and fulfills your needs. Or, you may be the parent of a child who would like to have a brother or a sister. Or, you may have always wanted a child, and having a stepchild fills the void that exists in your life.

On the other hand, you may discover that becoming a stepparent adversely affects your way of life. Or, you may have a difficult time dealing with your stepchild's other parent. Or, your own child may voice serious objections to your new stepparent role.

Thus, it is very important that you fully consider the consequences of becoming a stepparent.

Moreover, have you considered how you will be viewed by your significant other, your stepchild, your stepchild's other parent, and your child when you assume the role of a stepparent? All of these people have their own perceptions of who and what you are, and what your role should be in the life of your stepchild.

Let us briefly review how you might be viewed by these people.

To your stepchild and his or her other parent, you may be viewed as an unwelcome outsider who is not part of the family, or an intruder who only causes problems, or the wicked stepparent, or the person who has caused the breakup of the happy marriage, or the person who is preventing the parents from reuniting, or a person who is not fit to raise a child, or the person who interferes with the time that your significant other has to spend with his or her child, or the person who will deplete the financial resources that should be used for your stepchild.

To your significant other, you may be regarded as his or her accomplice, ally, and source of strength while he or she is involved in a custody battle, or the person who will be the primary caretaker and babysitter of his or her child.

To your own child, you may be viewed as a parent who is not going to be able to devote all of your time to the needs of your own child.

To me, a stepparent is a saint. He or she is:

A person who gives everything;

A person who asks for nothing in return;

A person who expects nothing in return; and

A person who is satisfied with receiving nothing in return.

But what about you? What do you think should be your role in your stepchild's life?

Hopefully, by examining your thoughts, feelings, and life situation, you may be able to determine whether or not you really want to be a stepparent.

You may decide that your life would be enhanced by having a stepchild live full-time with you. Or, after reading this book, you may decide to say, "WHO NEEDS IT?"

Whatever your decision is, you can at least feel that you are making a decision that is based on examining the facts about you, your lifestyle, your child, your significant other, and your stepchild.

Why This Book Is Necessary

There are many reasons why you should read this book in order to determine whether or not you really want to be a stepparent.

1) Some people think that it is easy to be a full-time stepparent and do not think about the problems that can occur.

These people may have grown up watching the Brady Bunch. In that television show, each stepparent appeared to have a warm, loving, and problem-free relationship with his or her stepchild. Well, that was television, not real life. In real life, there are many problems associated with being a stepparent. If you doubt that this is true, just ask any stepparent.

2) Some people are not prepared to assume the role of a stepparent, but they either do not acknowledge this fact or have never thought about it.

These people do not consider that being a stepparent means a long-term commitment to their stepchild. This commitment includes devoting many hours in the day toward the care and nurturing of their stepchild, sacrificing one's free time in order to accomplish the tasks required, and the willingness to do all of that with no expectation of praise or appreciation.

3) Some people have no objective way of determining whether or not they are stepparent material.

There are no guidelines to answer this important question. Unfortunately, when people are in love, they really don't want to consider the possibility that there may be problems in the future. Like Scarlet, "They'll think about that tomorrow."

4) Some people do not really know their stepchild.

These people do not get to know their stepchild until after they are married to their significant other. By then, it is too late. You can't return your stepchild like you can return wedding gifts.

5) Some people have no experience in raising a child.

These people have never been parents. They do not know what it means to take care of a child who is sick or to deal with a child who is not willing to do what is requested of him or her. However, these experiences are necessary if a stepparent is to survive the ordeal of raising a stepchild.

6) Some people are not prepared to cope with the daily needs of their stepchild.

The stepchild requires daily care and attention. He or she does not want to wait until you are ready to provide this care. He or she demands it NOW. For example, you may be required to transport your stepchild to and from school, activities, and doctors' appointments. While you may regard this transportation service as a favor to your stepchild, your stepchild considers it to be one of your many duties.

7) Some people are not prepared to deal with the constant criticisms that they will hear from their stepchild.

Be prepared to hear, "I don't have to listen to you; you are not my mommy (or daddy)." "My mommy (or daddy) is better and smarter than you are." "You can't cook as well as my mommy can." "You are not as pretty as my mommy." "My daddy is the best." "I don't want to live with you." "I want you to go away."

8) Some people do not consider the cost of raising their stepchild.

These people do not realize that they may have to contribute money toward their stepchild's living expenses because their significant other does not receive a sufficient amount of child support to pay all of their stepchild's expenses. In addition, they may have to pay some of their stepchild's college expenses because their significant other had agreed to be legally obligated to pay all or part of these expenses.

9) Some stepchildren are forced to live with stepparents who are mentally and physically abusive individuals.

Some stepchildren develop behavioral, mental, or physical problems because they are forced to live with stepparents who are mentally and physically abusive toward their stepchildren.

10) Some stepchildren resent living with a person who is a total stranger to them.

You and your significant other may be soul-mates, but you are a total stranger to your stepchild. Your stepchild may have only met you briefly before the wedding ceremony and, then, all of a sudden, you have moved into his or her house and into his or her life. Think about how you would feel if you were the child.

11) Some stepchildren resent sharing their parents with anyone.

These stepchildren feel that you are interfering with their time with their parents. This may breed anger, jealousy, and resentment.

12) Some children of stepparents resent sharing their parents with a stepchild.

This may not be a health situation for either your child or your stepchild.

Needless to say, it is extremely important that you discuss with your significant other all of the pros and cons of becoming a stepparent. And, don't be fooled into thinking that there are no cons to this situation because there are many. Obviously, I could not address all of the cons in this book. However, what you have to decide is whether the pros outweigh the cons.

I will start exploring this complex topic with a story.

The stories cited in this book are based on comments made by actual parents, stepparents, and stepchildren, but I have changed the names of all of the parties and the facts to protect the identity of such persons. Therefore, any resemblance to any person, living or dead, is purely coincidental.

The story of Sherry, Mark, and Barry

Sherry, a young secretary, met Mark, a handsome and charming salesman who traveled extensively for his company. Mark told Sherry that he was married, and that he was currently involved in a nasty divorce and custody battle. Mark was seeking sole custody of his five-year-old son, Barry.

Mark and Sherry began seeing each other almost every day. They were even considering moving in together before his divorce became final. It was not long before Sherry was committed to help Mark get custody of Barry. Even though she had never been a parent, she was sure that she could be a better mother to Barry than his own biological mother. Because she was in love and naive, she did not weigh the pros and cons of becoming a stepparent. Moreover, she did not really know that Barry could be a very demanding and difficult child. What Sherry encountered after Mark won custody, and Sherry and Mark were married, was not what she had expected. There were many problems between Sherry and Mark revolving around who would be primarily liable for Barry's care. Sherry was not emotionally ready to take on the responsibility of a small child or to deal with the day-to-day problems that occur in a young child's life. Sherry was angry and frustrated most of the time. She decided that she was tired of being Barry's principal caretaker as well as the primary person who was responsible for Barry's welfare. Because Mark was traveling most of the week, he was not there to be Barry's day-to-day parent. Moreover, Sherry did not like dealing with Barry's mother. Barry, however, had formed a close bond with Sherry. He relied on her for his daily needs, and he liked her to be there when he came home from school. After a year of arguing over Barry, Sherry divorced Mark. This was devastating to Barry, and he began to exhibit behavioral problems at school. Clearly, Sherry should have thought about whether she really wanted to be a stepparent before she married Mark and entered Barry's life.

12 DO YOU REALLY WANT TO BE A STEPPARENT?

Why It Is Important That Your Significant Other Be Involved In His Or Her Child's Life After The Divorce, Especially When The Child Is Under The Age Of Six

If you decide to marry a person who has a child, please accept the fact that this person should maintain his or her involvement with his or her child after the divorce, especially if the child is under the age of six. There is plenty of research to support the theory that the child under the age of six needs to feel secure and protected in order to develop into a healthy adult. Obviously, it is best for the child to have the love and protection of both parents.

There are some parents, however, who fail to realize that their child depends on both parents for love, nurturing, and security. These parents are often convinced that their child can thrive without the other parent's involvement. This is usually not the case, and the child suffers because of this misconception.

Some parents are actually surprised when their child suddenly exhibits behavioral problems, either at home or in school, after the other parent leaves the marital home and fails to maintain frequent and regular contact with the child.

Some parents mistakenly believe that the child under the

age of six will be able to anticipate and plan for the visitation time with the other parent. These parents explain at great length how they fill in calendars detailing the visitation for the month. These calendars are then put up on the refrigerator for the child to see every day. However, the calendar may be a terrible daily reminder that one parent is no longer living in the home.

Moreover, the child's perception of reality may be totally different from the parents' perceptions of what is real. For example, some very young children have no sense of time, and a day may appear to be a month, and a month seems to be somewhere in the distant future. Even though the parent may give the child made-up calendars to show when he or she will see Mommy or Daddy, the fact remains that what a calendar stands for may not be something that is real or meaningful to the child.

In the next section, you will review the opinions of several experts in the field of child development and child psychology. I have selected these authors because of their prominence, and because what they wrote made sense to me.

Please consider the opinions of these experts as you continue to decide whether or not you really want to be a stepparent.

Opinions Of Experts

Among these early pioneers in the area of child development are Arnold Gesell, M.D., Frances L. Ilg, M.D., and others who published a book entitled *Infant and Child in the Culture of Today*.[1] This book was based on many years of research conducted at the Yale University Clinic of Child Development, where hundreds of infants and children were studied. These researchers concluded that "It is culturally very essential that the whole period from birth to six years should be socially treated as a single area and in consecutive sequence. Even the elementary school teacher might profit by more familiarity with the psychological development of the first five years of life, the most fundamental and formative years in the cycle of the child's growth."

In discussing the growth of personality, Dr. Gesell preferred to think of the child's personality "as a structured end product of the child's developmental past. As such, it bears the imprint of the patterns of the culture in which he was born and reared. The early impression of the family life during the first five years leaves the most fundamental and enduring imprint. Acculturation begins in the home and the influence of the larger social groups is limited by the trends initiated through the family."

Dr. Gesell further emphasized his belief that "The first five years in the cycle of child development are the most fundamental and the most formative for the simple but sufficient reason that they come first. Their influence upon the years that follow is incalculable."

The next expert, Dr. Brian Sutton-Smith, authored a book entitled *Child Psychology*.[2] Dr. Sutton-Smith wrote that "Between the ages of 2 and 4, the toddler's physical and mental skills improve dramatically, and through them he gains an increasing sense of his own autonomy. The years between 2 and 4 are a critical time for the formation of personality characteristics and social behavior."

Gerald H. J. Pearson, M.D., who was the Director of the Philadelphia Psychoanalytic Institute, wrote a book entitled *Emotional Disorders of Children: A Case Book of Child Psychiatry*.[3] Dr. Pearson believed that "Between birth and the age of six or seven years, the child is dependent on the interplay of his feelings of love and hate toward his parents and on his identifications with them for the formation of his ego and superego." He concluded that the child "needs the security and backing of the visible presence of two parents - a father and a mother - in order to solve the problem of his conflicting feelings toward them. If a parent should be absent because of death, marital separation, or other necessary cause, the even developmental progress of the child's emotional life is severely affected."

Arthur Noyes, M.D. and Lawrence Kolb, M.D. wrote a book entitled *Modern Clinical Psychiatry*.[4] These authors believed that "The environment favorable to a wholesome growth of the personality is one in which are to be found the warm human relations of marriage, parenthood and the family. It is generally agreed that the influence of the child's environment is the most important factor in the development of neurotic symptoms or behavior problems. Death of a parent, or more frequently desertion, or divorce, preceded, usually, by a long period of domestic unhappiness, may be important in the production of personality disorders."

How Do You Feel About These Issues?
Instructions

Please answer only those questions that are applicable to you.

You do not have to give written answers to these questions. In fact, you should not write your answers until you have consulted with your attorney, if you choose to employ your own attorney, and the attorney who represents your significant other about whether you should or should not write your answers.

If your significant other is already involved in litigation, or if you anticipate that he or she will be, the opposing party, or his or her attorney, *may* have the right to subpoena your written answers. Of course, you do not want to incriminate yourself, or divulge information that you do not have to disclose. Therefore, please consult with the attorney(s) before you write your answers.

18 DO YOU REALLY WANT TO BE A STEPPARENT?

QUESTIONS

Do you feel that you have the right to consider what is in your best interest rather than what is in the best interest of your stepchild?

Please explain your answer.

Do you believe that you would resent your significant other's involvement in his or her child's life?

Please explain your answer.

How would you truly feel if your stepchild lived full-time with you? Would you be involved in his or her life?

Please explain your answer.

Summary

There are many good reasons for determining whether or not you really want to be a stepparent. Some have been explained in this chapter. Discovering whether or not you really want to be a stepparent is not an easy task. Much thought and a candid analysis of you and your unique situation are needed before deciding such an important issue. If you have any hesitancy at all about your position, please do not agree to become a stepparent until all doubt has been eliminated.

As you have read in the story of Sherry, Mark, and Barry, your decision affects many people, especially your stepchild. While most adults are able to eventually recover from a nasty divorce and custody battle, some children have a more difficult time coping with this situation. From the expert's comments, you can readily see that the child's early environment produces important and long-lasting consequences.

Please remember that you do not need to suffer the additional stress that will inevitably occur when you are not comfortable with how your life is structured. Moreover, it is not fair to your stepchild. He or she does not need the trauma of living with a person who resents being a stepparent.

CITATIONS

1. Gesell, A. and Ilg, F. *Infant and Child in the Culture of Today*. New York: Harper & Row, 1943.

2. Sutton-Smith, B. *Child Psychology*. New Jersey: Prentice-Hall, 1973.

3. Pearson, G. H.J. *Emotional Disorders of Children - A Case Book of Child Psychiatry*. New York: W. W. Norton, 1949.

4. Noyes, A.P. and Kolb, L.C. *Modern Clinical Psychiatry*. Philadelphia: W. B. Saunders, 1958.

CHAPTER TWO

THE FIRST STEP TOWARD DETERMINING WHETHER YOU REALLY WANT TO BE A STEPPARENT

Ascertaining How You Really Feel

Your first step toward determining whether or not you really want to be a stepparent is to ascertain how you really feel about becoming a stepparent. You need to answer this question honestly and selfishly, because if you are not happy being a stepparent, your significant other will not be happy, and certainly not your stepchild.

In order to ascertain how you really feel, you first need to know what your significant other expects you to do for your stepchild when your stepchild lives full-time in your home. Moreover, you need to feel confident that you will be able to discharge these duties and obligations in a competent manner without feeling imposed upon. Please realize that this is not a small favor that you are doing for someone. It is a major undertaking. You are committing yourself to revolve your life around a child who is only related to you by marriage. This commitment includes subordinating your priorities for a child who, more than likely, will not thank you for it. Therefore, this is your chance to tell your significant other that you do or do not want to accept this responsibility. Moreover, your significant other deserves to know how you really feel about becoming a stepparent.

Remember, you have the right to be fully informed of what is expected of you. You also have the right to express feelings that your significant other may not share or like to hear.

Among the things to consider is the age of your stepchild. The age of your stepchild can make a difference in your decision to become a stepparent. A young stepchild may become attached to you, and vice versa. An older stepchild may resent your intrusion into his or her parents' lives and may blame you for the breakup of the marriage between his or her parents.

In this chapter, I will discuss a few of the issues that have arisen in some of the cases that have been reported to me.

After you have reviewed and considered these issues, perhaps you may better understand why I believe that it is essential that you recognize that becoming a stepparent is a serious commitment to your significant other and your stepchild.

What The Stepparent Should Expect

Your Relationship With Your Significant Other May Be Strained

You can expect that there will be more arguments with your significant other when your stepchild comes to live full-time in your home. Even though parents frequently argue about how to raise the child who is born during the course of the marriage, these arguments are usually different when the child is the biological child of only one of the parties.

There may be a need for separate vacations with your significant other. When your stepchild lives with you, your stepchild may dictate where you will go for the family vacation. Moreover, you must be willing to participate in your stepchild's vacation plans, such as rafting, hiking, and similar activities.

You may have to see movies, plays, and other types of entertainment that were created for your stepchild, rather than seeing adult entertainment.

You should expect to go with your significant other and your stepchild to sporting events and other activities and have your stepchild insist upon sitting next to your significant other.

You should expect to be told by your stepchild that he or she wants to talk with your significant other in private, and not in your presence.

You should expect to suffer additional stress as a result of the constant and perhaps unreasonable demands of your stepchild.

You should expect to lose some of your private time with your significant other, especially the time in the bedroom. This may cause problems if there is not a strong marital relationship to begin with.

You should expect that any undesirable activities that take place in your home will likely be reported to your stepchild's other parent. This may include sexual activities as well as arguments that occur between you and your significant other.

You should expect that your stepchild's other parent may call the house frequently in order to speak with your significant other and your stepchild.

You should expect that your stepchild may try to cause trouble between you and your significant other because your stepchild may blame you for the breakup of his or her parents' "happy" marriage.

You should expect that your stepchild may lie about matters concerning you or your activities. This could be your stepchild's way of getting even with you.

The story of Jane, Ed, and Betty

Jane and Ed were recently married. Ed had been married before, and his former wife had been awarded custody of their daughter, Betty. Two years after his marriage to Jane, Ed decided to seek custody of Betty. Unfortunately, Ed never asked Jane if she wanted Betty to live with them. Jane had never been a parent and didn't particularly want to be a stepparent now. After a long custody battle, Ed was awarded custody of Betty.

A few years later, Jane, Ed and Betty went on a vacation. Betty kept playing with the blinds on the window until they broke. Jane saw Betty break the blinds. When Ed asked Betty if she had broken the blinds, Betty denied doing it, and blamed Jane. Jane denied breaking the blinds, but Ed believed Betty. Ed thought that Jane had lied because she did not want Betty to come with them. This was not the first time that Ed had taken Betty's side. Jane felt that she would have to spend the rest of her married life vindicating herself. After this incident, Jane did not believe that Ed trusted her. This caused an irreparable breach of trust between Jane and Ed. Jane was very angry with Betty, and she blamed Betty for breaking up her marriage. Jane and Ed subsequently divorced.

Your Personal Life May Be Exposed

If you are married to your significant other when he or she files a petition to modify custody of his or her child, the judge may order you to undergo a psychological or psychiatric evaluation. There may even be an investigation into your background.

If you have had a history of mental illness or you are being treated for a mental disorder, the judge may be concerned that your psychiatric condition may pose a danger to your stepchild.

If you are presently drinking excessive amounts of alcoholic beverages, or are using any sort of drugs, the judge may be concerned that your stepchild may be adversely affected by your alcohol and/or drug usage.

If your driving record includes major traffic violations, like a DUI, speeding, or reckless driving charge, there may be a question as to whether you should drive when your stepchild is in the car.

If you are in therapy or counseling, there may be a deposition of your therapist or counselor in order to determine if your condition poses any danger to your stepchild's well-being.

You should expect to be deposed by the other attorney, and cross-examined on the witness stand in court.

You should expect to be investigated by the guardian ad litem. In contested custody cases, the judge may appoint a guardian ad litem to represent the best interest of your stepchild.

There may be an investigation by the Department of Family and Children's Services. If you have been previously investigated by the Department of Family and Children's Services, that information may also be included.

You should expect to have the circumstances of your previous marriage(s) revealed, including the causes of the divorce(s), who was awarded temporary and permanent custody of your child, and whether there were any allegations of child abuse or neglect.

You should expect to have your relationship with your child, relatives, friends, and colleagues investigated, examined, and discussed.

You should expect to have your financial situation and work history investigated, examined, and discussed.

The story of Sarah, Paul, and Julie

Paul had been divorced for two years when he met Sarah. Paul's only child, Julie, was in the custody of his former wife.

Prior to meeting Paul, Sarah had been in therapy for severe depression, and had been taking medication. On one occasion, circumstances became too difficult for Sarah, and Sarah doubled her medication. She did not realize that her judgment was impaired when she drove to the store. On the way to the store, she was arrested. She was subsequently convicted for driving under the influence of drugs. She never told Paul about this incident.

Shortly after Paul and Sarah got married, Paul told her that he was going to seek custody of Julie. Sarah was not happy with his decision because she was afraid that if her severe depression and conviction were revealed, Paul might not get custody of Julie. Sarah was also afraid that if Paul did not get custody, he would blame her. During the custody trial, Sarah was called to testify. She had to admit that she had suffered from severe depression, and that she had been convicted for driving under the influence of drugs. After hearing all of the evidence, the judge ruled that Julie's mother should retain custody. Paul blamed Sarah for his failure to gain custody, and he became very resentful toward Sarah. He felt that if she would have been honest with him, he would not have sought custody in the first place. Eventually, he filed for a divorce.

There May Be Personal Attacks From All Sides

You should expect to be reminded by your stepchild that you are not his or her mother or father.

You should expect to be blamed for everything that goes wrong in your stepchild's life.

You should expect to be blamed because your significant other was not awarded custody in the first place.

You should expect to be criticized for the kind of food that is prepared in the home. This means that you may have to prepare a different meal for your stepchild, especially if your stepchild is allergic to certain foods or ingredients.

You should expect to be unfavorably compared to your stepchild's other parent.

You should expect to be told by your stepchild that his or her other parent has to work while you are allowed to stay at home and be supported by your significant other.

You should expect to be blamed by your stepchild's other parent for any changes in your stepchild's physical or mental condition.

You should expect that your stepchild's other parent may feel jealous about your relationship with your stepchild and may decide to do many things to thwart that relationship.

The story of Martha, Barry, and Crissy

Barry obtained custody of Crissy after it was proved in court that Crissy's mother was unfit. Because Barry had married Martha shortly after his divorce, Crissy always felt that Martha was the cause of the divorce.

Crissy had a lot of built-up anger and resentment toward Martha. Crissy constantly blamed Martha for everything that went wrong.

Barry was a traveling salesman, and left Crissy in Martha's care for most of the week. Because of Barry's work schedule, Martha was forced to raise Crissy without any help from Barry.

When Martha tried to discipline Crissy, Crissy would tell Martha that she was not her mother.

Crissy was continuously calling her mother to complain about Martha. Crissy's mother loved to tell Crissy that Martha was just no good.

Eventually, Martha told Barry that she was tired of being verbally abused by Crissy and her mother. Martha told Barry that he would have to relinquish custody, or she would file for a divorce.

You May Feel Like An Outsider

You should expect to be regarded as an outsider because your stepchild, his or her other parent, and your significant other were a family before you came on board.

You should expect to be excluded from certain family functions that are limited to your stepchild, his or her other parent, your significant other, and their relatives.

You should expect to have no contact with your stepchild in the event you and your significant other get divorced, regardless of how you feel.

The story of Dot, Morris, and Cynthia

Dot and Morris were married for two years when Dot was awarded custody of Cynthia, a child by a former marriage. Dot had a very close relationship with her former in-laws and was often invited by her former in-laws to family gatherings. Although Morris was included in the invitation, he felt very uncomfortable and out of place. When Morris asked Dot to decrease the number of times that she attended these functions, Dot became angry. She told Morris that it was very important that Cynthia continue to have a good relationship with her father's family. Although Dot limited her visits, she resented not having this time with her in-laws.

Your Financial Resources May Be Depleted

If your significant other is the custodial parent, he or she may receive an amount of child support that is not enough to pay all of your stepchild's living expenses. Therefore, you may have to contribute toward the living expenses of your stepchild.

If your significant other is the noncustodial parent, he or she may have to pay a large percentage of his or her net income as child support. Therefore, you may have to contribute toward the living expenses of your significant other.

The story of Jamie, Elijah, Albert, Ruth, and Rob

Jamie had custody of Albert and Ruth when Jamie married Elijah. Jamie was receiving $800 per month for the support of the two children. Shortly thereafter, Jamie's former husband, Rob, had an accident and was unable to work. Rob filed a modification action to reduce the amount of child support. The court reduced the child support to $200 per month.

In order for the children to continue with their extracurricular activities, Elijah had to pay most of these expenses from his own funds. Although Elijah loved his stepchildren, he resented having his savings account depleted. Moreover, the reduced amount of child support forced Jamie and Elijah to drastically change their lifestyle. Thereafter, Jamie and Elijah had many arguments over money.

Your Employment Or Activities May Be Disrupted

You should expect to be called at work to return home immediately when there is an emergency with your stepchild, or when your stepchild is sick and your significant other is not available.

You should expect to cancel any activity plans in order to stay at home when your stepchild is not in school, and your significant other is not available.

The story of Shannon, Floyd, and Kara

When Shannon married Floyd, Shannon had a daughter, Kara, who lived with Shannon's former husband. Shannon was an executive who traveled most of the time. When Kara was fourteen years old, she elected to live with Shannon. FLoyd was a full-time professor. He agreed to support Shannon in getting custody of Kara. After Shannon was awarded custody, it seemed to Floyd that every time Shannon was out of town, Kara would have a medical emergency. Since it was difficult for Floyd to get a substitute teacher, especially on short notice, he began dreading the time that Shannon was away from home. When Kara had to have allergy shots twice a week, Floyd realized that his schedule did not coincide with Kara's needs. He told Shannon that Kara would have to go back and live with her father, or he would file for a divorce.

Your Housekeeping Duties May Be Increased

You should expect to clean the house and keep it in good order, especially if you are a female.

You should expect to fix all of the meals, including those on holidays and weekends.

You should expect to do your stepchild's laundry.

You should expect to take care of your stepchild's pets, especially when your stepchild is very young.

Your Furniture May Be Damaged

Your house may not be decorated for your stepchild. Very expensive items, which are easily reachable by your stepchild, may be destroyed or damaged.

You should expect that some of your furniture and furnishings may be damaged or soiled as a result of the actions of your stepchild and his or her friends.

Your Relationship With Your Stepchild May Be Difficult

You may be reluctant to criticize your stepchild in private or in the presence of anyone. After all, aren't you constantly reminded that your stepchild is not really your child?

You should not criticize your stepchild's other parent when your stepchild is in your presence.

You should expect to stay neutral when there are disagreements between your stepchild and your significant other.

You are not allowed to usurp the authority or power of your stepchild's other parent. Even though your stepchild's other parent may not have physical custody of your stepchild, that parent has certain rights that must not be interfered with by you. These rights include visitation with your stepchild, and consulting and conferring with your significant other on certain matters relating to your stepchild.

You should expect to hear your stepchild say, "You can not tell me what to do; you are not my mother or father."

You should expect that your stepchild will threaten to live with the other parent if you do not abide by your stepchild's wishes.

You may have a close relationship with your stepchild until your stepchild slams the door in your face. A loving relationship may develop between you and your stepchild. However, your stepchild may feel that this close bond should be with his or her other parent, not you. Because your stepchild may not have a close relationship with his or her other parent, your stepchild may feel guilty about having a close relationship with you.

The story of Bret, Carol, Maggie, and Eric

When Bret and Carol got married, she had custody of her daughter, Maggie. Maggie's father, Eric, was very jealous and resentful of Bret, especially since Bret spent more time with Maggie than Eric did. Although Bret did not like Eric, Bret tried to never say anything negative about Eric. On the other hand, Eric constantly told Maggie that Bret was "a loser."

It was obvious that Bret and Maggie had a very close and loving relationship. Because Maggie loved Bret more than she did her own father, she began to feel guilty about their relationship. Eventually, Maggie distanced herself from Bret, and their relationship deteriorated.

You May Have To Perform Child Care Duties

You have the legal and moral responsibility to raise your stepchild in a proper environment.

You should expect to take your stepchild to his or her medical and dental appointments, including regular psychotherapy sessions.

You should expect to stay at home with your stepchild when your significant other is out of town.

You should expect to act as the referee when your stepchild is fighting with another child.

You should expect to transport your stepchild to and from school, to and from activities, and to and from the other parent's residence. If you have a child living with you, you may have to take your child to one activity and your stepchild to another.

You are expected to encourage your stepchild to love and respect both parents, regardless of how you feel toward the other parent.

You should expect to shop for your stepchild's clothes, even though you will probably be criticized for your selection.

You should expect to shop for groceries, including buying those groceries that only your stepchild wants to eat.

You should expect to be responsible for getting your stepchild up in the morning, on time, fed, and on the school bus.

You should expect to oversee your stepchild's homework, so that it is completed and ready to be turned in the next day.

You should expect to make sure that all permission slips are promptly returned to the school, so that your stepchild is able to go on field trips.

You should expect to take your stepchild to and from the tutor.

You should expect to attend your stepchild's functions at school and outside of school.

You should expect to volunteer for activities that are at your stepchild's school.

You should expect to shop for Mother's Day and Father's Day cards and gifts, even though you will probably not receive anything.

You should expect to be responsible for getting your stepchild ready for visits with the other parent.

Your Relationship With Your Child And Your Stepchild Will Be Monitored And Compared

You are not allowed to impose different rules for your child and your stepchild, such as rules relating to chores and privileges.

You must treat all of the children in the home equally. Therefore, you must not appear to be giving favorite status to your child, even though it is natural for you to feel differently about your child or your child may be a better behaved child.

You can not send your child to a private school without agreeing to send your stepchild to a private school.

You can not discipline your child differently from the way your stepchild is disciplined.

You can not spend more time or money on your child than you spend on your stepchild.

You Have To Know How To Discipline Your Stepchild

The law may provide that you are not allowed to spank your stepchild. Therefore, it is important that you know what you can and can not legally do with regard to disciplining another person's child. Even though your stepchild may be in your home and under your care, you may be criminally liable if you discipline your stepchild in a manner that is prohibited by law.

It is usually better to have your significant other discipline his or her child. However, your significant other should tell your stepchild that he or she is to obey you when your stepchild is in your care. Even so, you should expect to have your stepchild willfully disobey any demands made by you, unless those demands are authorized or seconded by your significant other.

The story of Joe, Linda, and Jeff

Linda had custody of her six-year-old son, Jeff, when she and Joe got married. Jeff was a hyperactive child, always getting into something. Jeff had been told repeatedly by Joe never to touch Joe's expensive stamp collection. Joe would show Jeff the stamps, but Jeff knew that he was not to touch the stamps without Joe's approval.

One day, Joe came home early from work and saw Jeff tearing individual stamps out of Joe's book. Joe was furious, and he gave Jeff a light spanking. This hurt Jeff's feelings more than it did his rear-end. However, Jeff swore to get even with Joe. Linda was angry at Joe when she learned that Joe had spanked Jeff. When Jeff went to school the next day, he told his teacher that his stepfather had beaten him, and that this was not the first time he had been beaten by his stepfather. The teacher told the principal, who then called the Department of Family and Children's Services (DFACS). The investigator from the department spoke with Jeff. The investigator then went to the house to speak with Joe. Joe was shocked that Jeff would say such a thing. Although Joe freely admitted that he had spanked Jeff, Joe denied that he had beaten Jeff. Regardless of Joe's denial, Joe was charged with child abuse.

Joe had to retain an attorney who required the payment of a substantial retainer. Joe had to take off from work in order to meet with his attorney and go to court. Joe almost lost his job.

It took approximately one year for Joe to clear his name. However, by that time, Joe had lost a promotion at work, and he had spent thousands of dollars on attorney's fees.

Even though he loved Linda, he was worried that something like this would happen again. He felt that he had no alternative but to file for a divorce.

Your Stepchild May Not Want A Relationship With Your Parents

You are expected to encourage your stepchild to love and respect his or her grandparents. However, your stepchild may not want to accept your parents as grandparents. Moreover, your parents may treat your stepchild differently from the way they treat your own child.

The story of Alexa, Norris, Peggy, and Rachel

When Alexa and Norris got married, Alexa had custody of her daughter, Rachel, who was then only two years old. Alexa and Norris were married for two years when Alexa learned that she was pregnant. Norris did not have any children, and he was delighted. Norris's parents were even more excited about having a grandchild. When Peggy was born, Norris' parents came to the hospital with many gifts for Peggy. Peggy and Rachel were only a few years apart in age, and they quickly formed a close bond. Both girls had a close relationship with Norris' parents. However, on birthdays and holidays, Norris' parents spent a lot of money on Peggy, but very little on Rachel. In the summer, Norris' parents would only take Peggy to their beach home. After awhile, Alexa told Norris that she did not like the way Rachel was being excluded by his parents, and that she was filing for a divorce.

What The Stepparent Should Not Expect
Any Expression Of Gratitude Or Appreciation

You should expect to perform the duties of a loving and devoted parent, but should not expect to be thanked or appreciated for what you do.

If you are lucky, you will have your stepchild acknowledge that you are performing all of the duties that biological parents should perform without having any of the legal rights that biological parents have.

Remember my moto, "Expect nothing from your stepchild and you will never be disappointed."

Finally, if you even dare to demand any expression of gratitude or appreciation for all of the sacrifices that you make for your stepchild, you should be prepared to hear your stepchild say,

"WHO ASKED YOU?"

THE STEPPARENT HAS RIGHTS

As the spouse of your significant other, you should have an absolute right to have your opinion considered when there are discussions concerning whether or not your significant other should seek primary physical custody of his or her child. The decision to seek primary physical custody directly and indirectly affects you. Your significant other should not casually mention to you that he or she has already filed for custody of his or her child. That is not fair to any of the parties, especially you.

You have the right to tell your significant other that you do not want to have your stepchild live full-time in your home.

You have the right to tell your significant other that if your significant other wants to seek custody, he or she does so without your assistance or participation.

You have the right to tell your significant other that if your significant other seeks custody of his or her child, you will seek a divorce.

Remember, you do have the right to say how you really feel about this issue.

Reviewing The Stepparent Issue
Instructions

Please answer only those questions that are applicable to you.

You do not have to give written answers to these questions. In fact, you should not write your answers until you have consulted with your attorney, if you choose to employ your own attorney, and the attorney who represents your significant other about whether you should or should not write your answers.

If your significant other is already involved in litigation, or if you anticipate that he or she will be, the opposing party, or his or her attorney, *may* have the right to subpoena your written answers. Of course, you do not want to incriminate yourself, or divulge information that you do not have to disclose. Therefore, please consult with the attorney(s) before you write your answers.

QUESTIONS

Do you have any experience in raising young children?
Please explain your answer.

Do you have any experience in raising teenagers?
Please explain your answer.

Do you have any mental or physical disorder that may affect your ability to care for your stepchild?
Please explain your answer.

Do you drink excessive amounts of alcohol or use illegal drugs?

Please explain your answer.

Is there anything in your background that may influence the judge not to award your significant other custody, such as your having been accused of child molestation or child abuse?

Please explain your answer.

How does your stepchild relate to you, and vice versa?

Please explain your answer.

If you have a child living with you, how does your child relate to your stepchild?

Please explain your answer.

Have you discussed with your significant other the pros and cons of his or her seeking custody? If so, what has been the position of your significant other? What has been your position regarding this issue?

Please explain your answer.

Why do you believe that you would make an effective stepparent?

Please explain your answer.

Why do you believe that you would not make an effective stepparent?

Please explain your answer.

Would you be supportive of your significant other's decision to seek custody of his or her child?

Please explain your answer.

What would you do if your significant other told you that he or she wanted to seek custody and you did not want him or her to do so?

Please explain your answer.

SUMMARY

Your first step toward determining whether or not you really want to be a stepparent is to ascertain how you really feel about taking care of a child who is not your biological child.

As you have read in this chapter, the cons outweigh the pros. Therefore, you should make your decision without being blinded by your love for your significant other.

It is important that your significant other consider your wishes and feelings. Your responsibility is awesome and your rewards are few. Regardless of how your significant other feels about seeking custody of his or her child, he or she must understand that you may not have the same emotional investment in his or her child as your significant other has.

Furthermore, it is important that you consider how you will cope with the additional duties and obligations that you will have when you are a stepparent. When you become a stepparent, you are obligated to perform all of the duties of a biological parent, even though you have none of the legal rights that a biological parent has.

CHAPTER THREE

THE SECOND STEP TOWARD DETERMINING WHETHER YOUR REALLY WANT TO BE A STEPPARENT

Why You Should Examine Your Motives For Wanting And Not Wanting To Be A Stepparent

Your second step toward determining whether or not you really want to be a stepparent is to examine your motives for wanting and not wanting to be a stepparent.

Why is it important for you to uncover what is motivating you? I believe the answer is obvious. How can you be sure that you are making a decision that is really in your best interest if you do not know *why* you are making that decision? In my view, discovering what your true motives are is essential.

The following two examples illustrate the point.

Do you want to be a stepparent because you are unable to have a child and you fear that your life is lacking something? However, will a stepchild really take the place of your own child?

Do you not want to be a stepparent because you do not want to compete with your stepchild for your significant other's love? However, isn't the love that your significant other has for his or her child different from the love that your significant other has for you?

Defining The Term Motivation

Let us begin the second step by reviewing two definitions of the term *motivation*. As you can see, these two definitions are somewhat similar.

Black's Law Dictionary defines motive as "a cause or reason that moves the will and induces action. Motive is that which incites or stimulates a person to do an act."[1]

In psychology, where motivation is studied, there are many varied definitions of the term motivation.

C. N. Cofer and M. H. Appley wrote 838 pages on the subject of motivation in a book entitled *Motivation: Theory and Research.*[2]

These authors wrote that "No matter where we begin the study of psychological processes or phenomena, we must sooner or later deal with the problem of motivation. Scientific psychology, as currently defined, studies behavior.

When we ask questions about the 'why' of behavior we are seeking information about processes not directly observable in an individual's overt actions, or even from his verbalizations about his covert actions.

When the hypothetical man on the street asks, 'What motivates behavior?' he is asking to have identified one or a combination of three kinds of things: (1) an environmental determinant which precipitated the behavior in question-the application of some irresistible force which of necessity led to this action; (2) the internal urge, wish, feeling, emotion, drive, instinct, want, desire, demand, purpose, interest, aspiration, plan, need, or motive which gave rise to the action; or (3) the incentive, goal, or object value which attracted or repelled the organism."

Your motives are important factors. However, before you examine your own motives, you might find it interesting to review what motivated other people who found themselves in your position.

WHY SOME PEOPLE WANT TO BE STEPPARENTS
People Who Fear That Their Lives Will Be Empty

Some people fear that their lives will be totally empty and miserable without the love and companionship of a child. These people sometimes have few friends, or may not be employed outside the home. These people want to devote their lives to a child, even a stepchild, in order to make their lives more meaningful.

The story of Verla, Scott, and Hannah

Verla was a forty-year-old, never-before-married, career woman who felt that something was missing in her life. She thought that not having a child was causing her to feel that her life was empty and meaningless.

She met Scott who was divorced and had custody of his two-year-old child, Hannah. Verla, Scott, and Hannah went out many times together. Verla loved Hannah and did a lot of things with Hannah. Hannah was very fond of Verla and came to regard Verla as a mother.

Verla and Scott got married. Because of Hannah, Verla felt that, for the first time, her life was complete. Verla became accustomed to performing the day-to-day chores that had to be done for a young child, and Verla loved every minute of it. At last, she was a mother.

People Who Want To Fit In

Some people believe that they have to be a parent or a stepparent in order to fit in with friends, neighbors, relatives, and colleagues.

It seems that in our society most people have a child. Parents display pictures of their child in the home and in the office. Parents talk about their child at parties. Parents love to compare notes with other parents on how their child is doing in school and in their activities. Therefore, many people who do not have a child feel left out. Many of these people feel that they have an obligation to produce a child, but because of something lacking in them, they have failed.

For many of these people, marrying a person who has a child is the answer. At least, they can say that they have a stepchild.

Even though they know intellectually that the stepchild will go with his or her parent in the event of a divorce, they still will be able to feel that they "fit in" with the rest of the parents.

People Who Are In Love With A Person Who Has A Child

Some people are so much in love with their significant other that nothing else matters. These people do not realize that when you fall in love with someone, you have to accept him or her for who and what he or she is now, which includes the fact that he or she is a parent. Therefore, when you tell someone that you want to marry him or her, you are also agreeing to love his or her child.

The story of Frances, Harold, and Vicki

Frances was an older woman who never had a child. She met Harold at a church social. Frances fell in love with Harold on their very first date. Harold was a successful physician whose wife had died two years before. Harold had one child, Vicki, age seven. Vicki lived with Harold.

Harold, Vicki, and Frances went on many outings together. Frances desperately wanted to marry Harold, and she was smart enough to know that Harold would not marry anyone who did not love and accept Vicki as an important part of the family unit. Even though Frances never really wanted a child, Frances decided that the sacrifice was worth it. She developed a loving relationship with Vicki. Harold and Frances were married. Everyone was happy, including Vicki who was very delighted to have a mother again.

People Who Are Parents And Believe That It Is Easy To Have A Blended Family

Some people believe that it is easy to have a blended family. They have deluded themselves into believing that there will be no problems when their child and the child of their significant other live together.

They do not accept the fact that each child is different. Even biological children are different from each other. Therefore, it may be difficult for some children from different families to blend harmoniously.

People Who Never Consider What They Are Getting Themselves Into

Some people do not consider the consequences of their actions, especially when it comes to marrying a person who has a child. These people are usually blindly optimistic about their future and very seldom consider the cons of any situation. Therefore, unless you lead a charmed life, which most people don't, you may want to take a realistic approach to life rather than an unrealistic one.

People Who Think That They Will Live Like The "Brady Bunch"

Some people who watch too much TV think that they will live like the "Brady Bunch." These people are very naive, and do not have a realistic approach to life. They should know that the television scriptwriters are writing fiction, and that their job is to appeal to an audience who is watching the show in order to escape from a reality that is usually unpleasant. Unfortunately, no home like the "Brady Bunch" home can be achieved without a lot of hard work, a lot of self-sacrifice on everyone's part, and an incredible amount of good luck.

People Who Believe That Their Significant Other Will Never Seek Custody Of His Or Her Child

Some people believe their significant other when he or she promises never to seek custody of his or her child. But, what happens if the other parent dies or your stepchild elects to live with your significant other? Do you really think that it would be fair to bind him or her to a promise not to seek custody? Would you really blame your significant other for circumstances that were beyond his or her control? Would you want to be bound by such a promise? My guess is that your answer would be, "No."

People Who Want To Show Their Significant Other That They Can Be Better Parents Than Their Stepchild's Other Parent

Some people want to show their significant other that they can be better parents than their stepchild's other parent. These people feel that they are in competition with their stepchild's other parent, and that it is necessary to prove themselves superior in every way, including being better parents.

The story of Margo, Harry, Karen, and Paula

Margo was only twenty years old when she first met Harry. Harry was an older man who had been divorced and had custody of his daughter, Paula, who was ten years old. Margo and Harry started dating, and eventually decided to get married. After Margo met Paula's mother, Karen, Margo just knew that she could be a better mother to Paula.

Margo felt very insecure about being a parent. In order to make herself seem superior, she never missed a chance to comment about how inadequate Karen was as a parent. These comments hurt Paula, and she told Margo to stop making statements against her mother.

The tension in the home became so unbearable for both Paula and Harry that Harry announced that he was filing for a divorce. Margo was heartbroken because she honestly did not know what she had done wrong.

People Who Need To Rescue Their Significant Other

Some people feel that their significant other depends totally on them for emotional support. These people feel compelled to rescue their significant other by doing whatever it takes to have their significant other declared the winner in the custody battle. These people do not consider that there may be consequences to themselves. All that matters is that they are the only people who can rescue their significant other from a fate worse than death. The only problem is that, sometimes, the significant other does not want to be rescued, and really does not want custody of his or her child.

The story of Helen and Maury

Helen was an executive when she met Maury who was in the midst of a nasty divorce and custody battle. Maury loved his daughter, but he really did not want physical custody of her. He only wanted joint legal custody and visitation. Almost immediately, Helen took charge of Maury's life, including his divorce and custody case. She demanded to see his attorney so that she could make sure that Maury was receiving the best legal representation. At first, Maury resisted, but then, he just gave up. Helen was determined to rescue Maury by having him awarded sole custody of his daughter, regardless of what Maury wanted.

WHY SOME PEOPLE DO NOT WANT TO BE STEPPARENTS

People Who Know That Some Marriages Fail When Their Stepchild Lives Full-Time In The Home

Some people are aware that some second marriages fail because of the problems created by the stepchild who lives full-time in the home. You have heard of the saying, "Until death do us part." Well, death is not the only cause of a couple parting. In fact, death seems to have very little to do with the break-up of a marriage these days.

Now, many people get divorced because of the constant fighting that exists in the home over whose rights are superior, who should be in control, how money should be spent, and how the children should be raised.

It is important to look into why these people felt the need to dissolve the bonds of marriage. Who or what caused the marriage to deteriorate? For example, when the stepchild comes to live full-time in the home, there are bound to be adjustments and conflicts. That is why some people choose to avoid being a stepparent. They know that there is much to lose, including their marriage, and very little to gain.

People Who Do Not Want To Financially Support Their Stepchild

Some people do not want to financially support a child who is not their biological child. In many cases, custodial parents do not receive a sufficient amount of child support to totally support their child. These custodial parents welcome the additional financial support provided by the stepparent. However, the stepparent may not want to make a voluntary contribution to the health and welfare of another person's child. Therefore, if a person feels that he or she is obligated to provide financial support to their stepchild, even if it is only paying for all of the expenses of the home, that person may feel used. As you already know, no one likes to be used.

Moreover, when the custodial parent is spending money on his or her child, the custodial parent is not contributing that money toward the payment of the household expenses.

People Who Do Not Want To Have Their Lives Interfered With

Some people resent it when a child, who is not their biological child, interferes with their lives. After all, the other parent is the *real* parent, not the stepparent. And yet, the stepparent is expected to behave like a real parent.

There are many examples that illustrate this point.

Some stepparents do not want to have their personal belongings damaged or touched by their stepchild, especially if they are afraid to discipline their stepchild.

Some stepparents do not want to be told that they can not go somewhere or do something because it interferes with the plans of their stepchild, or is not where their stepchild wants to go.

Some stepparents who have not had a good relationship with their stepchild really resent having to deal with their stepchild's children. Unfortunately, these children do not understand why they are not welcome.

Some stepparents feel that they have to watch how they dress in their own home when their stepchild is in the home. They feel uncomfortable if they have on clothes that may be revealing.

Some stepparents do not like to live with a stepchild who creates a lot of resentment and bitterness in the home and in the marriage.

Some stepparents do not like to have meals that are fixed primarily for the enjoyment of their stepchild.

Some stepparents do not like to go to their stepchild's movies, or attend ball games, especially when the games are played on the only free day that the stepparent has and when it is 95 degrees in the shade. This is even made worse when the stepparents and their stepchild have a poor relationship.

Some stepparents resent having to take their stepchild to a place of worship that is different from the stepparents'.

Some stepparents do not like to have their free time taken up with child-rearing duties, such as transporting their stepchild to various activities or doctor's appointments.

Some stepparents who have been an only child may have more of a problem with being a stepparent. These people are accustomed to being #1. Therefore, they may not have the sharing skills that a person who lived with other children might have.

People Who Are Afraid To Discipline Their Stepchild

Some people are afraid to discipline their stepchild. These people are afraid to get into a physical confrontation with their stepchild who may be bigger and stronger than the stepparents are. They have a realistic fear every day that they might be beaten up for attempting to discipline their stepchild.

Some people feel that they are not legally allowed to discipline their stepchild and, therefore, they feel helpless when their stepchild misbehaves. On the other hand, the stepparents may have to endure being mentally and physically abused by their stepchild.

The story of Horatio, Lois, and Dan

Horatio and Lois were married for five years when Dan, who was Lois's child, came to live with them. Before Dan arrived in the home, life was very good. After Dan entered the picture, their happy way of life changed to an unhappy one. Dan was now a teenager. He was disruptive, combative, and unruly. Lois had never known how to discipline Dan, which is why she gave her former husband custody of Dan. Lois turned to Horatio to do the disciplining, but Horatio was afraid of what Dan might do. Horatio felt that he needed to get out of this situation for his own safety, and he got a divorce.

People Who Fear That They Will Be Accused Of Child Abuse

Some people are afraid that they will be falsely accused of physically, mentally, or sexually abusing their stepchild. This is a realistic fear as many innocent stepparents are falsely accused of abusing or molesting their stepchild.

Because the child is protected by the biological parents, the courts, the police, and state agencies, any allegation of child abuse or molestation has to be investigated. It can be a nightmare for those stepparents who are innocent of any wrongdoing. Even though they are not guilty of any crime, they may have to explain what happened for the rest of their lives.

People Who Do Not Want To Be In Line Behind Their Stepchild

Some people resent having a significant other put his or her child ahead of them. These people know who comes first, and it is not them. They should understand and accept the fact that their significant other will always put the needs of his or her child ahead of their needs. That is why some people do not want to stand in line behind a child, especially when it is their stepchild.

Examining Your Motives For Wanting To Be A Stepparent And Not Wanting To Be A Stepparent

Instructions

Please answer only those questions that are applicable to you.

You do not have to give written answers to these questions. In fact, you should not write your answers until you have consulted with your attorney, if you choose to employ your own attorney, and the attorney who represents your significant other about whether you should or should not write your answers.

If your significant other is already involved in litigation, or if you anticipate that he or she will be, the opposing party, or his or her attorney, *may* have the right to subpoena your written answers. Of course, you do not want to incriminate yourself, or divulge information that you do not have to disclose. Therefore, please consult with the attorney(s) before you write your answers.

QUESTIONS

Do you believe that you have the ability to raise a child? If so, what specifically equips you to raise a child?

Please explain your answer.

Do you believe that you really want to have the responsibility of raising a child who is not your biological child?

Please explain your answer.

Do you really know why you want to be a stepparent?

Please explain your answer.

Do you really know why you do not want to be a stepparent?

Please explain your answer.

Does your lifestyle permit you to perform the duties of a stepparent? For example, are you willing to forego extensive traveling during the school year?

Please explain your answer.

Have you had the experience of being a babysitter, a caretaker of a child, or other similar types of experience? If so, how would you characterize your experience?

Please explain your answer.

Does the thought of being a stepparent scare you?

Please explain your answer.

Do you really enjoy being in the company of your significant other's child? If so, what specifically do you regard as enjoyable? If not, what specifically do you regard as not enjoyable?

Please explain your answer.

Would you feel more comfortable with the relationship between you and your significant other if he or she did not have a child? If so, have you discussed your feelings with your significant other?

Please explain your answer.

Are you jealous of the relationship between your significant other and his or her child?

Please explain your answer.

Do you feel anxious when you are around your significant other's child? If so, why do you feel this way?

Please explain your answer.

Do you think that it is fair to tell your significant other that you will not get married unless he or she promises you that he or she will never seek custody of his or her child?

Please explain your answer.

How do you like being with your significant other and his or her child?

Please explain your answer.

How do you feel about living with your significant other's child on a full-time basis?

Please explain your answer.

Do you feel threatened by the attention that your significant other gives to his or her child?

Please explain your answer.

Do you feel jealous when your significant other talks with his or her former spouse about matters concerning their child?

Please explain your answer.

Do you want to be a stepparent in order to prove to your significant other that you are a better parent than your stepchild's other parent?

Please explain your answer.

Do you want your significant other to obtain custody because you do not want him or her to pay child support, or because you want him or her to receive child support?

Please explain your answer.

Do you believe that the amount of child support that your significant other will be paying as child support will severely diminish your lifestyle?

Please explain your answer.

74 DO YOU REALLY WANT TO BE A STEPPARENT?

Do you believe that you will lose the respect of your friends, neighbors, relatives, and colleagues if you are not a parent, or at least a stepparent?

Please explain your answer.

Do you have a need to comply with society's expectation that a person should be a parent?

Please explain your answer.

Do you want to concentrate on your career? If so, do you have enough time to be a stepparent?

Please explain your answer.

Do you intend to further your education during the next few years? If so, do you have enough time to be a stepparent?

Please explain your answer.

Do you suffer from a chronic physical or mental condition that limits your ability to be a full-time stepparent?

Please explain your answer.

Do you have a criminal charge pending, or are you on parole or probation? If so, would your situation adversely affect your significant other's ability to gain custody of his or her child?

Please explain your answer.

Do you have an alcohol or drug problem? If so, would your problem affect your significant other's ability to gain custody of his or her child, or affect your ability to be a full-time stepparent?

Please explain your answer.

Does the age or sex of your significant other's child make a difference to you in wanting or not wanting to be a stepparent?

Please explain your answer.

What would you say were the pros and cons of being a stepparent?

Please explain your answer.

Summary

Your second step toward determining whether or not you really want to be a stepparent is to examine your motives for wanting to be a stepparent and not wanting to be a stepparent.

It is very important that you understand your motives. As you were reading this chapter, did you notice any similarities between any of your motives and the motives of the people in the chapter? Because this is only the second step in your analysis, you may not know what your true motives are at this point. If this is the case, please do not be too concerned. There are many more questions for you to answer as you continue to search for the right decision for you.

What you must realize is that you are about to make a decision that affects many people, especially you. That is why your decision to become a stepparent should not be dictated by society, your relatives, or anyone other than you. It is better to do what is in *your* best interest than to worry about what your neighbors, friends, or relatives think.

When I asked one parent whether she would want to be a stepparent, she immediately replied, "Why no, I can hardly tolerate being a parent."

CITATIONS

1. Black, Henry Campbell. *Black's Law Dictionary, Fifth Edition*. St. Paul, Minn.: West Publishing, 1979.
2. Cofer, C.N. and Appley, M.H. *Motivation: Theory and Research*. New York: John Wiley & Sons, 1964.

CHAPTER FOUR

THE THIRD STEP TOWARD DETERMINING WHETHER YOU REALLY WANT TO BE A STEPPARENT

THE KERMAN STEPPARENT QUESTIONNAIRE

Your third step toward determining whether or not you really want to be a stepparent is to examine your attitudes and abilities as they relate to your parenting skills.

Your parenting skills are important to not only your stepchild but to the judge who will be deciding the custody issue in your significant other's case. The judge is quite aware that you will have a significant influence on how your stepchild is raised in your home. If the judge is not convinced that the best interest of your stepchild would be served by having you as the stepparent, your significant other may not be awarded custody. Therefore, it is important that you indicate how you approach parenting, how you relate to your stepchild, how you relate to your stepchild's other parent as a co-parent, how you function as an individual, and how you are able to handle the duties of a stepparent.

80 DO YOU REALLY WANT TO BE A STEPPARENT?

The Kerman Stepparent Questionnaire (KSQ) was developed as a tool to help stepparents who are trying to determine whether or not they really want to be stepparents.

Your significant other may already be involved in custody litigation or there may be a chance that he or she will be in the future. It is important for you to be prepared for whatever happens, and that means knowing in advance whether or not you really want to be a stepparent.

The questionnaire contains ten major areas, with ten questions in each area.

The purpose of the KSQ is to identify some, but not all, of the attitudes and abilities that stepparents customarily exhibit in their relationship with their stepchild and with their stepchild's other parent.

The KSQ should be considered only as a source of additional information for you to use as you continue to explore whether or not you really want to be a stepparent.

Please read each question carefully. Some of the questions may have no relevance to you at all. After you have answered the questions in each area, you may discover how you really feel about the matters that are addressed in each area.

You should be aware that the KSQ is not a psychological test and has not been scientifically validated as a psychological instrument.

Hopefully, you may find that the questions and your answers will help you make an informed and intelligent decision about whether or not you really want to be a stepparent.

The Kerman Stepparent Questionnaire
Instructions

Please answer only those questions that are applicable to you.

You do not have to give written answers to these questions. In fact, you should not write your answers until you have consulted with your attorney, if you choose to employ your own attorney, and the attorney who represents your significant other about whether you should or should not write your answers.

If your significant other is already involved in litigation, or if you anticipate that he or she will be, the opposing party, or his or her attorney, *may* have the right to subpoena your written answers. Of course, you do not want to incriminate yourself, or divulge information that you do not have to disclose. Therefore, please consult with the attorney(s) before you write your answers.

After you have answered the ten questions in each area, add up all of the "Yes" responses and all of the "No" responses.

The total "Yes" responses and "No" responses may give you some indication as to how you have exhibited these attitudes and abilities. I have designated the parent who is not your significant other as your stepchild's other parent.

ISSUE ONE:

YOUR STEPCHILD'S DEVELOPMENT AS AN INDIVIDUAL

The purpose of these questions is to ascertain how you really feel about your stepchild's unique role as an individual, separate and apart from you.

As children grow and develop, they begin to express themselves in many increasingly unique and different ways. It is often difficult to be tolerant and understanding of a stepchild who demands that he or she has the right to dress the way his or her peers do, insists on associating with friends who may not be the type you would choose, or wants to behave in a manner that may seem strange to you. But, this is where you may be able to demonstrate your ability to adapt to the many phases of every child's life.

Some stepparents find it impossible to cope with their stepchild's unique way of behaving, while other stepparents seem to be able to adjust fairly well.

The judge who is making the custody decision in your significant other's case may want to know how you cope with these types of situations.

ISSUE ONE

Circle: "Y" for Yes "N" for No

1. Are you usually tolerant of the way your stepchild chooses to dress or wear his or her hair?   Y N
2. Do you usually encourage your stepchild to express his or her individuality?   Y N
3. Are you less likely to be constantly critical of your stepchild's appearance?   Y N
4. Do you encourage your stepchild to develop his or her natural abilities?   Y N
5. Do you understand your stepchild's need to choose his or her friends?   Y N
6. Are you able to accept your stepchild's lack of abilities in certain areas?   Y N
7. Are you likely to encourage your stepchild to pursue the career he or she wants?   Y N
8. Are you willing to help your stepchild choose activities and other outside interests?   Y N
9. Are you willing to consider your stepchild's input in matters pertaining to your stepchild?   Y N
10. Are you able to be sensitive to your stepchild's need to be accepted by his or her peers?   Y N

Enter the total number of times you circled "Y" or "N"
"Y"=   "N"=

ISSUE TWO:

YOUR STEPCHILD'S NEED FOR A STABLE HOME

The purpose of these questions is to determine your ability to provide your stepchild with a stable home environment. At this stressful time in your stepchild's life, your stepchild requires as much stability as possible.

One important issue for your stepchild is where he or she will live. Many children prefer to live in the house that they were living in prior to the divorce. To them, this provides some stability.

Another important consideration is where your stepchild will attend school. It has been my experience that the child wants to remain in the same school. That way, the child will not have the additional stress of coping with new teachers, counselors, and friends.

Lastly, many children feel safe and secure when there are certain routines that are followed every day. Therefore, it is necessary for you to be sufficiently organized in order to accommodate the needs of your stepchild at this critical stage in your stepchild's life.

ISSUE TWO

Circle: "Y" for Yes "N" for No

1. Do you intend to live in your stepchild's present school district? Y N
2. Do you intend to reside in your stepchild's current home? Y N
3. Do you intend to continue to have your stepchild treated by his or her current doctor and dentist? Y N
4. Do you believe that it is important to have your stepchild keep the same friends as a possible support network? Y N
5. Are you prepared to enforce a consistent routine for your stepchild, for example, bedtime and mealtime? Y N
6. Are you willing to prepare your stepchild for bed? Y N
7. Are you willing to prepare your stepchild's meals? Y N
8. Are you willing to help with homework? Y N
9. Are you willing to get your stepchild up and ready for school in the morning? Y N
10. Are you able to enforce the rules that are set up for your stepchild, such as chores? Y N

Enter the total number of times you circled "Y" or "N"
"Y"=   "N"=

ISSUE THREE:

COOPERATION WITH BOTH PARENTS

The purpose of these questions is to ascertain your ability and willingness to cooperate with both parents in matters regarding your stepchild's health, education, and welfare.

This is probably the most difficult area for some stepparents. Unfortunately, some stepparents feel some hostility toward their stepchild's other parent. However, communicating and cooperating with your stepchild's other parent is very important. For many reasons, it is important to have a good working relationship with your stepchild's other parent.

Until the child reaches the age of eighteen, some parents and stepparents spend years fighting with each other over nonsense. When the child is finally an adult, some parents and stepparents discover that they have lost precious time and a great deal of money, and may have also developed mental or physical symptoms due to the aggravation. A hostile relationship with your stepchild's other parent also causes a great deal of stress and tension for your stepchild as well. Therefore, cooperation with both parents is necessary and essential for you and your stepchild.

ISSUE THREE

Circle: "Y" for Yes "N" for No

1. Are you willing to consider the suggestions and opinions of your stepchild's other parent regarding issues involving your stepchild?   Y N

2. Are you able to set aside any negative feelings toward your stepchild's other parent and cooperate as a co-parent for the sake of your stepchild?   Y N

3. Do you believe that it is important to talk with your stepchild's other parent about child-related issues?   Y N

4. Are you willing to compromise with your stepchild's other parent on child issues when there are disagreements?   Y N

5. Are you willing to foster a good working relationship with your stepchild's other parent in matters regarding your stepchild's welfare?   Y N

6. Are you willing to abide by the decisions of the parents in matters affecting your stepchild?   Y N

7. Do you believe that both parents should be involved in your stepchild's life?   Y N

8. Are you willing to share information about your stepchild with your stepchild's other parent?   Y N

9. Are you willing to return phone calls from your stepchild's other parent when it concerns your stepchild?   Y N

10. Are you available for consultations with your stepchild's other parent?   Y N

Enter the total number of times you circled "Y" or "N"
"Y"=   "N"=

ISSUE FOUR:

Creating A Positive Relationship Between Your Stepchild And Extended Family Members

The purpose of these questions is to determine your ability to create a positive relationship between your stepchild and members of the extended family on both sides, yours and your stepchild's.

This task may be very difficult if your stepchild's relatives have been asked to side with one of the parents against the other.

Parents and stepparents should make every effort to make peace with all of the relatives, for the sake of the parents, the stepparents, and the stepchild.

ISSUE FOUR

Circle: "Y" for Yes "N" for No

1. Are you willing to encourage your stepchild to visit his or her maternal grandparents? Y N
2. Are you willing to encourage your stepchild to visit his or her paternal grandparents? Y N
3. Are you willing to encourage your stepchild to visit his or her other family members, such as aunts, uncles? Y N
4. Are you willing to encourage your stepchild to telephone extended family members? Y N
5. Do you have a good relationship with your parents? Y N
6. Do you have a good relationship with your significant other's parents? Y N
7. Are you able to refrain from making negative comments about your stepchild's other parent? Y N
8. Are you willing to allow your stepchild to spend time during the year with extended family members? Y N
9. Are you willing to assist your stepchild in purchasing cards and presents for all family members, including your stepchild's other parent? Y N
10. Do you want to maintain contact with all of your stepchild's extended family members? Y N

Enter the total number of times you circled "Y" or "N"
"Y"=   "N"=

ISSUE FIVE:
The Need to Refrain From Maligning Your Stepchild's Other Parent

The purpose of these questions is to ascertain your awareness of the need to refrain from maligning your stepchild's other parent. Some stepparents feel compelled to tell their stepchild what a bad person the other parent is. These remarks are very hurtful and harmful to the stepchild. Please do not make negative comments about your stepchild's other parent.

The following provisions are included in most agreements, restraining orders, temporary orders, and final decrees:

1) Each party is hereby enjoined and restrained from doing, or attempting to do, or threatening to do, any act injuring, maltreating, vilifying, molesting, or harassing the adverse party or the child of the parties.

2) Both parties do hereby mutually agree that it is of great importance that the child of the parties be taught and encouraged to love and respect both of his or her parents. Therefore, both parties covenant that neither of them will make derogatory remarks about the other in the presence of the child.

ISSUE FIVE

Circle: "Y" for Yes "N" for No

1. Do you accept the fact that your stepchild's other parent has rights? Y N
2. Are you able to think positively, and not negatively, about your stepchild's other parent? Y N
3. Are you willing to refrain from telling your stepchild that his or her other parent is evil or mean? Y N
4. Are you willing to tell your stepchild that his or her other parent is a good and loving parent? Y N
5. Do you believe that there should be a loving relationship between your stepchild and his or her other parent? Y N
6. Are you willing to tell your stepchild that his or her other parent has called to speak with your stepchild? Y N
7. Are you willing to remind your stepchild of the birthdays of both parents and help with the purchase of cards or gifts? Y N
8. Are you willing to encourage your stepchild to call his or her other parent "Mom" or "Dad"? Y N
9. Are you willing to refrain from telling your stepchild that his or her other parent does not love your stepchild? Y N
10. Will you refrain from telling your stepchild that his or her other parent does not financially support the child? Y N

Enter the total number of times you circled "Y" or "N"
"Y"=   "N"=

ISSUE SIX:

DEALING WITH YOUR STEPCHILD'S OTHER PARENT ON AN EQUAL BASIS

The purpose of these questions is to determine whether you are able to deal with your stepchild's other parent on an equal basis.

Some stepparents have a history of not treating their stepchild's other parent as an equal member of a team. All too frequently, the stepparent wants to pretend that the other parent does not exist or is no longer important in their stepchild's life. However, this is just not so.

In order to deal with your stepchild's other parent on an equal basis, you must respect him or her and must recognize that he or she has an important role in your stepchild's life and always will.

ISSUE SIX

Circle: "Y" for Yes "N" for No

1. Are you able to accept the fact that the parents have the final say in matters that are important to your stepchild? Y N
2. Are you able to accept the fact that you may not have any input in matters affecting your stepchild's life? Y N
3. Do you believe that your stepchild's welfare is more important than showing your stepchild's other parent who is boss? Y N
4. Can you accept the fact that your stepchild's other parent should have equal time with your stepchild? Y N
5. Do you want your significant other to obtain custody because you want to be a stepparent and not because you do not want your significant other to pay child support? Y N
6. Do you believe that it is not appropriate for your stepchild to act as an intermediary to resolve issues involving child support or visitation? Y N
7. Are you willing to allow your stepchild's other parent to have telephone contact with your stepchild? Y N
8. Are you willing to be flexible when it comes to your stepchild's other parent having more visitation time? Y N
9. Are you willing to consider seriously the suggestions made by your stepchild's other parent on how to parent your stepchild? Y N
10. Do you believe that both parents are necessary to raise your stepchild? Y N

Enter the total number of times you circled "Y" or "N"
"Y"=   "N"=

ISSUE SEVEN:

YOUR STEPCHILD'S NEED FOR A DAILY CARETAKER

The purpose of these questions is to determine whether or not you have the time to be the daily caretaker of your stepchild.

Stepparents who are committed to careers or professions quickly discover that taking care of a stepchild's daily needs is a very demanding job. It is not easy to tell an employer that you have to leave to pick up your stepchild when your significant other is out of town. While many employers want to be understanding of your situation, they may still want you to take care of their needs first.

Some stepparents are able to be highly effective in their work and in their capacity as the daily caretakers of their stepchild. However, stepparents need to be aware of their limitations in this area.

ISSUE SEVEN

Circle: "Y" for Yes "N" for No

1. Does your work schedule allow you to be available for your stepchild's needs?   Y N
2. Are you willing to take your stepchild to activities after school?   Y N
3. Are you willing to take your stepchild to doctor's and dentist's appointments?   Y N
4. Are you able to be available for your stepchild in the event of an illness or accident?   Y N
5. Are you willing to prepare your stepchild's meals?   Y N
6. Are you able to discipline your stepchild and set rules for your stepchild to follow?   Y N
7. Are you willing to get your stepchild ready for school in the morning?   Y N
8. Are you willing to arrange for birthday parties and other social activities for your stepchild?   Y N
9. Are you willing to encourage your stepchild to develop friendships in the neighborhood?   Y N
10. Are you able to effectively deal with your stepchild's emotional outbursts and behavioral problems?   Y N

Enter the total number of times you circled "Y" or "N"
"Y"=   "N"=

ISSUE EIGHT:

VIEWING YOUR LIFE AS SEPARATE FROM YOUR STEPCHILD'S

The purpose of these questions is to ascertain your ability to live your life without having to depend on your stepchild for emotional support.

Some therapists believe that it is healthy for you to be able to separate your life from the life of your stepchild. However, some stepparents are so enmeshed in their stepchild's life that these stepparents have no lives of their own. These are stepparents who participate in **all** of their stepchild's activities, attend **every** school function, and devote **all** of their time to their stepchild.

Moreover, it can be extremely traumatic for some stepparents when their stepchild is no longer living in the home, or he or she elects to live with his or her other parent, or there is a divorce and their stepchild lives with his or her parent. This may cause some stepparents to feel alone and abandoned.

ISSUE EIGHT

Circle: "Y" for Yes "N" for No

1. Do you participate in adult activities with other adults? Y N
2. Do you feel comfortable with hiring a babysitter when there is a social function? Y N
3. Are you able to devote time to your own health and appearance? Y N
4. Do you seek the company of adults on a regular basis for mature conversation? Y N
5. Do you consider having a personal life to be as important as being a stepparent? Y N
6. Do you socialize with friends outside of those you meet at your stepchild's school or activities? Y N
7. Do you recognize that your stepchild's needs are not the only focus in your life? Y N
8. Do you separate easily from your stepchild when it comes time to be apart? Y N
9. Do you recognize that your stepchild's needs can be fulfilled by others, and not just by you? Y N
10. Do you recognize that your stepchild has limitations when it comes to satisfying your needs? Y N

Enter the total number of times you circled "Y" or "N"
"Y"=   "N"=

ISSUE NINE:

THE NEED FOR ORGANIZATION

The purpose of these questions is to determine whether or not you are sufficiently organized to accomplish the tasks that need to be done each day. Bear in mind that you may have to shoulder most of the responsibility for the day-to-day care of your stepchild. This is especially true when your significant other travels a lot of the time or works long hours and weekends.

Most of us manage to do some, but not all, of the chores that we have on our daily list. Unfortunately, there are many child-related duties that can not be left for another day. For example, your stepchild may have to be picked up every day from either school or day care. Your stepchild needs to be fed every day. There are many housekeeping chores that must be performed each day, such as washing dishes or clothes.

Some stepparents who work full-time or part-time understand how difficult it is to deal with the many demands that are placed on them every day. That is why it is necessary for stepparents to be somewhat organized.

ISSUE NINE

Circle: "Y" for Yes "N" for No

1. Do you maintain a set schedule of daily activities that need to be accomplished?   Y N
2. Do you prioritize activities, so as to accomplish the most important tasks?   Y N
3. Do you make time during the day for everything that needs to be done?   Y N
4. Do you maintain a daily calendar or similar type of log?   Y N
5. Do you routinely make time during the day for child-related duties?   Y N
6. Are you usually well organized?   Y N
7. Do you routinely make time during the day for housekeeping duties?   Y N
8. Do you instruct your stepchild on how to utilize time, so that your stepchild is able to accomplish his or her tasks?   Y N
9. Are you able to balance the duties that are required to be done at work and at home?   Y N
10. Are you able to successfully deal with the demands of a career, a personal life, and your stepchild?   Y N

Enter the total number of times you circled "Y" or "N"
"Y"=   "N"=

ISSUE TEN:

MAINTAINING GOOD PHYSICAL AND MENTAL HEALTH

The purpose of these questions is to find out whether you recognize the importance of maintaining good physical and mental health.

You need to feel healthy, both physically and mentally, in order to be an effective stepparent and a productive individual.

Moreover, healthy and well-adjusted stepparents are better equipped to cope with the daily stresses of parenting, and can usually relate better to their stepchild and their stepchild's other parent.

ISSUE TEN

Circle: "Y" for Yes "N" for No

1. Do you exercise regularly, either at home or at a gym?	Y N
2. Are you generally a happy and contented person?	Y N
3. Do you usually handle stress and crises without falling apart?	Y N
4. Are you free from any alcohol or drug dependency?	Y N
5. Do you experience very few periods of depression or physical problems?	Y N
6. Are you willing to seek psychological help when there is a need?	Y N
7. Do you frequently examine your motives and actions in dealings with your stepchild as well as with your stepchild's other parent?	Y N
8. Do you recognize the importance of maintaining good physical and mental health?	Y N
9. Do you have a support system that will help you in the event of a crisis?	Y N
10. Do you usually have a positive outlook on life?	Y N

Enter the total number of times you circled "Y" or "N"
"Y"=   "N"=

SUMMARY

Your third step toward determining whether or not you really want to be a stepparent is to examine your attitudes and abilities as they relate to your parenting skills.

The Kerman Stepparent Questionnaire was developed as a tool to help people who may not know whether or not they really want to be stepparents.

The questionnaire contains ten areas, with ten questions in each area that are used to clarify important aspects of each area.

The purpose of the questionnaire is to identify your usual attitudes and abilities, and to enable you to better understand your own attitudes and abilities in each area.

You should be aware that the KSQ is not a psychological test. Moreover, there may be many other parenting skills that have not been addressed in the KSQ.

Issue One deals with how you feel about your stepchild's unique role as an individual, separate and apart from you. One of the most difficult aspects of raising a child is to acknowledge and understand that the child has many unique and different ways of relating to people in his or her world.

Issue Two deals with your ability to provide your stepchild with a stable home environment. It has been my experience that the child is opposed to a divorce because the child feels that a divorce will disrupt the child's secure existence. And, the child is usually correct. Therefore, it is very important to provide your stepchild with as much stability as possible during this time.

Issue Three deals with your ability and willingness to cooperate with your stepchild's other parent in matters regarding your stepchild's health, education, and welfare. In order to minimize the stress that occurs in a divorce situation, it is very important to communicate and cooperate with your stepchild's other parent in matters relating to your stepchild.

Issue Four deals with your ability to create a positive relationship between your stepchild and members of his or her extended family. Even though you may not be related to these people, your stepchild is.

Issue Five deals with your awareness of the need to refrain from maligning your stepchild's other parent. Criticizing him or her may make you feel better, but it is harmful and painful to your stepchild.

Issue Six deals with your ability to deal with your stepchild's other parent on an equal basis. You must recognize that he or she has an important role in your stepchild's life.

Issue Seven deals with whether you have the time to be the daily caretaker of your stepchild.

Issue Eight deals with your ability to live your life without having to depend on your stepchild for emotional support.

Issue Nine deals with whether you are sufficiently organized to accomplish the tasks that need to be done each day.

Issue Ten deals with your awareness of the need to maintain good physical and mental health.

Remember that this is an exercise for *your benefit.* Your answers may help you to evaluate where you stand in these areas. However, you should decide for yourself whether you possess those parenting skills that are necessary for raising your stepchild. You may decide that you can acquire those skills that you lack at this time, and that you can modify your behavior and attitudes.

It has been my experience that most stepparents are not perfect parents. Therefore, if you feel that you can not be a perfect stepparent, please do not despair. You are not alone. It is your willingness to be a good and dedicated stepparent that counts.

CHAPTER FIVE

THE FOURTH STEP TOWARD DETERMINING WHETHER YOU REALLY WANT TO BE A STEPPARENT

The Stepparent Data Record

Your fourth step toward determining whether or not you really want to be a stepparent is to complete The Stepparent Data Record (SDR).

The SDR includes questions that focus on many issues involving you and your stepchild. In addition, I have included in this chapter an explanation of why the questions are important and relevant. Your answers to these questions may help you to make an informed decision.

Some of these questions have been asked by caseworkers, judges, psychologists, psychiatrists, and other professionals in the course of making decisions about custody.

Remember that, contrary to our focus in this book, these professionals focus on what is in the best interest of your stepchild.

The Stepparent Data Record is divided into two sections:

The Stepparent's Information

The Stepchild's Information

THE STEPPARENT'S INFORMATION

<u>General Data:</u>

Some of the questions in this section are routinely asked.

In particular, the question about your citizenship status may be important if there is a question about your stepchild leaving the country.

<u>Educational Data:</u>

A college degree does not determine who will be awarded custody. However, you may be called upon to help your stepchild with his or her homework.

You may also benefit from a parenting course.

This section is particularly relevant because it details how many evenings you are in school. Obviously, if your significant other travels during the week, you may have to care for your stepchild. Therefore, the number of nights that you are away from your stepchild is relevant data to the judge who is making the child custody decision in your significant other's case.

Occupational Data:

The questions in this section are intended to determine your availability for your stepchild. If your significant other works nights and weekends, or is required to travel extensively, he or she may not be able to do what your stepchild requires on a daily basis. Therefore, your availability may be an important factor.

Judges are particularly impressed by the parent or stepparent who has a job that allows him or her to be at home when the child is there.

The stability factor is also important. The judge may be impressed by the person who has been employed by the same company for a period of years and has had no major problems at work.

Military Data:

These questions may be very relevant in your case.

If your significant other is in the military, the judge may want to know who will be taking care of your stepchild when your significant other is away.

If your significant other is on active duty or is in the military reserve, the judge may want to know how your stepchild will be cared for in the event your significant other is recalled.

Arrest And Citation Record Data:

Because arrest and citation records may not be sealed, the judge or an investigator may obtain them. Therefore, it is very important that you tell the attorney who represents your significant other and your attorney, if you choose to employ your own attorney, everything there is to know about any arrest or citation record. The attorney(s) must be prepared to deal with this information when it is brought out in any investigation of you, or in a deposition, or in court.

Needless to say, the stepparent who faces imprisonment for the commission of a crime, or who may be placed on probation for a period of time, may not be able to assume primary care of his or her stepchild when the parent is not available.

The type of crime that was committed is also important. Obviously, a crime of violence is more serious than a parking violation.

Please advise the attorney(s) if you have been charged with any crime, but have not yet been to trial. All of this information may be critical to your significant other's case.

If there is any other information that you feel is relevant and may be of concern to a judge, please let the attorney(s) know.

Tobacco, Alcohol, And Drug Use Data:

The attorney(s) should know if you smoke, drink alcohol to an excess, or use illegal drugs.

The most damaging testimony can come from your stepchild who reports to the judge or the guardian ad litem, who is the attorney appointed by the judge to represent your stepchild's best interest, that you get drunk every night, drive while intoxicated when your stepchild is in the car, or take drugs in the presence of your stepchild. If you have this kind of problem, the judge is likely to find that you are not capable of being the primary caretaker in the event your significant other is not available.

If your stepchild suffers from asthma or other respiratory disease, you should not smoke when your stepchild is in your care. Moreover, the judge may not believe that a person only smokes in the bathroom or outside of the house. The use of tobacco anywhere near your stepchild could be harmful. If you do smoke, there should be a sufficient amount of time from the date that you last smoked to the date of the court trial.

Prescription Medication Use Data:

Most of the population takes prescription medication. Therefore, there are no major problems with taking prescription medication, unless the medication affects your ability to be a caretaker of your stepchild. For example, if you can not drive an automobile when you take your medication, or if your medication forces you to sleep most of the day, you may have a difficult time in proving that you are capable of being a caretaker of your stepchild.

If you are only going to use the medication for a brief period of time, this information should be given to the attorney(s) before the question is asked in deposition or in court.

Physical Health Data:

The information concerning your present physical health condition relates to your ability to be a caretaker of your stepchild.

You should describe in detail your physical condition, especially how it may impact on your ability to be a caretaker of your stepchild.

Mental Health Data:

If you are presently being treated for a mental disorder, you should advise the attorney(s) of the nature of your illness. The judge may want to know if your mental condition affects your ability to care for your stepchild. Moreover, the attorney(s) may want to speak with your therapist who may be able to provide valuable testimony in court, if that becomes necessary.

If you are not presently being treated for a mental disorder, but are subject to periodic episodes of illness, the attorney(s) should know all of the information about this condition.

Parenting Skills Data:

Most people gain their parenting skills by having on-the-job training. However, some people have attended classes, seminars, or have read books on the subject. I am not sure which method is the best for developing effective parenting skills. However, if you have taken any parenting courses, have worked with children, or have a background in education, such as being a teacher, the attorney(s) may want to relate that information to the judge.

Relationship With Parents, Siblings, Extended Family Members, And In-Laws Data:

How you interact with your parents, siblings, extended family members, and in-laws may have an impact on your stepchild's relationship with these persons.

The judge may want to know what your relationship is with this group of people, since it is important that your stepchild develop a healthy relationship with his or her extended family. Therefore, if you have a strained relationship with any relative, you should advise the attorney(s) that there may be a problem in this area.

Be aware that a relative who testifies against you in court may be viewed by the judge as a very compelling and credible witness. However, you may have information that the attorney(s) may use in cross-examining the relative in order to minimize the damage to your significant other's case.

<u>Marriage Data:</u>

Information concerning your previous marriage(s) or your relationship with your own child may be relevant in your significant other's case. The judge may want to know the circumstances of your previous divorce(s), where your child is residing, who has custody, and your relationship with your child.

<u>Custodial Arrangement Data:</u>

You may be asked the following questions in a deposition or in court:

"Do you really want to be a stepparent?"

"Do you really want to have your stepchild live full-time in your home?"

"Do you have a good relationship with your stepchild?"

"If you do not have a good relationship with your stepchild, why don't you?"

"Are you prepared to be the primary caretaker of your stepchild in the event your significant other is not available?"

You must be prepared to answer these and many other questions that relate to your ability to be an effective stepparent.

THE STEPCHILD'S INFORMATION

General Data:

The questions under this category are rather basic, but relevant.

The age of your stepchild may make a definite difference in your relationship with him or her. For example, a young child may develop a positive bond with you because he or she is more dependent on you for his or her basic needs, such as taking him or her to and from school and other activities, preparing meals, and washing clothes.

On the other hand, a teenage child, who is not as dependent on you for all of his or her needs, may feel hostile towards you because he or she may blame you for breaking up his or her family.

Please note that your stepchild's citizenship status may be important if there has been a threat made by either parent to take your stepchild to another country.

If you have any other information about your stepchild that has not been asked, please supply that information.

Educational Data:

Many of the questions contained in this section may require some research.

You may have to go to your stepchild's school and obtain the names and telephone numbers of your stepchild's current teachers and counselors.

If your stepchild is enrolled in a special school for health or educational reasons, please explain in detail why the school is or is not meeting your stepchild's needs, and why your stepchild should or should not remain in the school.

Please bear in mind that you may not be consulted about where your stepchild attends school.

Occupational Data:

If your stepchild is employed, please state who takes your stepchild to work, and who picks up your stepchild after work.

Arrest And Citation Record Data:

It is also important to know the names and telephone numbers of any persons who are or have been involved with your stepchild, such as probation officers and counselors.

If your stepchild has been a repeat offender, the judge may want to know what has been done to remedy this situation. Please state in detail what you did to help your stepchild with his or her problem.

<u>Physical Health Data:</u>

Your stepchild's physical health history is extremely important.

If your stepchild has to go to a doctor, dentist, or therapist on a regular basis, are you available to take your stepchild to his or her appointments? You should be prepared to take your stepchild when your significant other is not available.

It is also critical that you know the names, addresses, and telephone numbers of your stepchild's physicians and dentists. You may have to take your stepchild for emergency medical or dental care, and you may not have the time to obtain this basic health information.

<u>Mental Health Data:</u>

If your stepchild has been treated for a mental disorder, or is currently being treated for a mental disorder, this section is very important.

If your stepchild sees a therapist on a regular basis, are you available to take your stepchild to his or her therapist?

You should have regular communication with your stepchild's therapist in order to be aware of your stepchild's current condition and progress.

You should also be prepared to attend the counseling sessions with your stepchild if the therapist deems it advisable. Some child psychologists and psychiatrists prefer to see all of the members of the child's family. As one of the primary caretakers of your stepchild, you may be included in this category.

Extracurricular Activities Data:

Some children are enrolled in too many activities. Please confer with your stepchild and both parents before you enroll your stepchild in any activity. While you may want to have your stepchild play a particular sport, your stepchild and his or her parents may think differently.

Sometimes, extracurricular activities may interfere with a parent's custodial or visitation times.

You may not have any input as to which activities your stepchild will participate in. However, you may have the primary obligation to attend the activities and provide the transportation to and from these activities.

Where The Stepchild Wants To Live:

In Georgia, a fourteen-year-old child has the right to elect to live with one of his or her parents. This decision is binding on the judge, unless the chosen parent is deemed to be unfit.

A child who is at least eleven years old but not yet fourteen years old may tell the judge where he or she wishes to live. The child's wishes are not binding on the judge.

If your stepchild does not want to live with you and your significant other, please try to understand the reasons for your stepchild's decision.

Your stepchild may be worrying that his or her other parent will be lonely, or will not be able to live alone. Or, your stepchild may think that you do not want him or her to live with you.

You must be prepared to accept your stepchild's decision, whatever that decision may be.

The Stepparent Data Record

Instructions

Please answer only those questions that are applicable to you.

You do not have to give written answers to these questions. In fact, you should not write your answers until you have consulted with your attorney, if you choose to employ your own attorney, and the attorney who represents your significant other about whether you should or should not write your answers.

If your significant other is already involved in litigation, or if you anticipate that he or she will be, the opposing party, or his or her attorney, *may* have the right to subpoena your written answers. Of course, you do not want to incriminate yourself, or divulge information that you do not have to disclose. Therefore, please consult with the attorney(s) before you write your answers.

THE STEPPARENT DATA RECORD
THE STEPPARENT'S INFORMATION:

GENERAL DATA:

What is your full name?

What is your home address?

What is your date of birth and age?

Where were you born?

What is your citizenship status?

EDUCATIONAL DATA:

Where did you attend high school and college, including vocational schools?

What was the last grade that you completed?

What degrees have you been awarded?

Are you currently enrolled in a school program, or do you anticipate enrolling in a school program this year? If so, will you have to attend classes during the day or in the evening?

How many evenings during the week will you be required to attend classes?

OCCUPATIONAL DATA: (Consider homemaking as employment with "employer" being yourself)

By whom are you employed?

What is your job title and description?

How many days during the week do you work?

What are your regular work hours?

Are you required to be on call?

Are you required to work evenings or weekends?

Are you required to travel?

When and how often are you required to be on call, work evenings or weekends, or travel?

Are you able to arrange your schedule at work to meet your stepchild's emergencies?

ARREST AND CITATION RECORD DATA:
PAST

Have you been charged with any felony or misdemeanor crime in the past? If so, what was the date of the offense, with what crime were you charged, what was the date of your trial, how did you plead to the charge, and, if you were found guilty, what was the sentence of the court?

PRESENT

Are you presently charged with any felony or misdemeanor crime, including the use or sale of any illegal drugs? If so, what was the date of the offense, with what crime were you charged, what is the date of your trial, how do you intend to plead, do you expect to be put on probation for this offense, and do you expect to serve time for this offense?

TOBACCO, ALCOHOL, AND DRUG USE DATA:

Do you smoke, drink alcohol to excess, or use illegal drugs? If so, how do you intend to deal with your problem?

Has any child seen you intoxicated? If so, what is the name of the child?

What is this child's relationship to you?

How often has this child seen you intoxicated?

Do you smoke? If so, are you obtaining treatment to curb your smoking?

Do you smoke in the house or in the car?

PRESCRIPTION MEDICATION USE DATA:

Do you use prescription medication? If so, what is the name of the medication(s)?

How frequently do you take the medication?

For what condition is the drug prescribed?

Does the medication interfere with the day-to-day care of your stepchild, such as preventing you from driving a car?

PHYSICAL HEALTH DATA:

Are you under the care of any health care provider? If so, what is the name, address, and telephone number of each health care provider?

What type of treatment are you receiving?

What was the date that you began treatment?

What is the present diagnosis of each health problem that you have?

Do you anticipate that you will need hospitalization?

Does your physical condition prevent you from caring for your stepchild on a full-time basis?

MENTAL HEALTH DATA:

Are you under the care of a psychiatrist, psychologist, or therapist? If so, what is the name, address, and telephone number of each therapist?

How often do you go for therapy?

What was the date that you began treatment?

What is your present diagnosis?

Do you believe that you will require hospitalization?

Does your mental condition prevent you from caring for your stepchild on a full-time basis?

MARRIAGE DATA:

Have you been married previously?

How many times have you been married?

What was the date of each divorce?

What was the cause(s) of each divorce?

What is your child's name and birth date?

Where, and with whom, has your child lived?

Did you and your former spouse enter into a settlement agreement that included custody, visitation, and child support provisions, or did the judge make these decisions?

If there was a settlement agreement, what were the custody, visitation, and child support provisions?

Have you complied with the custody, visitation, and child support provisions in the settlement agreement and/or order of the court? If not, what terms have you violated? What action did your former spouse take to enforce the agreement or order? What was the ruling of the court?

Has you former spouse complied with the custody, visitation, and child support provisions in the settlement agreement and/or order of the court? If not, what terms has he or she violated? What action did you take to enforce the agreement or order? What was the ruling of the court?

What is your current relationship with your child(ren)?

How much do you pay or receive per month as child support?

CUSTODIAL ARRANGEMENT DATA:

Have you discussed with your significant other the pros and cons of seeking custody of his or her child?

What do you believe are the pros?

What do you believe are the cons?

Will your life and your relationship with your significant other change when your significant other has custody?

What is your relationship with your stepchild?

What is your relationship with your stepchild's other parent?

What will be your role in your stepchild's life in the event your significant other is awarded custody?

Do you really want to be responsible for the day-to-day care of your stepchild?

Do you really want your significant other to seek custody of his or her child?

What is the relationship between your child and your stepchild?

How does your child feel about your becoming a full-time stepparent?

THE STEPCHILD'S INFORMATION:

<u>GENERAL DATA:</u> (List each child separately)

What is your stepchild's full name?

What is your stepchild's age and date of birth?

Where was your stepchild born?

What is your stepchild's citizenship status?

With whom has your stepchild lived in the last five years?

With whom does your stepchild live now?

<u>EDUCATIONAL DATA:</u>

What is the name and address of your stepchild's school?

What are the names and telephone numbers of your stepchild's teachers and school counselors?

What is your stepchild's current grade level?

What were the academic grades on the last report card?

What were the behavior grades on the last report card?

What were the teacher's and counselor's comments about your stepchild?

What are some of your stepchild's criticisms of the school?

What does your stepchild like about the school?

Does your stepchild receive any tutoring after school? If so, by whom, how frequently, and for what subject(s)?

Has your stepchild ever been suspended or expelled? If so, why was your stepchild suspended or expelled, when was your stepchild suspended or expelled, and how many days or weeks was your stepchild suspended or expelled?

If you have a child living with you, are you afraid that your stepchild may be a negative influence on your child?

Does your stepchild have any special needs, including physical or educational, that require a special school or class?

Are your stepchild's needs being met by the current school?

Are your stepchild's parents considering changing schools?

Are your stepchild's parents considering a private school?

How would you feel if your significant other decides that his or her child should attend a private school, especially if your child has to attend a public school?

Do you believe that you should have any financial responsibility in the event your stepchild attends a private school?

OCCUPATIONAL DATA:

Does your stepchild have a job? If so, where does your stepchild work?

What days and hours does your stepchild work?

When did the employment begin?

What does your stepchild do with the money that he or she earns?

How does your stepchild get to and from work?

Are you willing to transport your stepchild to and from work?

Do you believe that your stepchild should financially contribute to the household expenses? If so, what amount should your stepchild contribute?

ARREST AND CITATION RECORD DATA:
PAST

Has your stepchild been charged with any felony or misdemeanor crime in the past? If so, what was the date of the offense, with what crime was your stepchild charged, what was the date of the trial, how did your stepchild plead to the charge, and, if your stepchild was found guilty, what was the sentence of the court?

Was your stepchild incarcerated? If so, for how long, and where? Was your stepchild put on probation? If so, is your stepchild still on probation?

PRESENT

Is your stepchild presently charged with any felony or misdemeanor crime, including the use or sale of any illegal drugs? If so, what was the date of the offense, with what crime was your stepchild charged, what is the date of your stepchild's trial, how does your stepchild intend to plead, does your stepchild expect to be put on probation for this offense, and does your stepchild expect to serve time for this offense?

Are you willing to attend the counseling sessions with your stepchild and his or her parents?

PHYSICAL HEALTH DATA:
PAST

Has your stepchild had any major physical health problems? If so, what were your stepchild's health problem(s)?

What treatment did your stepchild receive?

When did the treatment begin?

For what period of time was the treatment provided?

What was the diagnosis of each condition?

What medication and dosage was prescribed, if any?

How long did your stepchild take the medication?

Do you know of any need for future treatment of this condition?

Which parent paid the expenses associated with the treatment?

Which parent primarily cared for your stepchild during this illness?

Was your stepchild left with any permanent condition or disability as a result of this illness?

Has your stepchild had any physical injuries as a result of an accident? If so, what were these physical injuries?

What treatment did your stepchild receive for these injuries?

PRESENT

Does your stepchild have any physical health problems? If so, what is your stepchild's health problem(s)?

What treatment does your stepchild receive?

When did the treatment begin?

What is the diagnosis of each condition?

What is the name and dosage of any medication prescribed?

How long does your stepchild have to take the medication?

What is the current state of your stepchild's condition?

Do you know of any need for future treatment of this condition?

Which parent pays the expenses associated with the treatment?

What is the yearly cost of the treatment?

Which parent maintains the health insurance for your stepchild?

Which parent pays those costs not covered by insurance?

Who takes your stepchild for treatment?

MENTAL HEALTH DATA:
PAST

Has your stepchild been treated for a mental disorder? If so, describe your stepchild's former condition.

Did your stepchild receive any psychological and/or psychiatric treatment? If so, what was the name, address, and telephone number of each therapist?

    What type of treatment did your stepchild receive?

    Was your stepchild hospitalized? If so, what was the name and address of the hospital?

    Which parent paid the expenses associated with the treatment?

    Are there any bills still outstanding? If so, what is the total amount due?

    Which parent is obligated to pay these bills?

PRESENT

    Is your stepchild being treated for a mental disorder? If so, describe your stepchild's mental condition?

    Is your stepchild being treated by a psychologist, psychiatrist, or other therapist? If so, what is the name, address, and telephone number of each therapist?

    What type of treatment is your stepchild receiving for his or her condition?

    Is your stepchild hospitalized? If so, what is the name and address of the hospital, the date that your stepchild was hospitalized, his or her diagnosis, and the name and dosage of the medication prescribed, if any?

Which parent pays the expenses associated with the treatment?

Are there any bills not covered by insurance? If so, what is the total amount due?

Which parent is obligated to pay these bills?

PARENTING SKILLS DATA:

Has your stepchild commented, either positively or negatively, about your parenting skills? If so, what has your stepchild said?

Has your stepchild commented, either positively or negatively, about the parenting skills of either of his or her parents? If so, what has your stepchild said?

RELATIONSHIP WITH SIBLINGS AND EXTENDED FAMILY MEMBERS DATA:

How does your stepchild relate to his or her biological siblings and to your child?

How does your stepchild relate to the members of his or her extended family, including your parents?

EXTRACURRICULAR ACTIVITIES DATA:

Does your stepchild participate in any extracurricular activities in school or outside of school?

How many activities does your stepchild participate in?

Who chose these activities?

When are these activities scheduled?

Which parent attends these activities on a regular basis?

Do you attend these activities on a regular basis?

Do any of your stepchild's activities interfere with a parent's custodial or visitation times?

Has your stepchild expressed a wish to limit the number of activities or to stop participating in an activity? If so, what has your stepchild said?

How have the parents complied with your stepchild's wishes?

Who transports your stepchild for most of these activities?

What are the usual expenses associated with these activities?

Which parent pays the expenses associated with these activities?

WHERE THE STEPCHILD WANTS TO LIVE:

Has your stepchild said where he or she wants to live? If so, where does your stepchild want to live during the school year? Did your stepchild give his or her reasons for choosing to live with one parent over another? If so, what are his or her reasons?

Where does your stepchild want to live during the summer? Did your stepchild give his or her reasons for choosing to live with one parent over another? If so, what are his or her reasons?

Does your stepchild want to live with both parents on an equal basis? If so, what is your stepchild's proposal?

Does your stepchild want to live with someone who is not a parent? If so, who is this person? Did your stepchild give his or her reasons for choosing to live with this person? If so, what are his or her reasons?

Has your stepchild said that he or she does not want to make the decision about where he or she will live? If so, what are the reasons given by your stepchild for not wanting to make this decision?

SUMMARY

Your fourth step toward determining whether or not you really want to be a stepparent is to complete The Stepparent Data Record (SDR).

Your answers to the questions that are included in the SDR may provide you with the information that you need to make this very important decision. Obviously, you are better prepared to make your decision if you know the pertinent facts about you and your stepchild. Hopefully, you already know the pertinent facts about your significant other.

The Stepparent Data Record is divided into two sections:

The Stepparent's Information

The Stepchild's Information

Each category includes some of the questions that may be routinely asked. However, each case is different, and so is the focus of the questions.

Included in The Stepparent Data Record are the following categories:

General Data
Educational Data
Occupational Data
Military Data

Arrest And Citation Record Data
Tobacco, Alcohol, And Drug Use Data
Prescription Medication Use Data
Physical Health Data
Mental Health Data
Parenting Skills Data
Relationship With Parents, Siblings, Extended Family Members, In-Laws Data
Marriage Data
Custodial Arrangement Data
Extracurricular Activities Data (Child's Record only)
Where The Child Wants To Live (Child's Record only)

You should really know your stepchild before you decide to become a stepparent. Because you are making a serious commitment to your stepchild, you need to know if you really want to be responsible for the welfare of another person's child.

Moreover, if you have a child of your own, you have an affirmative duty to protect your own child. Your child should not be forced to live with a child who has severe problems or may cause chaos and turmoil in the home.

CHAPTER SIX

THE FIFTH STEP TOWARD DETERMINING WHETHER YOU REALLY WANT TO BE A STEPPARENT

REVIEWING SOME GEORGIA CASES AND STATUTES RELATING TO CUSTODY ISSUES

Your fifth step toward determining whether or not you really want to be a stepparent is to review some of the Georgia cases and statutory laws relating to child custody issues. Whether you are from Georgia or a different state, you will want to discuss with your attorney, if you choose to employ your own attorney, and the attorney who represents your significant other those cases and laws that are applicable to your significant other's case.

Before you make your decision to become a stepparent, you should have some awareness of what your significant other may be legally required to do as a result of his or her decision to seek custody.

1) Your significant other may be ordered by the judge to undergo a psychological and/or psychiatric evaluation. You may also be included in the evaluation if you are the spouse of your significant other.

2) Your significant other may be investigated by the

Department of Family and Children's Services (DFACS), a Georgia agency, or a similar agency in your state. You may also be included in the investigation if you are the spouse of your significant other.

3) Your stepchild may be interviewed by the judge in his or her chambers.

4) Your significant other may be ordered to pay the guardian ad litem, who is the attorney appointed by the judge to represent the best interest of your stepchild, to investigate both of the parents, your stepchild, and you, if you are the spouse of your significant other.

5) Your significant other may be ordered to answer questions about his or her education, employment, past marriages, relationship with relatives, friends, and colleagues. You may also be included in this process if you are the spouse of your significant other.

6) Your significant other may have his or her financial status reviewed, including his or her tax returns and bank statements. You may also be included in this process if you are the spouse of your significant other.

7) Your significant other may have his or her criminal record, if any, including traffic offenses, examined. You may also be included in this process if you are the spouse of your significant other.

8) Your significant other may have his or her medical and mental health records examined. You may also be included in this process if you are the spouse of your significant other.

9) Your significant other may be investigated by a detective.

10) You and your significant other may have to give to the opposing attorney your diaries, love letters, gifts, photographs, and tape recordings.

11) Your significant other may have to testify at a deposition about his or her personal life and business interests. You may also be included in this process if you are the spouse of your significant other.

12) Your significant other may have to be present at the depositions of witnesses who are testifying for and against your significant other. These witnesses may include private investigators, relatives, doctors, employers, and friends.

13) You and your significant other may have to cancel your business trips because you have to go to court.

14) Your significant other may be awarded joint legal custody that requires him or her to consult and confer with the one person who aggravates him or her the most.

You have to decide for yourself whether you want to subject yourself to this process before you decide whether or not you really want to be a stepparent.

Remember, even if your significant other is awarded custody of his or her child, the award of custody may be changed at some later date under certain circumstances.

This chapter includes a few of the appellate court cases and statutory laws of Georgia that deal with child custody issues. Readers from states other than Georgia can utilize the book as a guide and then seek the advice of their local attorneys regarding the specific cases and statutory laws that apply to their significant other's case. This book is not intended to be a course in child custody law nor is it meant to be a substitute for seeking legal advice from an attorney.

In addition to the issues that are discussed in this chapter, there may be other issues and laws that are important to your significant other's case. Each case is unique because of its particular facts and circumstances. Therefore, the courts consider each case differently. Please make sure to discuss all of the issues and laws with the attorney(s) before you make any final decisions.

In this chapter, the statutory laws are included as single-spaced text and in bold type, and the decisions of the appellate courts are in bold type. The citations for both the statutory laws and the decisions of the appellate courts are at the end of the chapter. Please note that since the writing of this book, the statutory laws that are quoted may have been modified by subsequent acts of the legislature. Likewise, the appellate courts may have reversed previous decisions. Therefore, the laws and rulings cited in this book may be totally different at the time you are reading this book. That is why I emphasize that you must rely only on the attorney(s) for legal advice.

This chapter is divided into three sections.

- ***Before The Trial Issues*** are some of the issues that you and your significant other may want to consider before there is the trial of the case.

- ***During The Trial Issues*** are some of the issues that may be addressed during the trial of the case.

- ***After The Trial Issues*** are some of the issues that you and your significant other may or may not encounter later.

BEFORE THE TRIAL ISSUES
State's Policy Regarding Child Custody

It is always better for the parents to discuss and decide the custody issue. No one knows their child better than the parents. Because there is only a brief period of time to present a case in court, many facts about the parents and their child may never be heard by the judge. Moreover, some important information may never be presented in court because of a legal technicality.

Unfortunately, where the parents don't or won't come to an agreement about custody, the judge will render a decision. And, that decision will not be based upon the best interest of the parents, but what the judge considers to be in the best interest of the child, and which parent will be better able to promote the child's welfare and happiness.

The judge will consider the circumstances of the parties, the stepparents, and the child. Moreover, neither the mother nor the father has a prima facie right to the custody of the child.

> **"In all cases in which a divorce is granted, an application for divorce is pending, or a change in custody of a minor child is sought, the court, in the exercise of a sound discretion, may look into all the**

circumstances of the parties, including improvement of the health of a party seeking a change in custody provisions, and, after hearing both parties, may make a different disposition of the children, placing them, if necessary, in possession of guardians appointed by the judge of the probate court."[1]

"(1) In all cases in which the custody of any minor child or children is at issue between the parents, there shall be no prima-facie right to the custody of the child or children in the father or mother.
(2) The court hearing the issue of custody, in exercise of its sound discretion, may take into consideration all the circumstances of the case, including the improvement of the health of the party seeking a change in custody provisions, in determining to whom custody of the child or children should be awarded. The duty of the court in all such cases shall be to exercise its discretion to look to and determine solely what is for the best interest of the child or children and what will best promote their welfare and happiness and to make its award accordingly."[2]

The Parents May Enter Into Custody Agreements

Parents may enter into a settlement agreement that includes a provision that specifies which parent will have legal and physical custody. Although the judge will most likely ratify this provision in the agreement, he or she is not bound to do so.

> **"(a) It shall be expressly permissible for the parents of a minor child to present to the court an agreement respecting any and all issues concerning custody of the minor child. The term 'custody' shall include, without limitation, joint custody as such term is defined in Code Section 19-9-6.**
> **(b) The court shall ratify the agreement and make such agreement a part of the court's final judgment in the proceedings unless the court makes specific written factual findings as a part of the final judgment that under the circumstances of the parents and the child in such agreement that the agreement would not be in the best interests of the child. The court shall not refuse to ratify such agreement and to make such agreement a part of the final judgment based solely upon the parents' choice to use joint custody as a part of such agreement.**
> **(c) In its judgment, the court may supplement the agreement on issues not covered by such agreement."**[3]

Mediation Is Best For Resolving Custody Disputes

Mediation should be attempted in every custody dispute. In most cases, mediation saves time and money and helps define those issues that are contested.

Some judges make it mandatory for the parties to attend mediation before they are allowed to have their case heard in court. Mediation is a non-adversarial process whereby the parties meet with a trained neutral called a mediator. The parties may have their attorneys present or not. The mediation session is held in a room in the courthouse or in the mediator's office. It is a very informal meeting. The judge is not present. Everything that is said in mediation is confidential, unless there are threats of violence to self or others, or the mediator thinks that a child is abused, or the safety of any person is in danger. In mediation, the parties control whether they will settle the contested issues in the case or not. The mediator can not and will not force the parties to settle the issues in the case.

If the parties are able to settle all or some of the issues in the case, the mediator will prepare a memorandum of agreement that outlines which issues are settled and which issues remain to be decided by the judge. However, the mediation agreement must be written in great detail and must be specific as to all of the agreed-upon terms in order for the agreement to be enforceable.

The appellate court has held that **"'A divorce decree should accurately reflect a settlement reached by the parties, and a trial court is not authorized to adopt and incorporate into the final decree and judgment of divorce a purported memorialization of the settlement that contains more substantive terms than the settlement.'"**[4]

The Child Who Is Age 14 May Make An Election

In Georgia, the 14-year-old child may sign in the presence of a notary a document that is called an Election.

In this document, the child swears that the child is at least 14 years old, is making the election freely and voluntarily, and is electing to live with one of the child's parents.

The judge is bound by the child's election, unless the parent selected is not a fit and proper person to have custody of the child.

The child's election only affects where the child lives, not which parent shall have custody of the child.

Only the judge decides who shall have custody of the child.

"In all cases in which the child has reached the age of 14 years, the child shall have the right to select the parent with whom he or she desires to live. The child's selection shall be controlling, unless the parent so selected is determined not to be a fit and proper person to have the custody of the child. The court may issue an order granting temporary custody to the selected parent for a trial period not to exceed six months regarding the custody of a child who has reached the age of 14 years where the judge hearing the case determines such a temporary order is appropriate."[5]

Another provision of the law deals with cases involving a change in custody.

> **"In all custody cases in which the child has reached the age of 14 years, the child shall have the right to select the parent with whom he or she desires to live. The child's selection shall be controlling unless the parent so selected is determined not to be a fit and proper person to have the custody of the child."**[6]

Even though a 14-year-old child may elect to live with one of his or her parents, the trial court may find that the selected parent is not a fit and proper parent to have custody. However, the trial court must have a basis for its decision.

The appellate court has held that **"'If the court's judgment is based upon a stated fact for which there is no evidence, it should be reversed.'"**[7]

The Child Who Is Age 11 May Tell The Judge Where The Child Wants To Live

Some children under the age of fourteen have very definite opinions about where they want to live. They have expressed their wishes to parents, lawyers, and guardians. However, these children had no right to make their wishes known to the judge who was ruling on the issue of custody.

Now, these children can tell the judge where they want to live. Effective July 1, 2000, Georgia has a statute that provides that the judge shall consider the desires of the child who has reached the age of 11 but not 14 years in determining which parent should be awarded custody.

The statute also provides that the judge shall also consider the educational needs of the child.

The child's desires, however, are not controlling or binding on the judge. The judge still has the discretion to disregard the wishes of the child if the judge determines that where the child wants to live is not in the best interest of the child.

Moreover, the mere fact that the 11-year-old child wishes to live with one of his or her parents does not, in and of itself, constitute a material change of conditions or circumstances.

As provided in the statute, the judge also has the authority to change custody on a temporary basis.

The first section of the statute provides:

> "**In all cases in which the child has reached the age of 14 years, the child shall have the right to select the parent with whom he or she desires to live. The child's selection shall be controlling, unless the parent so selected is determined not to be a fit and proper person to have the custody of the child.**
>
> **In all cases in which the child has reached the age of at least 11 but not 14 years, the court shall consider the desires, if any, and educational needs of the child in determining which parent shall have custody. The court shall have complete discretion in making this determination, and the child's desires are not controlling. The court shall further have broad discretion as to how the child's desires are to be considered, including through the report of a guardian ad litem. The best interest of the child standard shall be controlling.**
>
> **The desire of a child who has reached the age of 11 years but not 14 years shall not, in and of itself, constitute a material change of conditions or circumstances in any action seeking a modification or change in the custody of that child.**

The court may issue an order granting temporary custody to the selected parent for a trial period not to exceed six months regarding the custody of a child who has reached the age of at least 11 years where the judge hearing the case determines such a temporary order is appropriate."[8]

The second section provides:

"In all custody cases in which the child has reached the age of at least 11 but not 14 years, the court shall consider the desires and educational needs of the child in determining which parent shall have custody. The child's selection shall not be controlling. The best interests of the child standard shall apply."[9]

The Child Who Is Age 14 May Affect The Custody Of The Younger Sibling

If the 14-year-old child elects to live with one of his or her parents, and the selected parent is a fit and proper parent to assume custody, the judge may award the selected parent custody of the younger sibling as well.

Children who are very close in age, have a close relationship to one another, and are dependent on one another for emotional support may want to live together in the same household.

Often, children express their desire to be together because they have shared the same room, attended the same school, and protected each other since they were very young. Younger children may feel that an older sibling will provide the protection that the parents may not be providing because they are too busy waging war against one another.

The appellate court has held that **"'A child's selection of the parent with whom he desires to live, where the child has reached 14 years of age, is controlling absent a finding that such parent is unfit. Without a finding of unfitness the child selection must be recognized and the court has no discretion**

to act otherwise.' The award of custody of the 14-year-old child...was a sufficient change in condition to warrant change of custody of the younger child...as well."[10]

The story of Patty, Dan, Carol, Markham, and Bea

Patty and Dan were divorced many years ago when their children, Carol and Markham, were very young. In the settlement agreement, Patty was given sole custody of the children. Patty never remarried. She supported the children from the money that she earned from her job and the child support that she received every month from Dan.

Dan enjoyed the single life until he met Bea. Two months after their first date, they got married. Every other weekend, Carol and Markham would come over to Dan's house for the visitation period. Dan had a beautiful home with all of the amenities, including a swimming pool.

When Carol became 14 years old, she told her mother that she wanted to live with Dan. Dan was eager to have custody of Carol. However, he neglected to discuss with Bea whether he should have Carol live with them. Bea never thought that Dan would have custody of his children. Moreover, Bea never anticipated that Markham, who was very close to Carol, would also want to be in Dan's custody. Bea never quite adjusted to having two children in her house, and because Bea was unhappy, everyone was unhappy.

DURING THE TRIAL ISSUES

The Judge Decides The Custody Issue Unless The Parents Decide

If the parents can not decide the custody issue, the superior court judge in Georgia has the legal authority to make this decision.

The superior court judge may transfer the case to the juvenile court for investigation only, or for investigation and determination, as to the issues of custody, visitation, and child support.

> "**The superior courts have authority:**
> **(1) To exercise original, exclusive, or concurrent jurisdiction, as the case may be, of all causes, both civil and criminal, granted to them by the Constitution and laws;**
> **(2) To exercise the powers of a court of equity;**"[11]

The following code section also applies:

> "**Where custody is the subject of controversy, except in those cases where the law gives the superior courts exclusive jurisdiction, in the consideration of these cases the juvenile court shall have concurrent jurisdiction to hear and determine the issue of custody and support when the issue is transferred by proper order of the superior court.**"[12]

The Judge May Order An Evaluation And Investigation

The judge may order a psychological and/or psychiatric evaluation of both parents, the child, and you, if you are the spouse of your significant other. The judge may also order an investigation by the Department of Family and Children's Services (DFACS), or a similar agency.

Moreover, either party may file a motion requesting a mental evaluation and/or an investigation by the Department of Family and Children's Services.

> **"The court is authorized to order a psychological custody evaluation of the family or an independent medical evaluation."[13]**

> **"On motion of either party in any action or proceeding involving determination of the award of child custody between parents of the child, when such motion contains a specific recitation of actual abuse, neglect, or other overt acts which have adversely affected the health and welfare of the child, the court may direct the appropriate family and children services agency or any other appropriate entity to investigate the home life and home environment of each of the parents. In any action or proceeding involving determination of the award of child custody between parents of the child when during such proceedings a specific recitation of actual abuse, neglect, or other overt acts which have adversely affected the health and welfare of the child has been**

made the court shall also have authority on its own motion to order such an investigation if in the court's opinion the investigation would be useful in determining placement or custody of the child."[14]

The appellate court has held that **"In attempting to reach a determination regarding the best interest of the child, the superior court has the power, in any proceeding where the issue of child custody is contested, to compel either or both parents to submit to examination and evaluation by a court-appointed clinical psychologist or psychiatrist. The mental health of the parents is an inherent and vital part of their overall 'state of health,'...and can be a critical factor in determining the best interest of the child."**[15]

The Judge May Appoint A Guardian Ad Litem

The judge may appoint a guardian ad litem to represent the child's best interest. The judge may also include in the order who shall pay the guardian's fees.

Usually, the guardian interviews each parent before seeing the child. Then, each parent and the child are interviewed together. The visits usually take place at the home of the parents. If the parents have remarried, their spouses will be interviewed.

In most cases, the guardian will request specific information from the parents or their attorneys.

In addition to furnishing the guardian with statements, documents, and pictures, each parent can submit his or her list of witnesses for the guardian to contact. It is important to list only those witnesses who can provide the most relevant information. Some parents make the mistake of listing all the people they know. However, the guardian may only have a limited time in which to complete the investigation. Therefore, the guardian may only contact a few of the witnesses who are listed.

In addition, the guardian talks with the child's teachers, neighbors, and doctors as well as any other witnesses who are familiar with the child and/or the parents.

After the guardian has completed his or her investigation, the guardian will prepare a report for the judge.

Some judges will permit the attorneys to have copies of the report. Other judges will only permit the attorneys to make notes from the report. However, the attorneys are entitled to review the completed guardian's report, which may include the guardian's recommendation as to which parent should have sole custody or primary physical custody.

Please do not despair if the guardian recommends that the other parent should have custody. Your significant other may still be awarded custody. The judge makes the final decision about custody, and the judge is not bound by the guardian's recommendation.

At the trial of the case, the attorneys for both parents may have the right to cross-examine the guardian about how the investigation was conducted, the contents of the report, the guardian's biases, his or her credentials, and any other relevant matter.

> **"When a minor is interested in any litigation pending in any court in this state and he has no guardian or his interest is adverse to that of his guardian, such court may appoint a guardian ad litem for the minor."[16]**

Factors The Judge May Consider Before Awarding Custody

The judge may consider many factors before making a custody determination, including some of the following:

- With which parent does the child have a stronger bond?
- Which parent is more affectionate toward the child?
- Which parent provides a stable, safe, and moral environment?
- Which parent is emotionally stable and is not suffering from a mental disorder?
- Which parent does not have a drug and/or alcohol problem?
- Which parent encourages the child to relate to extended family members and siblings?
- Which parent takes the child to the doctor, dentist, and other health care providers for the child's scheduled appointments?
- Which parent encourages the child to develop a positive, loving relationship with the other parent?
- Which parent will refrain from making disparaging comments about the other parent in the presence of

the child?

- Which parent's work schedule is flexible so that the parent is available in case of an emergency?
- Which parent gets the child to school and events on time?
- Which parent attends the child's extracurricular activities and school functions?
- Which parent is able to effectively discipline and supervise the child?
- Which parent is going to continue to live in the state in order that the other parent will not be deprived of frequent contact with the child?
- With which parent has the child expressed a desire to live?
- Which parent is not on parole or on probation or does not have a pending criminal charge?
- Which parent is not seeking custody for the purpose of obtaining revenge against the other parent?
- What have friends, relatives, and experts said about each parent's ability to be the primary caretaker of the child?

- Has the psychiatric and/or psychological evaluation revealed any conditions that would limit a parent's ability to be the primary caretaker of the child?
- Have there been any allegations that a parent has sexually or physically harmed the child?
- Has there been a history of one parent causing physical harm to the other?
- Has there been a history of one parent making threats of bodily injury toward the child or toward the other parent?
- Has a parent displayed inappropriate behavior while the child was present, for example, engaging in acts of sexual intercourse in the child's presence?
- Has a parent abandoned or neglected the child?

The Child Shall Be Available For Consultation

"Except by leave of court, the minor child/children of the parties shall not be permitted to give oral testimony at temporary hearings; such child/children will be excluded from the courtroom or other place of hearing. When custody is in dispute, if directed by the court, minor child/children of the parties shall be available for consultation with the court. At any such consultation, attorneys for both parties may be in attendance but shall not interrogate such child/children except by express permission from the court. Upon request, the proceedings in chambers shall be recorded."[17]

The appellate court has held that **"USCR 24.5(B) specifically provides that when child custody is in dispute in domestic relations actions, at any consultation between the court and the child, both the attorneys may be present and 'upon request, the proceedings in chambers shall be recorded.'"**[18]

The Judge May Award Temporary Custody

The judge may award temporary custody to one of the parents before making the final custody determination.

> **"Upon the filing of an action for a change of child custody, the court may in its discretion change the terms of custody on a temporary basis pending final judgment on such issue. Any such award of temporary custody shall not constitute an adjudication of the rights of the parties."[19]**

> **"Joint custody may be considered as an alternative form of custody by the court. This provision allows a court at any temporary or permanent hearing to grant sole custody, joint custody, joint legal custody, or joint physical custody where appropriate."[20]**

The Judge May Change Temporary Custody

The judge may change temporary custody after there has been an award of temporary custody to one parent.

The appellate court has held that **"The discretion of the judge is broad as long as the case is in the bosom of the court and no permanent custody has been granted as in the final divorce. The temporary custody hearing does not decide any final issues between the parties. We held the child may be given to one person at one hearing and another person at another hearing."**[21]

The Judge Must Consider Awarding Joint Custody If Both Parents Are Fit And Proper

The appellate court has held that **"The Court of Appeals correctly pointed out that the Legislature's enactment of O.C.G.A. Section 19-9-6- providing the court with the option of awarding joint legal or joint physical custody or both- and the 1990 amendments to O.C.G.A. Section 19-9-3(a) stating that neither parent has a prima facie right to custody and that joint custody may be considered- indicate a state policy favoring shared rights and responsibilities between both parents. We also agree with the Court of Appeals that where ...the trial court finds both parents fit and proper, the trial court must give due consideration to the feasibility of a joint custody arrangement. However, the 1990 legislation did not change the trial court's primary duty in any custody determination between parents, which is to 'determine solely what is for the best interest of the child or children and what will best promote their welfare and happiness.'"**[22]

Various Types Of Custody That May Be Awarded

The judge may award joint legal custody, joint physical custody, joint legal custody and joint physical custody, or sole custody.

The appellate court has held that **"Where, as here, the trial court determines that both parents are fit and equally capable of caring for the child, the court must consider joint custody but is not *required* to enter such an order unless it specifically finds that to do so would be in the best interest of the child."**[23]

> "(1) 'Joint custody' means joint legal custody, joint physical custody, or both joint legal custody and joint physical custody. In making an order for joint custody, the court may order joint legal custody without ordering joint physical custody.
> (2) 'Joint legal custody' means both parents have equal rights and responsibilities for major decisions concerning the child, including the child's education, health care, and religious training; provided, however, that the court may designate one parent to have sole power to make certain decisions while both parents retain equal rights and responsibilities for other decisions.
> (3) 'Joint physical custody' means physical custody is shared by the parents in such a way as to assure the child of substantially equal time and contact with both

parents.

(4) 'Sole custody' means a person, including, but not limited to, a parent, has been awarded permanent custody of a child by a court order. Unless otherwise provided by court order, the person awarded sole custody of a child shall have the rights and responsibilities for major decisions concerning the child, including the child's education, health care, and religious training, and the noncustodial parent shall have the right to visitation. A person who has not been awarded custody of a child by court order shall not be considered as the sole legal custodian while exercising visitation rights."[24]

" 'Legal custodian' means a person, including, but not limited to, a parent, who has been awarded permanent custody of a child by a court order. Where custody of a child is shared by two or more persons or where the time of visitation exceeds the time of custody, that person who has the majority of time of custody or visitation shall be the legal custodian."[25]

"Joint custody may be considered as an alternative form of custody by the court. This provision allows a court at any temporary or permanent hearing to grant sole custody, joint custody, joint legal custody, or joint physical custody where appropriate."[26]

In a Louisiana case involving the issue of joint custody, the appellate court of Louisiana has held that **"Among the factors to be considered...in determining whether joint custody is in the best interest of the child are:**

(a) The love, affection, and other emotional ties existing between the parties involved and the child.

(b) The capacity and disposition of the parties involved to give the child love, affection, and guidance and to continue the education and raising of the child in his religion...or creed, if any.

(c) The capacity and disposition of the parties involved to provide the child with food, clothing, medical care, and other material needs.

(d) The length of time the child has lived in a stable, satisfactory environment, and the desirability of maintaining continuity.

(e) The permanence as a family unit, of the existing or proposed custodial home or homes.

(f) The moral fitness of the parties involved.

(g) The mental and physical health of the parties involved.

(h) The home, school, and community record of the child.

(i) The reasonable preference of the child, if the court deems the child to be of sufficient age to express a preference.

(j) The willingness and ability of each of the parents to facilitate and encourage a close and continuing parent-child relationship between the child and the other parent.

(k) The distance between the respective residences of the parties.

(l) Any other factor considered by the court to be relevant to a particular child custody dispute. However, the classification of persons according to race is neither relevant nor permissible."[27]

In Joint Legal Custody, One Parent Is Usually Designated To Make The Final Decision

In a joint legal custody arrangement, the judge usually designates one parent to make the final decision in the event the parents disagree about an issue involving their child's health, education, and welfare. In the settlement agreement, the parents may designate which parent shall have the final decision-making power.

Some parents who do not have the final say express their fear that the other parent will dominate the child's life. That is usually not the case. For example, if the parents disagree about the child's medical or dental care, the child's doctor usually makes the decision. If either parent disagrees with that decision, either parent can obtain a second opinion. If the parents disagree about the child's education, the parent who wants the child to attend a private school has the option of paying for it. If the parents disagree about the child's extracurricular activities, the parents may decide that each parent can have the final say as to one activity per year. If the parents have a major difference of opinion as to a really important matter, they should seek the advice of a professional.

The Judge May Order Joint Legal Custody Without Ordering Joint Physical Custody

"In making an order for joint custody, the court may order joint legal custody without ordering joint physical custody."[28]

Custody May Be Awarded To A Third Party

"In any action involving the custody of a child between the parents or either parent and a third party limited to grandparent, great-grandparent, aunt, uncle, great aunt, great uncle, sibling, or adoptive parent, parental power may be lost by the parent, parents, or any other person if the court hearing the issue of custody, in the exercise of its sound discretion and taking into consideration all the circumstances of the case, determines that an award of custody to such third party is for the best interest of the child or children and will best promote their welfare and happiness. There shall be a rebuttable presumption that it is in the best interest of the child or children for custody to be awarded to the parent or parents of such child or children, but this presumption may be overcome by a showing that an award of custody to such third party is in the best interest of the child or children. The sole issue for determination in any such case shall be what is in the best interest of the child or children."[29]

MODIFICATION OF CUSTODY

The Parent Who Has Been Awarded Custody Is Favored

The appellate court has held that **"A parent who has been awarded custody pursuant to a divorce decree has a prima facie right to retain such custody, and a trial court in a modification action should ordinarily favor such parent."**[30]

Power And Duty Of The Court In Modification Cases

> **"In all cases in which...a change in custody of a minor child is sought, the court, in the exercise of a sound discretion, may look into all the circumstances of the parties, including improvement of the health of a party seeking a change in custody provisions, and, after hearing both parties, may make a different disposition of the children...This subsection shall not limit or restrict the power of the court to enter a judgment relating to the custody of a minor in any new proceeding based upon a showing of a change in any material conditions or circumstances of a party or the minor."**[31(a)]

> **"The duty of the court in all such cases shall be to exercise its discretion to look to and determine solely what is for the best interest of the child or children and what will best promote their welfare and happiness and to make its award accordingly."**[31(b)]

What The Court Must Find In Order To Change Custody

The appellate court has held that **"In order to change custody, the trial court 'must affirmatively find...either that the original custodian is no longer able or suited to retain custody or that conditions surrounding the child have so changed that modification of the original judgment would have the effect of promoting his welfare. It is a change for the worse in the conditions of the child's present home environment rather than any purported change for the better in the environment of the non-custodial parent that the law contemplates under this theory.'"**[32]

The appellate court has held that **"'As between natural parents, a change in custody of a minor child may be awarded only upon a showing of a change in material conditions or circumstances of the parties or the child, subsequent to the original decree of divorce and award of custody, and that the change of custody would be in the best interests of the child.'"**[33]

The appellate court has held that **"A petition to change child custody should be granted only if the trial court finds that there has been a material change of condition affecting the welfare of the child since the last custody award. If there has been such a change, then the court should base its new custody decision on the best interest of the child. If the record contains any reasonable evidence to support the trial judge's decision on a petition to change custody, it will be affirmed on appeal."**[34]

The appellate court has held that **"'Whether there are changed conditions affecting the welfare of the child occurring after the rendition of a former final custody judgment which will warrant changing custody is essentially a fact question in each individual case. And if there is reasonable evidence in the record to support the decision made by the...court in changing or in refusing to change custody or visitation rights, then the decision of that court must prevail.'"**[35]

No Legal Definition Of "Changed Condition"

The appellate court has held that **"There has been no legal definition of the new or changed condition necessary to warrant a change of custody, but it must be such as substantially affects the welfare of the minors."**[36]

New Evidence After The Filing Of The Petition Is Admissible

The appellate court has held that **"'The trial court must consider all facts and conditions which present themselves up to the time of rendering the judgment and not merely facts and conditions which occur prior to the filing of the petition.' We adhere to the rule that where the issue is a material change in conditions affecting the welfare of a child, it is error to refuse to hear any evidence which might have some bearing upon that issue. Where the welfare of a child is involved, relevant information must be received up until the very time that the court rules."**[37]

Examples Of Evidence That Will Not Warrant Changing Custody:

1) No New And Material Conditions That Affect The Welfare Of The Child

The judge is not authorized to change custody "where there is no evidence to show new and material conditions that affect the welfare of the child."

The appellate court has held that "'**Though the trial judge is given a discretion, he is restricted to the evidence and is unauthorized to change the custody where there is no evidence to show new and material conditions that affect the welfare of the child.' Whether conditions, which affect the welfare of the child, have changed since the rendition of a former final custody judgment depends on the facts of the case. Without new and material conditions that substantially affect the welfare of the child, a change of custody is not authorized.**"[38]

2) Moving And Remarriage

The custodial parent may move out of the state with the minor child. The custodial parent may remarry. These events are not in and of themselves sufficient to change custody.

The appellate court has held that **"Relocating and remarrying are not in and of themselves sufficient changes in conditions to authorize a change in custody."**[39]

3) Best Interest And Welfare Alone

The judge may not change custody merely because it is in the best interest of the child to do so.

The appellate court has held that **"The trial court awarded custody of the child...solely upon the conclusion that it was in the 'best interest and welfare of the child' without first finding 'a change in material conditions or circumstances of the parties or the child, subsequent to the original decree of divorce and award of custody.' Although the evidence presented in the trial court may have been sufficient to support a change of custody, it appears that the trial court failed to apply the complete correct legal standard in this case."**[40]

Examples Of Evidence That Will Warrant Changing Custody:

1) New And Material Conditions That Affect The Welfare Of The Child

The petitioner must prove that there are new and material conditions that affect the welfare of the child.

The appellate court has held that **"'The award of custody of a child of the parties in a divorce decree is conclusive unless there have been subsequently to the decree new and material changes in the conditions and circumstances** *substantially affecting the interest and welfare of the child.'* **The question is not whether there has been a change of conditions, but whether there has been a** *material* **change, i.e., one that affects the welfare of the child. That necessarily means the change of conditions must be one which is adverse or detrimental to the child's welfare."**[41]

2) Award Of Custody Of The 14-Year-Old Child

The 14-year-old child has the right to decide that he or she wants to live with one of the parents. The child's selection of a parent is controlling, unless the selected parent is found not to be a fit and proper person to have custody.

The appellate court has held that "'**A child's selection of the parent with whom he desires to live, where the child has reached 14 years of age, is controlling absent a finding that such parent is unfit. Without a finding of unfitness the child selection must be recognized and the court has no discretion to act otherwise.' The award of custody of the 14-year-old child...was a sufficient change in condition to warrant change of custody of the younger child...as well.**"[42]

3) *Stress Due To Joint Physical Custody*

Some parents want to have joint physical custody of their child.

In these cases, the child spends an equal, or almost equal, number of days in each parent's home. The parents may decide that the child should spend one week with one parent and one week with the other parent. Or, the parents may decide that one parent has the child the first half of the month and the other parent has the child the second half of the month. However, it may be very stressful for the child to constantly travel in order to reside with the mother and the father.

The appellate court has held that "'Once a permanent child custody award has been entered, the test for use by the trial court in change of custody suits is whether there has been a change of conditions affecting the welfare of the child.' Since potential change of custody is always considered in light of the best interests of the child, an order changing custody may be based on evidence of a positive or adverse change in the circumstances of either of the joint custodial parents, or any change in the circumstances of the child substantially affecting the welfare and best interests of the child. In its order changing custody, the trial court found that 'there has been a material change of conditions since the time of the [divorce decree implementing the joint custody agreement] in that the child is being transferred back and forth between the two parent's homes, under circumstances which cause the child confusion and distress with the frequency of changing homes.' We find there was reasonable evidence showing that, since the joint custody agreement was entered into..., there has been an adverse change in conditions affecting the welfare of the child. The evidence was sufficient under this test even in the absence of evidence establishing that the adverse conditions affecting the child had a measurable adverse effect on the child."[43]

4) *Smoking May Be A Relevant Factor*

The custodial parent who smokes may lose custody of the child who suffers with asthma.

The appellate court has held that "**A parent who has been awarded custody pursuant to a divorce decree has a prima facie right to retain such custody, and a trial court in a modification action should ordinarily favor such parent. 'Whether there are changed conditions affecting the welfare of the child occurring after the rendition of a former final custody judgment which will warrant changing custody is essentially a fact question in each individual case. And if there is reasonable evidence in the record to support the decision made by the court in changing or in refusing to change custody or visitation rights, then the decision of that court must prevail.' The fact that the child was diagnosed with asthma after the divorce clearly constitutes a change in circumstances making...smoking a factor relevant to the child's welfare. Neither party contests the fact that smoking**

can be an irritant to an individual with asthma. It is not our function to second-guess the trial court in cases such as this, which turn largely on questions of credibility and judgments as to the welfare of the child. The trial court is in the best position to make determinations on these issues. The fact that the guardian ad litem recommended against a transfer of custody does not change this result, since there was evidence to support the trial court's judgment."[44]

5) *Living With A Person Who Is Not A Spouse*

The judge may award the noncustodial parent custody of the child where the custodial parent lives with a person in a husband-wife relationship without being married. However, every case is different, and the custodial parent may not lose custody.

The custodial parent has the obligation to maintain a moral environment for the child. An immoral environment usually includes living with a person in a husband-wife relationship where the parties are not married.

Some parties in today's society live together without the benefit of marriage. Sometimes, they live together for a few months in order to determine if they are compatible. That may be a good solution for the parties. However, where there are children involved, the custodial parent may have to defend his or her position in court if the noncustodial parent files for custody.

The appellate court has held that **"...changes of custody have been upheld where a parent cohabits with another individual without benefit of marriage while the child is living with the parent."**[45]

6) *Repeated Denial Of Visitation Rights*

The custodial parent who repeatedly interferes with or denies the noncustodial parent's visitation rights may lose custody. The judge has the discretion to award the noncustodial parent custody of the minor child in cases where the custodial parent repeatedly denies the noncustodial parent his or her visitation rights. Visitation is a right that belongs to the noncustodial parent.

The custodial parent should encourage the child to visit with the noncustodial parent as often as possible. As you have read in a previous chapter, the child needs both parents in order to develop into a healthy adult.

The custodial parent who purposely plans outings for the child when it is the noncustodial parent's visitation period is interfering with that parent's rights.

Usually, visitation is limited to a few days in the month and that means every minute is precious.

Under most agreements or court orders, the noncustodial parent has visitation with his or her child every other weekend, which amounts to only four days a month. Of course, that is in addition to the holiday and summer visitation time and, usually, one night for dinner per week. Most noncustodial parents look forward to the time when they can be with their children. These parents plan their time around seeing their children.

Moreover, most children want to see and interact with both parents, not just one of their parents.

It is obvious that the repeated interference with the noncustodial parent's visitation rights adversely affects the child's relationship with the noncustodial parent.

That is why it is not in the best interest of either the noncustodial parent or the child for the custodial parent to interfere with this period of time.

The appellate court has held that "'**The repeated denial of the noncustodial parent's visitation rights authorizes a change in custody.' Where there is evidence of a change of condition affecting the child's welfare, a change in custody is justified without a showing that the adverse condition had a measurable effect on the child.**"[46]

The story of Chris, Delores, and Sam

Chris and Delores had a bitter divorce and custody battle that lasted two years. Sam, who was their only child, was four years old. At the end of the trial, the judge awarded custody to Delores, and Chris was awarded visitation rights. Shortly thereafter, Chris met and married Lulu. Lulu had never been married, had no children, and never wanted any. She loved Sam, but she never really wanted to be a stepparent. Chris faithfully exercised every minute of his visitation time with Sam. However, Delores could not forget what Chris had put her through during the trial. She never missed an opportunity to interfere with Chris' visitation rights. For example, Sam was either too sick to go with Chris, or Delores had to go out of town, or Sam had other plans.

Chris decided to seek custody, even though Lulu did not support his decision. Chris was awarded custody. Lulu was not happy, and she often made her feelings known to Chris.

MISCELLANEOUS PROVISIONS

The Judge May Not Change Custody By Modifying Visitation

Because of the evidence, the judge may not have the legal authority to change custody. The judge, however, may not do indirectly what he or she may not do directly. The judge may not modify visitation rights in such a way as to allow the noncustodial parent to have the child the majority of the time.

The appellate court has held that **"Since the time of visitation...under the new visitation schedule exceeds the time of custody...there can be no doubt that the new visitation schedule is in substance a change of custody. It was error for the trial court to indirectly effect a change in custody by modifying the visitation schedule."**[47]

The Judge May Not Change Custody In A Contempt Proceeding

Although custody may not be modified in a contempt action, visitation rights may.

The appellate court has held that **"Visitation rights may now be modified on motion of either party or on motion of the trial judge in a contempt action. The legislature did not provide that a change of custody could be made by motion. A**

petition for change of custody must still 'be accomplished through new proceedings.'"[48]

Self-Executing Provision In The Agreement Is Permissible

The parties' agreement may provide that, under certain circumstances, custody will be transferred to the noncustodial parent who will then be entitled to receive child support.

The appellate court has held that **"A self-executing change serves the interest of judicial economy by effecting the change of custody and the establishment of child support obligations without the necessity of court proceedings in a case...where there are no allegations of parental unfitness."**[49]

Attorney's Fees Are Not Awarded

The appellate court has held that **"Georgia courts have repeatedly held that attorney fees are not recoverable in an action where the noncustodial parent seeks a change of custody."**[50]

The appellate court has held that the trial court judge may award attorney's fees in a case where the action involved the modification of visitation rights as well as child support and contempt.[51]

AFTER THE TRIAL ISSUES

The Custodial Parent Must Notify The Noncustodial Parent Of A Change In The Child's Address

"In any case in which a judgment awarding the custody of a minor has been entered, the court entering such judgment shall retain jurisdiction of the case for the purpose of ordering the custodial parent to notify the court of any changes in the residence of the child. In any case in which visitation rights have been provided to the noncustodial parent and the court orders that the custodial parent provide notice of a change in address of the place for pickup and delivery of the child for visitation, the custodial parent shall notify the noncustodial parent, in writing, of any change in such address. Such written notification shall provide a street address or other description of the new location for pickup and delivery so that the noncustodial parent may exercise such parent's visitation rights. Except where otherwise provided by court order, in any case under this subsection in which a parent changes his or her residence, he or she must give notification of such change to the other parent and, if the parent changing residence is the custodial parent, to any other person granted visitation rights. Such notification shall be given at least 30 days prior to the anticipated change of residence and shall include the full address of the new residence."[52]

Civil And Criminal Remedies For Violating Custodial Rights

Both civil and criminal remedies are available to the custodial parent if the noncustodial parent violates the rights of the custodial parent.

> "The powers of the several courts to issue attachments and inflict summary punishment for contempt of court shall extend only to cases of disobedience or resistance by any party to any lawful order, rule, decree, or command of the courts."[53]

> "The grant of attorney's fees as a part of the expenses of litigation, made at any time during the pendency of the litigation, whether the action is for contempt of court orders involving child custody, and child visitation rights, shall be within the sound discretion of the court, except that the court shall consider the financial circumstances of both parties as a part of its determination of the amount of attorney's fees, if any, to be allowed against either party."[54]

> "A person commits the offense of interference with custody when without lawful authority to do so the person (A) Knowingly or recklessly takes or entices any child away from the individual who has lawful custody of such child; (B) Knowingly harbors any child who has absconded; or (C) Intentionally and willfully retains possession within this state of the child upon the expiration of a lawful period of visitation with the child."[55]

The Surviving Parent, Not The Stepparent, Has Custody

The surviving parent, not the stepparent, is the legal custodian the moment the custodial parent dies, unless there has been a prior termination of the surviving parent's rights. Even though the stepparent has become emotionally attached to his or her stepchild, and vice versa, the surviving parent has all of the rights. Therefore, any action to change custody must be filed in the surviving parent's county of residence.

> **"Upon the death of either parent, the survivor is entitled to custody of the child; provided, however, that the court, upon petition, may exercise discretion as to the custody of the child, looking solely to the child's best interest and welfare."[56]**

The story of Bill, Judy, Susie, and Brenda

Bill and Judy were divorced when Susie was only three years old. Judy agreed that Bill should have custody of Susie. Bill married Brenda, a wonderful woman who really loved Susie. Brenda became very attached to Susie, and Susie was very close to Brenda. A few years later, Bill died, and Judy came for Susie. Brenda was devastated. She had just lost Bill and now she was losing Susie. Judy understood Brenda's pain, but Judy told Brenda that Susie was not Brenda's daughter. Brenda swore that she would never again give her heart to a stepchild.

THE GRANDPARENT'S CUSTODY RIGHTS

In Some Cases, Custody May Be Awarded To Grandparents

Effective July 1, 2000, the following code section was amended to provide that the great-grandparent may seek custody of the minor child.

> "In any action involving the custody of a child between the parents or either parent and a third party limited to grandparent, great-grandparent, aunt, uncle, great aunt, great uncle, sibling, or adoptive parent, parental power may be lost by the parent, parents, or any other person if the court hearing the issue of custody, in the exercise of its sound discretion and taking into consideration all the circumstances of the case, determines that an award of custody to such third party is for the best interest of the child or children and will best promote their welfare and happiness. There shall be a rebuttable presumption that it is in the best interest of the child or children for custody to be awarded to the parent or parents of such child or children, but this presumption may be overcome by a showing that an award of custody to such third party is in the best interest of the child or children. The sole issue for determination in any such case shall be what is in the best interest of the child or children."[57]

REVIEWING THE CUSTODY OPTIONS
INSTRUCTIONS

Please answer only those questions that are applicable to you.

You do not have to give written answers to these questions. In fact, you should not write your answers until you have consulted with your attorney, if you choose to employ your own attorney, and the attorney who represents your significant other about whether you should or should not write your answers.

If your significant other is already involved in litigation, or if you anticipate that he or she will be, the opposing party, or his or her attorney, *may* have the right to subpoena your written answers. Of course, you do not want to incriminate yourself, or divulge information that you do not have to disclose. Therefore, please consult with the attorney(s) before you write your answers.

Questions

Is your significant other seeking sole custody? If so, why should the judge award your significant other sole custody?

In this type of custodial arrangement, your significant other would have the right to make all of the decisions affecting the child's health, education, and welfare.

This may be a better option for your significant other, especially if he or she decides that a joint custody arrangement would not be in his or her best interest. Often, divorcing parents have difficulty in communicating about any issue. That explains why they got divorced in the first place. Your significant other might decide that having the legal obligation to discuss issues with his or her former spouse may be too stressful.

Please explain your answer.

Is your significant other seeking joint legal custody? If so, why should the judge award the parents joint legal custody?

In this type of custodial arrangement, your significant other and your stepchild's other parent consult and confer about all significant matters respecting the child's health, education, and welfare. However, the parents must be able to communicate effectively, and be able to work together for the sake of the child. In the event of a disagreement, one parent would be designated to make the final decision.

If your significant other is seeking joint legal custody in which both parents consult and confer about important matters respecting the child, whom do you think should have the final say as to matters involving education, medical and dental care, extracurricular activities, and other significant matters?

Please explain your answer.

Is your significant other seeking joint physical custody? If so, why should the judge award the parents joint physical custody?

In this type of custodial arrangement, both parents share the custodial time on an equal, or almost equal, basis. One parent may be designated as the primary physical custodian, i.e., the parent who has the child the majority of the time, and the other parent may be designated as the secondary physical custodian.

The parents must live relatively close to one another. The parents may decide that each parent would have custody of the child every other week, one-half of the month, or alternating months. However, many judges do not favor having the child go back and forth every other week from one parent's house to the other parent's house, like a ping pong ball. Often, the child does not consider either home as his or her home.

As a stepparent, you must also agree to live relatively close to your stepchild's other parent. You may or may not find this arrangement to be objectionable.

Please explain your answer.

Is your significant other seeking joint legal custody and joint physical custody? If so, why should the judge award the parents joint legal custody and joint physical custody?

In this type of custodial arrangement, both parents are truly parenting the child together, and the child has the opportunity to be with both parents on an equal, or almost equal, basis.

The parents must be able to communicate effectively, share ideas, and agree to live relatively close to one another.

This type of arrangement may cause many problems. For example, the parents have to be in constant contact with each other, and the child will have to adjust to two different parenting styles and rules.

Please explain your answer.

202 DO YOU REALLY WANT TO BE A STEPPARENT?

Do you think that the parents should incorporate into their settlement agreement a self-executing clause that provides that custody would be transferred to the noncustodial parent in the event the custodial parent moves from the state, or if the minor child makes an election to live with the noncustodial parent?

Please explain your answer.

How would you arrange the custodial or visitation time periods for your significant other?

Please explain your answer.

It may be helpful to use a chart similar to the one below, indicating M for mother and F for father.

SUN.	MON.	TUES.	WED.	THURS.	FRI.	SAT.

As to the weekends, what is your proposal as to when the first weekend begins, and what should be the specific times from the beginning of the weekend to the time the weekend ends?

Do you believe that there should be make-up weekends in the event the child is sick, or the parent can not visit that weekend?

Please explain your answer.

As to weekday times, what is your proposal as to when the weekday time begins and ends? Should the weekday time include overnight?

Please explain your answer.

As to holidays and special days, what is your proposal as to how the holidays and special days should be allocated?

Should these days be alternated, so that one parent has the first holiday or special day, and the other parent has the next holiday or special day? If so, what is the first holiday or special day, and which parent gets this day? Should one parent have certain holidays and special days in even-numbered years, and the other parent have certain holidays and special days in odd-numbered years? Should each parent have one-half of the holiday or special day, with the parents alternating the beginning half? Which day and what time should each holiday and special day begin and end?

Do these time allocations meet your needs and those of your own child?

Please explain your answer.

What is your proposal for sharing holidays and special days, including MLK Day, Valentine's Day, Washington's Birthday, Easter Sunday, Spring Break, Memorial Day, Mother's Day, Father's Day, 4th of July, Labor Day, Halloween,

Thanksgiving, Christmas or Winter Break (1-2 weeks), New Year's Day, Jewish Holidays, Christian Holidays, Non-Christian Holidays, Child's Birthday, Parent's Birthday, Relative's Birthday, Grandparents' Day, Teacher Workdays, and other days off from school?

Should holidays and special occasion days take precedence over weekend visitation?

Should there be make-up holidays and special occasion days if the child is sick, or one parent can not visit? Should these days be forfeited?

Please explain your answer.

As to the time during the summer, what is your proposal as to how many weeks each parent should have the child? Should these weeks be consecutive or non-consecutive? Should the noncustodial parent get additional weeks in the summer as the child gets older? If so, what age should the child have to be in order for the number of weeks to increase? How many weeks should be added to the existing number of weeks? Should these additional weeks be non-consecutive or consecutive? When should notice be given by each parent as to the weeks he or she prefers? If both parents choose the same weeks, who should have the first choice of weeks? Which day and what time should the week or weeks begin and end? Should there be make-up weeks in the summer if the child is sick, one parent can not visit, or the child goes to camp or summer school?

Do you want your significant other to have his or her child during the same time period that you have your own child?

Please explain your answer.

As to the responsibility for transporting the child for custodial or visitation times, who should be responsible for picking up and returning the child to his or her residence? Should the parents meet half-way, or at a location other than the residence? May you, a relative, or a friend transport the child? If either party moves from the state, or moves more than a certain number of miles from the other parent, who should be responsible for paying the costs of transportation? Which parent should be responsible for making all travel arrangements? Should one parent have to accompany the child on public transportation, and if so, until what age?

Please explain your answer.

Do you think that the parents should include a provision in their settlement agreement that neither party shall drink, smoke, or use drugs while that party has custody or visitation?

Please explain your answer.

Do you think that the parents should include a provision in their settlement agreement that the child may telephone the home of the other parent on certain days and during specified times, and who should pay for long distance calls and a private line?

Please explain your answer.

Do you think that the parents should include a provision in their settlement agreement that each parent and his or her spouse may visit the child in school or at day care?

Please explain your answer.

Do you think that the parents should include a provision in their settlement agreement that each parent has the "right of first refusal" to have the child if the other parent is unable to care for the child, or if the other parent is traveling?

Please explain your answer.

Do you think that the parents should include a provision in their settlement agreement that each parent will provide the other with the address and telephone number where the child may be reached when he or she is away from his or her residence for more than a certain number of nights?

Please explain your answer.

Do you think that the parents should include a provision in their settlement agreement that each parent will provide any day care center or babysitter with the name, address, and telephone number of the other parent and his or her spouse?

Please explain your answer.

Do you think that the parents should include a provision in their settlement agreement that, when the custodial parent is unavailable, any day care center or babysitter may contact the other parent and his or her spouse in the event of any emergency?

Please explain your answer.

Do you think that the parents should include a provision in their settlement agreement that each parent and his or her spouse will have the name, address, and telephone number of any day care center or babysitter who is caring for the child?

Please explain your answer.

Do you think that the parents should include a provision in their settlement agreement that each parent and his or her spouse will have the name, address, and telephone number of any doctor, dentist, psychologist, therapist, psychiatrist, or any other health care provider who is treating the child?

Please explain your answer.

Do you think that the parents should include a provision in their settlement agreement that each parent will give the other parent telephone notice by a certain date and time if the visiting parent is unable to exercise his or her visitation time?

Please explain your answer.

Do you think that the parents should include a provision in their settlement agreement that the parent who does not exercise his or her visitation time will pay for babysitting charges?

Please explain your answer.

Do you think that the parents should include a provision in their settlement agreement that neither party nor his or her spouse shall make negative or derogatory remarks about the other parent or stepparent in the presence of the child nor allow other household members to do so?

Please explain your answer.

Do you think that the parents should include a provision in their settlement agreement that, as soon as possible, each parent or his or her spouse will notify the other parent if there has been an accident involving the child or if the child is seriously ill?

Please explain your answer.

212 DO YOU REALLY WANT TO BE A STEPPARENT?

Do you think that the parents should include a provision in their settlement agreement that each parent and his or her spouse has the right to discuss the child with any health care provider, including hospital personnel, psychiatrists, psychologists, dentists, and physicians, and the right to receive copies of all reports, bills, and other documents concerning the child?

Please explain your answer.

Do you think that the parents should include a provision in their settlement agreement that each parent and his or her spouse has the right to discuss the child with any teacher, school counselor, or other school official, and the right to receive copies of all report cards and schedules?

Please explain your answer.

Do you think that the parents should include a provision in their settlement agreement that each parent and his or her spouse has the right to participate in and attend the child's activities, including being a coach or an instructor?

Please explain your answer.

Do you think that the parents should include a provision in their settlement agreement that each parent and his or her spouse has the right to confer with the child's coaches or instructors?

Please explain your answer.

Do you think that the parents should include a provision in their settlement agreement that each parent and his or her spouse has the right to attend all school functions, and the right to participate in any school activities?

Please explain your answer.

214 DO YOU REALLY WANT TO BE A STEPPARENT?

Do you think that the parents should include a provision in their settlement agreement that neither parent shall permit a party of the opposite sex, except for a family member or spouse, to stay overnight when the child is present in the home?

Please explain your answer.

Do you think that the parents should include a provision in their settlement agreement that neither parent shall take the child to any place that is not suitable for children, such as a bar or night club?

Please explain your answer

Do you think that the parents should include a provision in their settlement agreement that both parents must agree to include his or her spouse in any discussion concerning the health, education, or welfare of the child?

Please explain your answer.

SUMMARY

Your fifth step toward determining whether or not you want to be a stepparent includes your review and consideration of some of the issues relating to child custody.

This chapter focuses on only a few of the Georgia cases and laws that deal with the custody issues. Please discuss with your own attorney, if you choose to employ an attorney, and the attorney who represents your significant other the appellate court cases and statutory laws that relate to your significant other's case.

If you decide to become a stepparent, there are many issues that you need to consider, including the likelihood that the judge will determine that it is in the best interest of your stepchild for custody to be awarded to your significant other, and how the type of custody that is awarded coincides with your present lifestyle.

The purpose of this review is obvious. If you choose to become a stepparent, you should be aware of what your significant other may be legally ordered to do. That is why it is imperative that you discuss with the attorney(s) all of the pros and cons of becoming a stepparent.

You should be aware that custody litigation is very costly, time-consuming, and causes the parents, the stepparents, and the child to suffer a lot of emotional pain.

You may have your life investigated and revealed. You may not want to have your personal life and your financial situation discussed and examined by strangers.

Your answers to the questions that are included in this chapter may help you decide whether or not you really want to be a stepparent.

KEY TO THE CITATIONS

In order to understand the terms and abbreviations used in this chapter, the following explanation should be helpful to you.

O.C.G.A. stands for the Official Code of Georgia Annotated, which contains the statutory laws of Georgia.

Ga.App. stands for a Georgia Court of Appeals case in which one party is appealing the lower court's decision, and the case does not involve a divorce issue.

Ga. stands for a Georgia Supreme Court case in which one party is appealing the lower court's decision, and the case involves a divorce issue as well as a custody issue.

Citation stands for the manner in which a case is cited, for example, Don Smith, Plaintiff v. Mary Smith, Defendant.

The notation 216 Ga. 521, 118 S.E.2d 82 (1961) indicates that the case is found in volume 216 of the Georgia Supreme Court cases on page 521, and in volume 118 of the South Eastern Reporter Second Series on page 82, and the appellate court's decision was written in 1961.

In this book, I have used only the first initial of the last name in each citation rather than the full last name, which you will find in the case books.

CITATIONS

1. O.C.G.A. Section 19-9-1(a)(1)
2. O.C.G.A. Section 19-9-3(a)(1),(2)
3. O.C.G.A. Section 19-9-5
4. D v. D, 269 Ga. 480, 499 S.E.2d 317 (1998)
5. O.C.G.A. Section 19-9-1(a)(3)
6. O.C.G.A. Section 19-9-3(a)(4)
7. S v. S, 207 Ga.App. 471, 428 S.E.2d 376 (1993)
8. O.C.G.A. Section 19-9-1(a)(3)
9. O.C.G.A. Section 19-9-3(a)(4.1)
10. P v. P, 167 Ga.App. 265, 306 S.E.2d 97 (1983)
11. O.C.G.A. Section 15-6-8
12. O.C.G.A. Section 15-11-5(c)
13. O.C.G.A. Section 19-9-3(a)(6)
14. O.C.G.A. Section 19-9-4(a)
15. R v. R, 195 Ga.App. 493, 393 S.E.2d 750 (1990)
16. O.C.G.A. Section 29-4-7
17. Uniform Superior Court Rule 24.5(B)
18. W v. S, 221 Ga.App. 338, 471 S.E.2d 284 (1996)
19. O.C.G.A. Section 19-9-3(e)
20. O.C.G.A. Section 19-9-3(a)(5)

21. M v. M, 230 Ga. 779, 199 S.E.2d 179 (1973)

22. B v. B, 265 Ga. 465, 458 S.E.2d 126 (1995)

23. B v. B, 265 Ga. 465, 458 S.E.2d 126 (1995)

24. O.C.G.A. Section 19-9-6

25. O.C.G.A. Section 19-9-22(2)

26. O.C.G.A. Section 19-9-3(a)(5)

27. L v. L, No. 90 CA 0087, Court of Appeal of Louisiana, First Circuit, 563 So.2d 1273; 1990 La. App.

28. O.C.G.A. Section 19-9-6(1)

29. O.C.G.A. Section 19-7-1(b.1)

30. D v. D, 235 Ga.App. 184, 509 S.E.2d 117 (1998)

31(a). O.C.G.A. Section 19-9-1

31(b). O.C.G.A. Section 19-9-3

32. D v. D, 235 Ga.App. 184, 509 S.E.2d 117 (1998)

33. J v. H, 175 Ga.App. 169, 333 S.E.2d 21 (1985)

34. M v. G, 225 Ga.App. 752, 484 S.E.2d 789 (1997)

35. D v. D, 235 Ga.App. 184, 509 S.E.2d 117 (1998)

36. E v. E, 206 Ga. 297, 57 S.E.2d 83 (1950)

37. S v. S, 253 Ga. 183, 318 S.E.2d 57 (1984)

38. M v. M, 241 Ga.App. 109, 522 S.E.2d 772 (1999)

39. J v. H, 175 Ga.App. 169, 333 S.E.2d 21 (1985)

40. O v. O, 217 Ga.App. 780, 459 S.E.2d 439 (1995)

41. T v. T, 208 Ga.App. 375, 430 S.E.2d 659 (1993)

42. P v. P, 167 Ga.App. 265, 306 S.E.2d 97 (1983)

43. In re S.D.J., 215 Ga.App. 779, 452 S.E.2d 155 (1994)

44. D v. D, 235 Ga.App. 184, 509 S.E.2d 117 (1998)

45. B v. K, 224 Ga.App. 179, 480 S.E.2d 230 (1996)

46. H v. L, 232 Ga.App. 376, 501 S.E.2d 879 (1998)

47. K v. A, 218 Ga.App. 120, 460 S.E.2d 540 (1995)

48. B v. B, 247 Ga. 548, 277 S.E.2d 655 (1981)

49. W v. J, 260 Ga. 493, 396 S.E.2d 890 (1990)

50. In re S.K.R., 229 Ga.App. 652, 494 S.E.2d 558 (1997)

51. M v. O, 260 Ga. 849, 400 S.E.2d 310 (1991)

52. O.C.G.A. Section 19-9-1(c)(1),(2),(3)

53. O.C.G.A. Section 15-1-4(a)(3)

54. O.C.G.A. Section 19-6-2(a),and (1)

55. O.C.G.A. Section 16-5-45(b)(1),and (A),(B),(C)

56. O.C.G.A. Section 19-9-2

57. O.C.G.A. Section 19-7-1

CHAPTER SEVEN

THE SIXTH STEP TOWARD DETERMINING WHETHER YOU REALLY WANT TO BE A STEPPARENT

REVIEWING SOME GEORGIA CASES AND STATUTES RELATING TO VISITATION ISSUES

Your sixth step toward determining whether or not you really want to be a stepparent is to review some of the Georgia cases and statutory laws relating to visitation issues. Whether you are from Georgia or a different state, you will want to discuss with your attorney, if you choose to employ your own attorney, and the attorney who represents your significant other those cases and laws that are applicable to your significant other's case.

Before you make your decision to become a stepparent, you should have some awareness of what your significant other may be legally required to do as a result of his or her decision to be awarded visitation rights, rather than custody.

1) The judge will determine your significant other's visitation rights based upon the best interest of his or her child.

2) Your significant other is not considered the legal custodian while he or she is exercising his or her visitation rights.

3) Your significant other may not have input in matters regarding the health, education, or welfare of the child.

4) Your significant other may not have the right to have his or her child treated in a hospital or by a physician in the event of an emergency.

5) Your significant other may be denied access to his or her child's medical, dental, hospital, and other records.

6) Your significant other may have his or her visitation rights modified when the custodial parent moves to another state or locality.

7) Your significant other may be ordered to provide all of the transportation for his or her visitation period. Therefore, he or she may have to pick up the child at his or her residence and return the child to his or her residence.

8) A 14-year-old child may petition the court to terminate your significant other's visitation rights.

9) Your significant other may have his or her visitation rights supervised under certain circumstances.

10) Your significant other may be ordered to post a bond before he or she may exercise his or her visitation rights if there is some doubt about whether your significant other

will return the child to the custodial parent.

You have to decide for yourself whether you can accept the possibility that these conditions may be imposed upon your significant other before you decide whether or not you really want to be a stepparent.

This chapter includes a few of the appellate court cases and statutory laws of Georgia that deal with visitation issues. Readers from states other than Georgia can utilize the book as a guide and then seek the advice of their local attorneys regarding the specific cases and statutory laws that apply to their significant other's case. This book is not intended to be a course in child visitation law nor is it meant to be a substitute for seeking legal advice from an attorney.

In addition to the issues that are discussed in this chapter, there may be other issues and laws that are important to your significant other's case. Each case is unique because of its particular facts and circumstances. Therefore, the courts consider each case differently. Please make sure to discuss all of the issues and laws with the attorney(s) before you make any final decisions.

In this chapter, the statutory laws are included as single-spaced text and in bold type, and the decisions of the appellate courts are in bold type. The citations for both the statutory laws and the decisions of the appellate courts are at the end of the chapter. Please note that since the writing of this book, the statutory laws that are quoted may have been modified by subsequent acts of the legislature. Likewise, the appellate courts may have reversed previous decisions. Therefore, the laws and rulings cited in this book may be totally different at the time you are reading this book. That is why I emphasize that you must rely only on the attorney(s) for legal advice.

This chapter is divided into three sections.

- *Before The Trial Issues* are some of the issues that you and your significant other may want to consider before there is the trial of the case.

- *During The Trial Issues* are some of the issues that may be addressed during the trial of the case.

- *After The Trial Issues* are some of the issues that you and your significant other may or may not encounter later.

TWO BASIC PRINCIPLES

There are two basic principles that apply to visitation issues.

1) It is extremely important that both parents see their child as much as possible; and

2) The judge will only consider *what is in the best interest of the child* in awarding visitation rights.

Again, the judge is not interested in what is in the best interest of the parents.

BEFORE THE TRIAL ISSUES

Visitation Rights Differ From Custodial Rights

Black's Law Dictionary defines visitation rights as "the right of one parent to visit children of the marriage under order of the court."

The parent who has visitation rights has the right to visit the child but has no control over the life of the child.

The parent who has been awarded custody has the right to determine how the child will be raised. That right includes the power to make all of the decisions affecting the child's health, education, and welfare.

Visitation is a *right*, not merely a privilege. This right may be enforced by the judge if the custodial parent interferes with the visitation rights of the noncustodial parent.

> **"The term 'custody' includes visitation rights."[1]**

> **"A person who has not been awarded custody of a child by court order shall not be considered as the legal custodian while exercising visitation rights."[2]**

State's Policy Regarding Visitation Rights

> **"It is the express policy of this state to encourage that a minor child has continuing contact with parents and grandparents who have shown the ability to act in the best interest of the child and to encourage parents to share in the rights and responsibilities of raising their children after such parents have separated or dissolved their marriage."[3]**

Please note that a stepparent has no right to visit his or her stepchild in the event of a divorce from the child's parent. Therefore, a stepparent has all of the duties and responsibilities of a parent and none of the legal rights when it concerns a stepchild.

DURING THE TRIAL ISSUES

The Judge Decides Visitation Rights

Even though the parents may decide that the noncustodial parent should have certain visitation rights, the judge makes the final decision in this matter.

The appellate court has held that **"We construe OCGA Sections 19-9-1(a) and 19-9-3(a) to preserve the authority of the trial court to set visitation rights based upon the best interests of the child."**[4]

Standard Provisions For Visitation

The usual standard visitation times for the noncustodial parent is every other weekend from Friday at 6:00 p.m. until Sunday at 6:00 p.m., one night during the week for dinner, two to four weeks in the summer, and alternating holidays. However, the parents can agree to expand the usual visitation times so that the noncustodial parent can have more visitation time with the child.

There may be additional provisions in the court's order or in the settlement agreement, including some of the following provisions.

The parents agree that the child should maintain a close relationship with the other parent, and to that end, the parents agree to foster and encourage a free, liberal, and reasonable exercise of the visitation rights.

The parents agree to refrain from making disparaging or insulting remarks about the other parent in the presence of the child and not tolerate such actions by others.

The parents agree to refrain from undermining the relationship between the child and the other parent and not tolerate actions by others that are designed to undermine, or that result in undermining, said relationship.

The custodial parent shall have the child ready to be picked up by the noncustodial parent at the specified time and have the appropriate clothing packed.

The noncustodial parent shall be entitled to obtain copies of all school records.

The noncustodial parent shall be entitled to attend all parent-teacher conferences and school functions.

The noncustodial parent shall be entitled to discuss with any teacher or school counselor all matters regarding the child.

The noncustodial parent shall be entitled to attend and participate in all extracurricular activities of the child.

The noncustodial parent shall be entitled to consult and confer with any doctor, dentist, therapist, or other person treating the child, and shall be entitled to receive any reports, notes, charts, and records from such providers.

Each parent shall notify the other parent in the event the child becomes seriously ill and requires medical attention.

Each parent shall notify the other parent in the event the child is involved in an accident.

Both parents shall have the right to telephone the child during reasonable hours when the child is at the home of the other parent.

The Divorced Parent's Visitation Rights

The divorced parent has a *right* to visit his or her child. That *right* will not be interfered with by the judge, unless it is proven that visitation would not be in the best interest of the child. However, the judge usually rules that both parents should see the child as much as possible.

If there is evidence that the noncustodial parent's actions and behavior are detrimental to the health, safety, and well-being of the child, the judge has the power to order that the noncustodial parent's visitation should be limited, supervised, or suspended.

Where visitation is limited, the noncustodial parent may have only a limited time during the month to visit his or her child.

Where visitation is supervised, the supervisor may be the other parent or another party appointed by the judge or chosen by the parties. The supervisor has to be present during the entire time that the noncustodial parent has visitation with his or her child.

Where visitation is suspended, the noncustodial parent may not have visitation with his or her child for a definite period of time or for an unspecified period of time.

The appellate court has held that "'**A divorced parent has a natural right of access to (the) child awarded to the other parent, and only under exceptional circumstances should the right or privilege be denied.' Less extreme arrangements, including limited and supervised visitation, could be instituted to satisfy the trial court's concerns...**"[5]

The story of Chara, David, Sally, and Paula

Chara and David were finally divorced after many years of fighting in court. Chara was awarded custody of their only child, Sally. David was awarded liberal visitation rights. David exercised every minute of his visitation period. After a few years, Chara and David began to have a better relationship with one another. Chara even allowed David to spend additional time with Sally. Everything was fine until David married Paula.

Paula convinced David that he needed to fight for more visitation. David talked with Chara about more visitation. Chara resented Paula's interference. After this conversation, Chara began to make excuses as to why David should not have as much access to Sally. While Chara did not violate the court's order regarding David's visitation rights, she no longer permitted David to exercise the extended visitation time that she had once allowed. Because of Paula's actions, David became bitter toward Paula, and he filed for a divorce.

The Parent's Immoral Conduct Might Warrant Limitations

The appellate court has held that **"In some instances a parent's 'immoral conduct' might warrant limitations on the contact between parent and child; but, only if it is shown that the child is exposed to the parent's undesirable conduct in such a way that it has or would likely adversely affect the child. The primary consideration in determining custody and visitation issues is not the sexual mores or behavior of the parent, but whether the child will somehow be harmed by the conduct of the parent. 'Visitation rights must be determined with reference to the needs of the child rather than sexual preferences of the parent. The best interests of the child remain paramount. Too long have courts labored under the notion that divorced parents must somehow be perfect in every respect. The law should recognize that parents, married or not, are individual human beings; each with his or her own particular virtues and vices. In domestic relations cases the courts should recognize that all parents have faults, and look not to the faults of the parents, but to needs of the child.'"**[6]

The Parent Who Is Guilty Of Family Violence May Have Visitation With Certain Stipulations

"A court may award visitation by a parent who committed one or more acts involving family violence only if the court finds that adequate provision for the safety of the child and the parent who is a victim of family violence can be made. In a visitation order, a court may:

(1) Order an exchange of a child to occur in a protected setting;

(2) Order visitation supervised by another person or agency;

(3) Order the perpetrator of family violence to attend and complete, to the satisfaction of the court, a program of intervention for perpetrators or other designated counseling as a condition of the visitation;

(4) Order the perpetrator of family violence to abstain from possession or consumption of alcohol, marijuana, or any Schedule 1 controlled substance listed in Code Section 16-13-25 during the visitation and for 24 hours preceding the visitation;

(5) Order the perpetrator of family violence to pay a fee to defray the costs of supervised visitation;

(6) Prohibit overnight visitation;

(7) Require a bond from the perpetrator of family violence for the return and safety of the child; and

> **(8) Impose any other condition that is deemed necessary to provide for the safety of the child, the victim of family violence, or another family or household member.**
>
> **If a court allows a family or household member to supervise visitation, the court shall establish conditions to be followed during visitation."[7]**

"Whether or not visitation is allowed, the court may order the address of the child and the victim of family violence to be kept confidential."[8]

"The court shall not order an adult who is a victim of family violence to attend joint counseling with the perpetrator of family violence as a condition of receiving custody of a child or as a condition of visitation."[9]

The Judge May Order The Noncustodial Parent To Post A Bond

Where there is a risk that the noncustodial parent may not return the child to the custodial parent, the judge may order the noncustodial parent to post a bond in order to guarantee the return of the child to the custodial parent at the expiration of the visitation period.

The appellate court has held that **"The bond does not prevent...leaving the state, but merely assures that...(the noncustodial parent) will comply with the terms of the court's order and return the children to Georgia at the expiration of the visitation period."**[10]

The Judge May Not Overburden The Parent Who Moves

The judge may not place a heavy burden on the custodial parent who moves to another state.

The appellate court has held that **"The trial court abused its discretion in placing such burdensome responsibilities... They not only present formidable obstacles...and severe restrictions...with respect to the expense and inconvenience of frequent travel, the opportunity to move, and the ability to secure and maintain employment, but also subject the children to a rigorous travel scheme which is likely to interfere with school and other activities."**[11]

Visitation Provision In A Settlement Agreement Must Not Be Contrary To Public Policy

The judge may not uphold a visitation provision in a settlement agreement that is contrary to the public policy of the State of Georgia.

The appellate court has held that **"The trial court improperly upheld the validity of the visitation provision which prohibited the child's contact with any African-American males. This provision is unenforceable as against public policy . 'The only authentic and admissible evidence of public policy of a State is its constitution, laws, and judicial decisions.' The visitation provision here violated the express public policy against racial classification, and the public policy encouraging a child's contact with his noncustodial parent. The visitation provision of the divorce decree sanctioned arbitrary racial classification in determining visitation rights in violation of the Equal Protection Clause of the state and federal constitutions. The trial court held that the provision was enforceable because it was a matter of private contract. However, after that private agreement was incorporated into the trial court's order, enforcing the** private agreement became state action. 'Private biases may be outside the reach of the law, but the law cannot, directly or indirectly, given them effect.' The courts of this State cannot sanction such blatant racial prejudice, especially where it also interferes with the right of a child in the parent/child relationship. The agreement between the parties clearly violated the State's public policy to promote the best interest of the child. Although a court may validly provide, under appropriate circumstances, that a child is to have no contact with particular individuals who are deemed harmful to the child, such provision cannot be based solely upon racial considerations, as such ruling violates the public policy of the State of Georgia."[12]

The Noncustodial Parent Usually Provides The Transportation

The noncustodial parent usually picks up the child for visitation and returns the child to the residence of the custodial parent when the visitation period ends. However, the parties may agree to meet half-way, meet at a designated place, or share in the transportation. The judge will usually order any arrangement agreed to by the parties so long as it is in the child's best interest.

MODIFICATION OF VISITATION

Visitation May Be Modified

"In any case in which a judgment awarding the custody of a minor has been entered, on the motion of any party or on the motion of the court, that portion of the judgment effecting visitation rights between the parties and their minor children may be subject to review and modification or alteration without the necessity of any showing of a change in any material conditions and circumstances of either party or the minor, provided that the review and modification or alteration shall not be had more often than once in each two-year period following the date of entry of the judgment."[13]

Test For Modification Of Visitation

The test for modification of visitation is based upon the best interests of the child.

The appellate court has held that **"The determination to modify visitation is governed by the best interests of the child."**[14]

The Therapist Does Not Have The Authority To Modify Visitation

The judge may not delegate to the therapist the judge's authority to modify or suspend visitation.

The appellate court has held that "'**Visitation privileges are, of course, part of custody.' It is the trial court's responsibility to determine whether the evidence is such that a modification or suspension of custody/visitation privileges is warranted, and the responsibility for making that decision cannot be delegated to another, no matter the degree of the delegatee's expertise or familiarity with the case. While the expert's opinion may serve as evidence supporting the trial court's decision to modify or suspend visitation, the decision must be made by the trial court, not the expert.**"[15]

The Child Who Is Age 14 May Cease Visitation With A Court Order

The appellate court has held that "**14-year-olds do have the right to elect not to visit with their noncustodial parents; however, to allow them to make such election without a court order would violate the previously cited statutory provisions and would permit, if not encourage, custodial parents to vent** their spite for their former mates by pressuring, directly or indirectly, the children to make such an election. The fact that a child of 14 can select his or her custodial parent, does not require the conclusion that such a child can be allowed to elect to not visit with the noncustodial parent. Just as the selection of the custodial parent is subject to the judge's determination that the parent so selected is 'a fit and proper person to have the custody of the child,' so must the modification or alteration of visitation rights established by the divorce decree or a subsequent modification or alteration thereof be done by order of the court."[16]

The appellate court has held that "Court supervision of a fourteen-year-old's decision not to visit protects the child and the noncustodial parent against any coercion by the custodial parent."[17]

Some older children may refuse to visit with the noncustodial parent. However, the appellate court has held that the judge may not put children in jail for refusing to visit with the noncustodial parent.[18]

The Judge May Not Change Custody By Modifying Visitation

The judge may not change custody under the judge's power to modify the noncustodial parent's visitation rights.

The appellate court has held that **"Since, as the trial court concluded, there was no showing of a material adverse effect on the minor child, a change of custody was not authorized. Therefore, it was error for the trial court to indirectly effect a change by modifying the visitation schedule."**[19]

The Judge May Modify Visitation Rights In A Contempt Proceeding

The appellate court has held that **"Visitation rights may now be modified on motion of either party or on motion of the trial judge in a contempt action."**[20]

AFTER THE TRIAL ISSUES

Remedies For Enforcing A Visitation Order

Visitation rights may be enforced by filing a motion to punish for contempt in the superior court that issued the order.

The appellate court has held that **"The proper administration of justice demands that courts have power to enforce their orders and decrees by contempt proceedings, and since disobedience to lawful order of court is obstruction of justice, courts may punish for contempt in order to compel respect or compliance."**[21]

The Noncustodial Parent May Not Withhold Child Support As A Method Of Enforcing Visitation Rights

The noncustodial parent may not withhold the payment of child support as a method of enforcing his or her visitation rights.

The appellate court has held that **"The trial court erred in ordering the withholding of child support payments as a method of enforcing the visitation provisions of the decree. This Court has held that the payment of support cannot be 'made contingent on allowance of visitation privileges.'"**[22]

The Custodial Parent May Not Unilaterally Decide Visitation Rights

The judge makes the final decision regarding the noncustodial parent's visitation rights. The custodial parent may not dictate the visitation rights of the noncustodial parent. The custodial parent should not allow the child to dictate the visitation rights of the noncustodial parent.

The custodial parent has a duty to encourage and promote the visitation rights of the noncustodial parent. Any attempt by the custodial parent to thwart the visitation rights of the noncustodial parent may result in a contempt action.

The appellate court has held that the judge abused his discretion where the judge ordered that the noncustodial parent was to have **"'no rights of visitation with the child except that (the noncustodial parent) may visit with the child at such times and places and on such conditions as are agreed to in writing by parties.' The trial court's order has the effect of denying (the noncustodial parent) any right to visitation..., leaving the visitation completely at the unfettered discretion of (the custodial parent)."**[23]

The Custodial Parent Who Moved To Another State Was Not In Contempt Of The Court's Order

The appellate court has held that a **"...move to another state necessarily involved some inconvenience to...exercise of...visitation rights with the child. However, there was no evidence that (the custodial parent) wilfully interfered with ...visitation or maliciously moved the child out of the state so that (the noncustodial parent) could not see her."**[24]

The Custodial Parent May Or May Not Be Found In Contempt For Denying Visitation Rights

The appellate court has held that **"To hold in contempt, the court must find that there was a willful disobedience of the court's decree or judgment. However, a change of condition 'subsequent to the making of a court order may constitute sufficient justification for disregarding such order.'"**[25]

The story of Clara, Don, and Peter

Clara and Don were divorced many years ago. In their settlement agreement, they agreed that Don would have liberal visitation rights with their son, Peter. Peter loved his father and really enjoyed the times that they spent together. Two years later, however, Don began to exhibit signs of mental illness.

At times, Don thought that he was in Vietnam, and he became violent. On one occasion, Don thought that Peter was the enemy, and Don almost wounded Peter.

When Sally learned of what had happened, she told Don that was going to stop Don's visitation with Peter, regardless of the court's order.

Don became angry, and he filed an action in court to hold Sally in contempt of the court's order. After the judge heard the evidence, Sally was not found to be in contempt of the court's order, and Don's visitation was thereafter supervised.

Instances Where Attorney's Fees May Be Awarded

The noncustodial parent may be awarded attorney's fees in order to enforce his or her visitation rights.

> **"The grant of attorney's fees as a part of the expenses of litigation, made at any time during the pendency of the litigation, whether the action is for contempt of court arising out of a divorce and alimony case, including but not limited to contempt of court orders involving child visitation rights, shall be within the sound discretion of the court."[26]**

Reviewing The Visitation Issue

Instructions

Please answer only those questions that are applicable to you.

You do not have to give written answers to these questions. In fact, you should not write your answers until you have consulted with your attorney, if you choose to employ your own attorney, and the attorney who represents your significant other about whether you should or should not write your answers.

If your significant other is already involved in litigation, or if you anticipate that he or she will be, the opposing party, or his or her attorney, *may* have the right to subpoena your written answers. Of course, you do not want to incriminate yourself, or divulge information that you do not have to disclose. Therefore, please consult with the attorney(s) before you write your answers.

QUESTIONS

Do you want your significant other to have visitation rights with his or her child instead of custody?

Please explain your answer.

Do you believe that your significant other should have visitation rights with his or her child because visitation rights would not interfere with your lifestyle?

Please explain your answer.

Do you believe that your significant other should have visitation rights with his or her child because visitation rights would not interfere with your significant other's career demands?

Please explain your answer.

Do you believe that your significant other should have visitation rights with his or her child because of the time that you and your significant other have available for his or her child?

Please explain your answer.

In addition to the visitation rights, do you want your significant other to include the following provisions in his or her settlement agreement?

a. The right to have access to all of the child's records, including school, medical, psychological, and dental records.

b. The right to discuss the child with the child's doctors, teachers, therapists, or any other person who has seen the child in a professional capacity.

c. The right to obtain a second opinion for any serious medical, dental, or other health-related matters.

d. The right to attend school functions and to participate in any of the child's extracurricular activities.

Please explain your answer.

250 DO YOU REALLY WANT TO BE A STEPPARENT?

Do you believe that your chances of having a meaningful relationship with your stepchild will be diminished because your significant other has visitation rights and not custody?

Please explain your answer.

Do you really want your significant other to be the custodial parent?

Please explain your answer.

Do you believe that your life as a couple would be adversely affected if your significant other is awarded custody?

Please explain your answer.

SUMMARY

Your sixth step toward determining whether or not you really want to be a stepparent includes your review and consideration of some of the visitation issues.

This chapter focuses on only a few of the Georgia cases and laws that deal with the visitation issues. Please discuss with your attorney, if you choose to employ an attorney, and the attorney who represents your significant other the appellate court cases and statutory laws that relate to your significant other's case.

If you decide to become a stepparent, there are many issues that you need to consider, including the likelihood that the judge will determine that it is in the best interest of your stepchild that your significant other should have visitation rights that may not suit your present lifestyle.

The purpose of this review is obvious. If you choose to become a stepparent, you should be aware of what your significant other may be legally ordered to do. That is why it is imperative that you discuss with the attorney(s) all of the pros and cons of becoming a stepparent.

The parents can discuss and decide the noncustodial parent's visitation rights. However, the judge reviews any agreement made by the parents, and the judge makes the final decision regarding the noncustodial parent's visitation rights.

The judge will not restrict the noncustodial parent's visitation rights, unless it is in the best interest of the child to do so.

As per the statute, visitation rights may be reviewed and modified at a later date.

The test for modification of visitation is based upon the best interest of the child.

Visitation rights are enforced by the judge. The noncustodial parent may file a motion to punish for contempt in the event his or her visitation rights are wrongfully withheld. The noncustodial parent may even be entitled to collect attorney's fees for having to file the motion.

Your answers to the questions that are included in this chapter may help you decide whether or not you really want to be a stepparent.

KEY TO THE CITATIONS

The terms and abbreviations used in this chapter have been explained in the previous chapter.

CITATIONS

1. O.C.G.A. Section 19-9-22(1)
2. O.C.G.A. Section 19-9-22(2)
3. O.C.G.A. Section 19-9-3(d)
4. W v. W, 261 Ga. 218, 403 S.E.2d 799 (1991)
5. C v. C, 261 Ga. 598, 409 S.E.2d 203 (1991)
6. In re R.E.W., 220 Ga.App. 861, 471 S.E.2d 6 (1996)
7. O.C.G.A. Section 19-9-7 (a) and (d)
8. O.C.G.A. Section 19-9-7 (b)
9. O.C.G.A. Section 19-9-7 (c)
10. D v. R, 235 Ga. 457, 219 S.E.2d 704 (1975)
11. K v. K, 264 Ga. 440, 445 S.E.2d 531 (1994)
12. T v. B, 235 Ga.App. 243, 510 S.E.2d 532 (1998)
13. O.C.G.A. Section 19-9-1(b)
14. H v. B, 217 Ga.App. 567, 459 S.E.2d 170 (1995)
15. W v. W, 266 Ga. 493, 467 S.E.2d 578 (1996)
16. P v. W, 253 Ga. 649, 322 S.E.2d 892 (1984)
17. W v. W, 261 Ga. 218, 403 S.E.2d 799 (1991)

18. H v. P, 242 Ga. 688, 251 S.E.2d 308 (1978)
19. M v. B, 185 Ga.App. 702, 365 S.E.2d 866 (1988)
20. B v. B, 247 Ga. 548, 277 S.E.2d 655 (1981)
21. G v. B, 239 Ga. 244, 236 S.E.2d 599 (1977)
22. L v. L, 270 Ga. 409, 509 S.E.2d 926 (1999)
23. H v. C, 261 Ga. 598, 409 S.E.2d 203 (1991)
24. H v. H, 199 Ga.App. 132, 404 S.E.2d 276 (1991)
25. B v. O, 176 Ga.App. 518, 336 S.E.2d 375 (1985)
26. O.C.G.A. Section 19-6-2(a)

CHAPTER EIGHT

THE SEVENTH STEP TOWARD DETERMINING WHETHER YOU REALLY WANT TO BE A STEPPARENT

REVIEWING SOME GEORGIA CASES AND STATUTES RELATING TO CHILD SUPPORT ISSUES

Your seventh step toward determining whether or not you really want to be a stepparent is to review some of the Georgia cases and statutory laws relating to child support issues. Whether you are from Georgia or a different state, you will want to discuss with your attorney, if you choose to employ your own attorney, and the attorney who represents your significant other those cases and laws that are applicable to your significant other's case.

Before you make your decision to become a stepparent, you should have some awareness of what your significant other may be legally required to pay as child support if he or she is not the custodial parent, or what he or she may receive as child support if he or she is the custodial parent.

1) In Georgia, the judge may order the noncustodial parent to pay to the custodial parent an amount equal to between 17% and 23% of the noncustodial parent's gross income as child support if there is one (1) child.

2) The custodial parent is entitled to claim the child as a dependent on his or her federal and state income tax returns. However, the custodial parent can voluntarily give that right to the noncustodial parent.

3) A parent may be ordered to pay child support even though he or she is awarded joint legal custody or joint physical custody.

4) A parent may have the right to file a motion to modify the amount of child support, up or down, but he or she has no right to demand a modification.

5) A parent may be required to produce his or her tax returns, bank statements, statements from brokerage houses, 1099's, W-2's, and all other records that evidence his or her income, assets, and liabilities.

6) A parent may be ordered to maintain health and life insurance for the benefit of his or her child.

7) A parent may be ordered to pay more child support as his or her gross income increases.

8) A parent's property may be awarded as part of child support.

9) A parent may be ordered to pay more child support if his or her spouse contributes to the parent's living expenses even though the parent's income has not increased.

10) A parent may be ordered to pay the same amount of child support even though he or she is subsequently awarded more visitation rights or is awarded custody of one of the children.

You have to decide whether you can accept the possibility that these conditions may be imposed upon your significant other before you decide whether you really want to be a stepparent.

This chapter includes a few of the appellate court cases and statutory laws of Georgia that deal with the child support issues. Readers from states other than Georgia can utilize the book as a guide and then seek the advice of their local attorneys regarding the specific cases and statutory laws that apply to their significant other's case. This book is not intended to be a course in child support law nor is it meant to be a substitute for seeking legal advice from an attorney.

In addition to the issues that are discussed in this chapter, there may be other issues and laws that are important to your significant other's case. Every case is unique because of its particular facts and circumstances. Therefore, the courts consider each case differently. Please make sure to discuss all of the issues and laws with the attorney(s) before you make any final decisions.

In this chapter, the statutory laws are included as single-spaced text and in bold type, and the decisions of the appellate courts are in bold type. The citations for both the statutory laws and the decisions of the appellate courts are at the end of the chapter. Please note that since the writing of this book, the statutory laws that are quoted may have been modified by subsequent acts of the legislature. Likewise, the appellate courts may have reversed previous decisions. Therefore, the laws and rulings cited in this book may be totally different at the time you are reading this book. That is why I emphasize that you must rely only on the attorney(s) for legal advice.

This chapter is divided into three sections.

- *Before The Trial Issues* are some of the issues that you and your significant other may want to consider before there is the trial of the case.

- *During The Trial Issues* are some of the issues that may be addressed during the trial of the case.

- *After The Trial Issues* are some of the issues that you and your significant other may or may not encounter later.

The story of April, Albert, and James

April, an unmarried, middle-aged woman met Albert, an executive with a major corporation. Albert had been previously married, and had one twelve-year-old child, James, who lived with his mother. Albert had an income of $75,000 per year. April was a school teacher, and had an income of approximately $30,000 per year. Albert and April found that they had everything in common, except that she had no children. They decided to get married. April was very happy because she thought that she had someone who could provide her with a lifestyle that she had always wanted. However, April did not count on Albert's substantial child support obligations. Albert had been court-ordered to pay the sum of $1,250 per month as child support. He was also ordered to provide medical insurance and to pay all of the uncovered medical, dental, and hospital expenses for James. He was also ordered to provide life insurance. Albert's total child support obligations were approximately $1,900 per month, for a total of $22,800 per year. Moreover, the amount that Albert paid as child support was not deductible by him on his income tax returns. Albert had approximately $2,200 per month left to pay his own expenses. Albert's car payment alone was $400 per month. Unfortunately, April had not calculated Albert's child support obligations when she agreed to marry him.

In addition, April had to take care of James when he came over for visitation, including washing and ironing his clothes and buying him his food. April was not a happy camper.

April quickly realized that Albert was not financially able to provide her with a luxurious lifestyle. She told Albert that love was not enough. She also told him that she was filing for a divorce.

James really liked April, and he felt sad because he thought that he was the cause of their divorce.

BEFORE THE TRIAL ISSUES

Definitions Of Some Terms:

Age Of Majority
"The age of legal majority in this state is 18 years; until that age all persons are minors."[1]

Child Support Obligee
"Child support obligee means an individual to whom the payment of a child support obligation is owed and includes a custodial parent or caretaker of a child to whom such support obligation is to be paid or a governmental agency entitled by law to enforce a child support obligation on behalf of such parent, caretaker, or child."[2]

Child Support Obligor
"Child support obligor means an individual owing a duty of support to a child or children, whether or not such duty is evinced by a judgment, order, or decree."[3]

Child Support Order
"Child support order means a judgment, decree, or order of a court or authorized administrative agency requiring the payment of child support in periodic amounts or in a lump sum and includes (A) a permanent or temporary order and (B) an initial order or a modification of an order."[4]

Emancipation

"Emancipation of a child is the relinquishment by parent of control and authority over child, conferring on him the right to his earnings and terminating parent's legal duty to support child. A child can be emancipated by acts of either the parent or the child. Marriage, with or without the consent of the parents, emancipates the child."[5]

Modification Of A Child Support Order

"Modification means a change in a child support order that affects the amount, scope, or duration of the order and modifies, replaces, supersedes, or otherwise is made subsequent to a child support order or foreign child support order."[6]

State's Policy Regarding Child Support

The appellate court has held that **"The public policy of this state is to require parents to provide adequate support for their children."**[7]

The Parent's Obligation To Support The Child

The appellate court has held that **"Prior to the revision of our domestic-relations laws in the wake of the landmark United States Supreme Court decision in Orr v. Orr (1979), OCGA Section 19-7-2 made it the duty of the father only to provide for the support of the children until majority. At** present, the effect of Section 19-7-2 is two-fold: First, it codifies the basic, legal principle now making it the joint and several duty of each parent to provide child support until the child reaches the age of majority; second, it authorizes this joint and several duty to be altered 'to the extent that the duty of one parent is otherwise or further defined by court order.'"[8]

> "It is the joint and several duty of each parent to provide for the maintenance, protection, and education of his or her child until the child reaches the age of majority, dies, marries, or becomes emancipated, whichever first occurs, except as otherwise authorized and ordered pursuant to subsection (e) of Code Section 19-6-15 and except to the extent that the duty of the parents is otherwise or further defined by court order."[9]

Child Support Belongs To The Child

The appellate court has held that "The right to bring an original action to recover child support payments, as well as the right to institute a modification action, are rights belonging to the child or children and are not waivable by the custodial parent."[10]

Controlling Factors To Be Applied

The appellate court has held that **"The necessities of the children and the Husband's ability to pay are the controlling factors."**[11]

The appellate court has held that **"Regardless of the cause of the separation between the parents, their children are entitled to be supported during their minority commensurate with their proven customary needs and the father's financial ability to provide for them. These needs are collectively referred to as necessaries and include all material and educational expenses shown to be appropriate to the children's situation and needs in their experience as a part of the family of their parents and not merely funds for those needs regarded as the minimum requisites of a bare subsistence."**[12]

Please note that the appellate court cases that are cited here refer to the husband's ability or the father's ability because these cases were decided prior to the enactment of legislation that changed the law.

The parent may be required to pay the child's extraordinary expenses, such as private school or therapy.

The appellate court has held that **"'Children are entitled to be support by the father...commensurate with their proven custody needs and the father's ability to provide for them.'A father cannot provide a bare subsistence existence for his children and consider that he has done his duty. His support, as far as he is able, must be appropriate to the children's situation."**[13]

The Judge Has The Authority To Approve Or Not Approve The Parents' Agreement As To The Amount Of Child Support

The parties may always decide the amount of child support. However, the judge has the authority to approve or not approve the child support provision in the parties' agreement. The judge may decide that the amount of child support does not meet the needs of the child, or the amount of child support is not within the child support guidelines.

The appellate court has held that **"Where the parties have resolved collateral issues in divorce litigation and, thereby, have presented a settlement agreement to be incorporated into the final divorce decree, the trial court is not bound by** the agreement, particularly with respect to custody of, and support for, minor children. Thus, in reviewing a settlement agreement, the trial judge should determine whether the child support payments established therein are commensurate with the customary needs of the children, as limited by the financial ability of the payor parent. Where the child-support-payment amounts do not conform to the foregoing parameters, although the agreed-upon child support is adequate to meet the subsistence needs of the children and keep them from becoming deprived, the trial judge acts well within his discretion in refusing to approve the agreement."[14]

The story of Betty, Paul, and Jane

Betty and Paul decided to have an amicable divorce, and they wanted to settle all of the issues of custody, visitation, child support, property, and debts. They really did not have that many assets, and they only had a few debts. They worked very hard to reach an agreement that was fair to both of them. Betty and Paul decided that they would equally share custody of their son, **Andy**. Andy would spend half of the year with Betty and half of the year with **Paul**, and neither parent would pay child support to the other. Betty and Paul earned approximately the same amount of money per year. Their attorneys drew up the agreement and Betty and Paul signed the agreement.

Paul was very happy about the agreement since he had promised Jane, his girlfriend, that he would not have to pay child support. Jane and Paul were counting on using all of Paul's income for their own expenses when they got married.

Betty and Paul and their attorneys went to the courthouse to have the judge review and approve their agreement. All four of them went into the judge's chambers. The judge looked at the agreement and said that because there was no provision for the payment of child support, he could not approve the agreement. Betty and Paul were astonished that the judge would not approve their agreement. The attorneys just shook their heads as they thanked the judge and left the judge's chambers.

Because they knew that they had to comply with the judge's order, Betty and Paul were forced to put into the agreement an amount of child support that Paul had to pay Betty. Betty and Paul were not happy with this child support provision.

Morever, Jane was disappointed when Paul told her the news. She told Paul that maybe they ought to wait to get married.

DURING THE TRIAL ISSUES

Child Support Guidelines Statute

The judge or the jury must consider the child support guidelines in determining the amount of child support, but the trier of fact may vary the amount. The statute provides that "The trier of fact shall vary the final award of child support, up or down,...upon a written finding that the presence of one or more of the following special circumstances makes the presumptive amount of support either excessive or inadequate."

The following is the child support guidelines statute. I have italicized those parts of the statute that I believe are of particular significance.

> "(a) In the final verdict or decree, *the trier of fact shall specify in what amount and from which party the minor children are entitled to permanent support.* The final verdict or decree shall further specify as required by Code Section 19-5-12 *in what manner, how often, to whom, and until when the support shall be paid.* The final verdict or decree shall further include *a written finding of the gross income of the father and the mother and the presence or absence of special circumstances* in accordance with subsection (c) of this Code section. The trier of fact must also determine *whether the accident and sickness insurance for the child or the children involved is reasonably available at reasonable costs*

through employment related or other group health insurance policies to an obligor. For purposes of this Code section, accident and sickness coverage shall be deemed available if the obligor has access to any policy of insurance authorized under Title 33 through an employer or other group health insurance plan. *If the accident and sickness insurance is deemed available at reasonable cost, the court shall order the obligor to obtain the coverage*; provided, however, *if the obligee has accident and sickness insurance for the child or children reasonably available at reasonable costs through employment related or other group health insurance policies, then the court may order that the child or children be covered under such insurance and the obligor contribute as part of the child support order such part of the cost of providing such insurance or such part of any medical expenses incurred on behalf of the child or children not covered by such insurance as the court may deem equitable or appropriate. If currently unavailable or unreasonable in cost, the court shall order the obligor to obtain coverage when it becomes available at a reasonable cost, unless such insurance is provided by the obligee as provided in this subsection.* When support is awarded, the party who is required to pay the support shall not be liable to third persons for necessaries furnished to the children embraced in the verdict or decree. In any contested case, the parties shall submit to the court their proposed findings regarding the gross income of the father and the mother and the presence or absence of special circumstances. *In any case in which child support is determined by a jury, the court*

shall charge the provisions of this Code section and the jury shall be required to return a special interrogatory similar to the form of the order contained in Code section 19-5-12 regarding the gross income of the father and the mother and the presence or absence of special circumstances. Furthermore, *nothing contained within this Code section shall prevent the parties from entering into an enforceable agreement to the contrary which may be made the order of the court pursuant to the review by the court of child support amounts contained in this Code section; provided, however, any such agreement of the parties shall include a written statement regarding the gross income of the father and the mother and the presence or absence of special circumstances* in accordance with subsection (c) of this Code section.
(b) The child support award shall be computed as provided in this subsection:

(1) *Computation of child support shall be based upon gross income;*
(2) For the purpose of determining the obligor's child support obligation, *gross income shall include 100 percent of wage and salary income and other compensation for personal services, interest, dividends, net rental income, self-employment income, and all other income, except need-based public assistance;*
(3) *The earning capacity of an asset of a party available for child support may be used in determining gross income.* The reasonable earning potential of an asset may be determined by multiplying its equity by a reasonable rate of

interest. The amount generated by that calculation should be added to the obligor's gross monthly income;
(4) *Allowable expenses deducted to calculate self-employment income that personally benefit the obligor, or economic in-kind benefits received by an employed obligor, may be included in calculating the obligor's gross monthly income;* and
(5) *The amount of the obligor's child support* obligation shall be *determined by multiplying the obligor's gross income per pay period by a percentage based on the number of children for whom child support is being determined.*

The applicable percentages of gross income to be considered by the trier of fact are:

Number of Children	Percentage Range of Gross Income
1	17 percent to 23 percent
2	23 percent to 28 percent
3	25 percent to 32 percent
4	29 percent to 35 percent
5 or more	31 percent to 37 percent

Application of these guidelines shall create a rebuttable presumption that the amount of the support awarded is the correct amount of support to be awarded. A written finding or specific finding on the record for the award of child support that the application of the guidelines would be unjust or inappropriate in a particular case shall be sufficient to rebut the presumption in that case. Findings that rebut said presumption must state the amount of support that would have been required under the guidelines and include justification of why the order varies from the guidelines. *These guidelines are intended by the General Assembly to be guidelines only and any court so applying these guidelines shall not abrogate its responsibility in making the final determination of child support based on the evidence presented to it at the time of trial.*

(c) *The trier of fact shall vary the final award of child support, up or down,* **from the range enumerated in paragraph (5) of subsection (b) of this Code section** *upon a written finding that the presence of one or more of the following special circumstances makes the presumptive amount of support either excessive or inadequate*:

(1) Ages of the children;

(2) A child's extraordinary medical costs or needs, in addition to accident and sickness insurance, provided that all such costs or needs shall be considered if no insurance is available;

(3) Educational costs;

(4) Day-care costs;

(5) Shared physical custody arrangements, including extended visitation;

(6) A party's other support obligations to another household;

(7) Income that should be imputed to a party because of suppression of income;

(8) In-kind income for the self-employed, such as reimbursed meals or a company car;

(9) Other support a party is providing or will be providing, such as payment of a mortgage;

(10) A party's own extraordinary needs, such as medical expenses;
(11) Extreme economic circumstances, including but not limited to:
- (A) Unusual high debt structure; or
- (B) Unusually high income of either party or both parties, which shall be construed as individual gross income of over $75,000.00 per annum;

(12) Historical spending in the family for children which varies significantly from the percentage table;
(13) Considerations of the economic cost-of-living factors of the community of each party, as determined by the trier of fact;
(14) In-kind contribution of either parent;
(15) The income of the custodial parent;
(16) The cost of accident and sickness insurance coverage for dependent children included in the order;
(17) Extraordinary travel expenses to exercise visitation or shared physical custody; and
(18) Any other factor which the trier of fact deems to be required by the ends of justice.

(d) The guidelines shall be reviewed by a commission appointed by the Governor to ensure that their application results in the determination of appropriate child support award amounts. The commission will complete its review and submit its report within four years following July 1, 1989, and shall continue such reviews every four years thereafter. Nothing contained in such report shall be considered to authorize or require a change in the guidelines without action by the General Assembly having the force and effect of law.

(e) *The duty to provide support for a minor child shall continue until the child reaches the age of majority, dies, marries, or becomes emancipated, whichever first occurs; provided, however, that, in any temporary or final order for child support with respect to any proceeding for divorce, separate maintenance, legitimacy, or paternity entered on or after July 1, 1992, the trier of fact, in the exercise of sound discretion, may direct either or both parents to provide financial assistance to a child who has not previously married or become emancipated, who is enrolled in and attending a secondary school, and who has attained the age of majority before completing his or her secondary school education, provided that such financial assistance shall not be required after a child attains 20 years of age. The provisions for support provided in this subsection may be enforced by either parent or the child for whose benefit the support is ordered.*

(f) The provisions of subsection (e) of this Code section shall be applicable only to a temporary order or final decree for divorce, separate maintenance, legitimation, or paternity entered on or after July 1, 1992, and *the same shall be applicable to an action for modification of a decree entered in such an action entered on or after July 1, 1992, only upon a showing of a significant change of material circumstances.*"[15]

Guidelines Statute Offers A Computational Reference

The appellate court has held that **"Under the terms of the statute, the finder of fact is free to apply the guidelines, or to fix child support on the basis of appropriate factors other than those reflected in the guidelines. The judge's duty is to allocate resources based upon need and ability to pay. That duty is unchanged by the new statute. At the most, the statute offers a computational reference, which the finder of fact may apply if it chooses."**[16]

Initial Percentage Is Based On Number Of Children For Whom The Trier Of Fact Is Determining Support

The child support guidelines statute requires that "the guideline calculation be based only on the number of children for whom the child support is being determined."

The appellate court has held that "'**The guideline percentage of child support...cannot be based upon the total number of children the obligor must support.' The statute requires that the guideline calculation be based only on the number of children for whom the child support is being determined. Once the guideline percentage is determined, the trial court may vary the range upon a written finding that the presence of one or more enumerated special circumstances makes the presumptive amount of support excessive or inadequate. One of the enumerated circumstances is a party's support obligations to another household. The mere fact of additional children, however, will not justify a reduction in the guideline range. The essential question is whether this additional support obligation renders the presumptive amount of support excessive. The trial court may answer this question only be examining all the relevant circumstances** including the sources of support for the new household. By considering not only the fact of additional children, but also the circumstances relevant to the support needs of those children, the trial court will be able to make a determination of support that best balances the children's needs and the parent's ability to pay."[17]

The Parties, Judge, Or Jury May Vary The Amount Of Child Support

The parties, judge, or jury may vary the amount of child support called for in the guidelines.

> "(a) Nothing contained with this Code section shall prevent the parties from entering into an enforceable agreement to the contrary which may be made the order of the court pursuant to the review by the court of child support amounts contained in this Code section; provided, however, any such agreement of the parties shall include a written statement regarding the gross income of the father and the mother and the presence or absence of special circumstances in accordance with this Code section.
> (c) The trier of fact shall vary the final award of child support, up or down, from the range enumerated in this Code section upon a written finding that the presence of one or more of the following special circumstances makes the presumptive amount of support either excessive or inadequate."[18]

Calculating The Amount Of Child Support

1) Payment Of Medical Premiums

The cost of the medical insurance premium is not to be considered in the initial calculation. However, once the amount of child support is determined, the judge or the jury may deduct the amount of the premium from the amount of child support.

The appellate court has held that **"Once the child support award is determined pursuant to the formula set forth in O.C.G.A. Section 19-6-15(b), the trier of fact can then vary the 'final award,' upon a consideration of 'any factor which (it) deems to be required by the ends of justice.' A list of the factors warranting such variations is set forth in OCGA Section 19-6-15(c). It includes 'medical costs,' 'educational costs,' 'extended visitation,' and, pursuant to the 1994 amendment to the statute, 'accident and sickness insurance coverage.' The trier of fact can give consideration to indirect costs paid by the obligor, e.g., health insurance premiums, in departing from the guidelines. Indirect payments can be considered only to 'vary the final award of child support...'"**[19]

2) *The Obligor's Other Child Support Obligations*

After the initial guideline calculation is made, the judge or the jury may consider the obligor's other child support obligations.

The appellate court has held that **"In determining the final child support award, the trier of fact can consider an obligor's 'other support obligations to another household.' Thus, the existence of other children may be considered in calculating the level of support. But, this is not to say that the initial guideline calculation is to be made on the basis of 'other support obligations.' On the contrary, the guideline calculation is to be 'based on the number of children for whom child support is being determined.' After that calculation is made, the final award can be adjusted on the basis of other children to whom the obligor owes support."**[20]

3) *Gross Income Of The Recipient*

Where there is a change in custody, the amount of child support that was received by the obligee should not be included in his or her gross income for the purpose of calculating his or her child support obligation.[21]

4) *Joint Legal Custody*

Being awarded joint legal custody does not automatically mean that the parent will not have to pay child support.

The appellate court has held that **"A parent may be required to support a child, notwithstanding the existence of 'joint legal custody,' as defined in OCGA Section 19-9-6."**[22]

5) *Social Security Benefits*

Under certain circumstances, social security disability payments paid for the benefit of the child may be credited toward the amount of child support.

The appellate court has held that **"It is well established that under certain circumstances, social security disability payments paid for the benefit of a child can be credited toward the court-ordered support obligation of the person from whose account they are paid. A survey of these cases reveal that the issue has been decided in the context of a disability that arises subsequent to the time the support obligation begins."**[23]

282 DO YOU REALLY WANT TO BE A STEPPARENT?

The Judge Or Jury May Not Ignore The Evidence Regarding The Obligor's Gross Income

The judge or the jury may not ignore the evidence presented at trial and find a different gross amount of income.

The appellate court has held that **"The Child Support Guidelines laid down in OCGA Section 19-6-15(b) and (c) are mandatory and must be considered by any trier of fact setting the amount of child support. Application of the guidelines creates a rebuttable presumption that the amount of support calculated within the correct percentages...is the correct amount of support, OCGA Section 19-6-15(b)(5), and deviation from the percentages requires a written finding of special circumstances. The jury in this case found no special circumstances existed to vary the amount of child support under the guidelines. The record in this case establishes that the jury failed to calculate correctly the gross income..."**[24]

The Obligor May Be Ordered To Obtain Health Insurance

"The trier of fact must also determine whether the accident and sickness insurance for the child or the children involved is reasonably available at reasonable costs through employment related or other group health insurance policies to an obligor. For purposes of this Code section, accident and sickness coverage shall be deemed available if the obligor has access to any policy of insurance authorized under Title 33 through an employer or other group health insurance plan. If the accident and sickness insurance is deemed available at reasonable cost, the court shall order the obligor to obtain the coverage; provided, however, if the obligee has accident and sickness insurance for the child or children reasonably available at reasonable costs through employment related or other group health insurance policies, then the court may order that the child or children be covered under such insurance and the obligor contribute as part of the child support order such part of the cost of providing such insurance or such part of any medical expenses incurred on behalf of the child or children not covered by such insurance as the court may deem equitable or appropriate. If currently unavailable or unreasonable in cost, the court shall order the obligor to obtain coverage when it becomes available at a reasonable cost, unless such insurance is provided by the obligee as provided in this subsection."[25]

The Parent May Be Ordered To Pay Medical And Dental Expenses

The parent may be ordered to pay the child's medical and dental expenses.

The term *medical bills* and *doctor bills* includes dentist bills and bills for the child's optical needs, such as eye-glasses.

The appellate court has held that **"The statute is expressive of the public policy that every child should have the right to receive at the hands of parents such health services as reasonably shall be required to maintain the child in good physical and mental health, and as reasonably shall be required to correct or ameliorate any dysfunction of mind or body. Accordingly, the term 'medical bills' is construed to include those reasonable charges of professionals in generally recognized fields of health care that reasonably are required to maintain this child in good health, and to correct or alleviate any physical or mental dysfunction. That includes, obviously, the reasonable cost of services reasonably required for the child's dental health, and the reasonable costs of providing corrective devices, such as eye-glasses, as reasonably shall be required by the child's optical needs."**[26]

The term *medical expenses* does include the fees charged by a psychologist who rendered the service in a psychiatric hospital under the direction of a psychiatrist.[27]

The term *dental expenses* has been held to include orthodontic expenses.[28]

The Parent May Be Ordered To Obtain Life Insurance

Either parent or both parents may be ordered to obtain and maintain life insurance for the benefit of the child.

> **"(a) In any case before the court involving child support the court may include in the order of support provision for life insurance on the life of either parent or the lives of both parents for the benefit of the minor children. The court may order either parent or both parents to obtain and maintain the life insurance.**
> **(b) The amount of the premium for such life insurance shall be counted as a part of the support ordered, provided that the court shall review the amount of the premium for reasonableness in the circumstances of the child, the parent ordered to pay support, and the other parent.**
> **(c) An order for child support shall not require maintenance of life insurance for a child's benefit after the child reaches the age of majority and shall not require that the proceeds of life insurance be available for the benefit of a child after the child reaches the age of majority.**

**(d) The trier of fact may direct either or both parents to maintain life insurance for the benefit of a child who has not previously married or become emancipated, who is enrolled in and attending a secondary school, and who has attained the age of majority before completing his or her secondary school education, provided that maintenance of such life insurance for the benefit of the child shall not be required after a child attains 20 years of age.
(e) Nothing shall prevent parents from entering into an agreement for the provision of life insurance that differs from or exceeds the terms of this Code section."**[29]

Child Support May Be Increased As The Obligor's Gross Income Increases

The judge may order that the amount of child support is to be reviewed annually and increased if the obligor's annual gross income increases.

The appellate court has held that **"Such an adjustment provision does not preclude either party from seeking modification. We conclude that the future-modification provision of the trial court's order is proper."**[30]

How Child Support Is Paid

The amount of child support may be paid in periodic payments, such as monthly, or in a lump sum that is paid in one payment or in installments.

The appellate court has held that the trier of fact may determine how child support is to be paid. The court has held that **"The amount found may be in a lump sum which they (the jury) may provide shall be paid at once or in installments."**[31]

The Judge Or Jury May Award The Use Of Property As Part Of Child Support

The judge or the jury may order the obligor to provide a home for the use and benefit of the child until the child reaches the age of majority.

The appellate court has held that **"The provision in both the jury verdict and the final judgment requiring (obligor) to provide a home for his children is in the nature of child support."**[32]

After the child has reached the age of majority, the property must revert back to the obligor.

The appellate court has held that **"'A divorce court can not award any part of the father's property to his children.**

He is not required to settle an estate upon them.' However, the father is responsible for the support of his minor children. Construing this trust provision with the other child support provision, we conclude that the trust property is to be used for the 'use, benefit, education and support of the child' until he becomes 18 years of age. The court has no authority to give the trust corpus to the children after they have reached majority and the uses have terminated. Therefore, by implication, the trust corpus here reverts to the husband."[33]

The Obligor's Voluntary Expenditures May Not Be Taken As A Credit Toward Child Support

The parent may not deduct from his or her child support any voluntary expenditures.

The appellate court has held that **"The father is not entitled to credit on his child support obligation under the decree for any voluntary payments directly to the child or for items of food, clothing, etc. which he may have given to him. In other states having similar statutes it has been held that the purchase of toys, bicycles, clothes, and other gifts to the child do not amount to support within the requirements of the decree of the court."[34]**

Payment Of Child Support Is Not Contingent On Visitation

The noncustodial parent who is being denied his or her visitation rights by the custodial parent must obey the court's child support order.

Some noncustodial parents feel that it is not fair that they are forced to pay guideline child support to the custodial parent who is depriving them of their visitation rights.

The appellate court has held that **"This court, recognizing that other states are divided on the question, held as a matter of first impression in this state that child-visitation rights should not be made contingent on payment of child support, and, conversely, payment of support should not be made contingent on allowance of visitation privileges."**[35]

The Parent's Obligation To Pay The College Expenses

Neither parent is legally obligated to pay the college expenses of the child.[36]

The story of Mark, Lillian, Dee, and Olivia

Mark and Lillian were divorced many years ago. They had one child, Dee, who was five years old when Mark and Lillian divorced. Mark worked almost every day, and he had been earning a sizeable amount of money each year. At the time of their divorce, Lillian insisted that Mark pay for Dee's college expenses. Mark willingly agreed to do so since he was sure that he could afford it when the time came. Their settlement agreement provided that Mark had to pay Dee's college expenses, including room, board, books, tuition, and all other related expenses.

When Dee graduated from high school, she interviewed many colleges, including some very expensive ones. Because there was no restriction in the settlement agreement as to which college Dee could choose, she chose the most expensive college and notified Mark of his obligation to her.

At this time, Mark was married to Olivia, and they had two children. Mark had lost most of his money in the stock market. He told Dee that he could not afford to pay for her college expenses, especially when she chose the most expensive college. Olivia was very concerned about their finances since they were just barely making ends meet as it was.

Dee told Mark that his situation was his problem, not hers. She told Mark that if he did not pay her college expenses, she would sue him. He told her to do just that. Dee hired an attorney and sued Mark. The judge enforced the college provision in the settlement agreement, and Mark had to pay.

The Judge May Not Award The Dependency Exemption

The appellate court has held that **"The Sixteenth Amendment to the United States Constitution provides that only Congress has the power to impose a tax on income. 'Custodial parent gets exemption.' This subsection grants custodial parents, with earned income, a reduction in income tax liability. One of the exceptions within the statute allows a custodial parent to release the exemption. All the state courts that have considered the issue have agreed that the exemption belongs to the custodial parent, unless that parent signs the release. If a state forcibly takes the tax exemption from a custodial parent, with earned income, that parent's income becomes subject to unauthorized tax liability. The state would be exerting the power of taxation, and that power 'is not subject to state control.' Congress has declared that the exemption belongs to the custodial parent and Georgia will not endeavor to frustrate the 'specific statutory language.'"**[37]

Duration Of The Child Support Obligation

"**The duty to provide support for a minor child shall continue until the child reaches the age of majority, dies, marries, or becomes emancipated, whichever first occurs; provided, however, that, in any temporary or final order for child support with respect to any proceeding for divorce, separate maintenance, legitimacy, or paternity entered on or after July 1, 1992, the trier of fact, in the exercise of sound discretion, may direct either or both parents to provide financial assistance to a child who has not previously married or become emancipated, who is enrolled in and attending a secondary school, and who has attained the age of majority before completing his or her secondary school education, provided that such financial assistance shall not be required after a child attains 20 years of age. The provisions for support provided in this subsection may be enforced by either parent or the child for whose benefit the support is ordered.**"[38]

Death Of The Obligor Terminates The Child Support Obligation

The legal obligation to pay child support terminates upon the death of the obligated parent.

The appellate court has held that "**Generally, the duty of a father to support his children ceases upon his death, and the duty then devolves upon another, usually the mother, during the minority of the children. The law does not require that a**

father provide for the support of his children after his death. A father is not required by law to create an estate for his minor children."[39]

Provisions In Child Support Orders

There are three provisions that may be included in child support orders.

One provision is the continuing garnishment provision that provides that if the amount of the unpaid child support is equal to or greater than the amount that is due for one month, the payments may be collected by the process of continuing garnishment.

> **"(a) Any order of support of a child entered or modified on or after July 1, 1985, shall contain the following provision:**
> **'Whenever, in violation of the terms of this order there shall have been a failure to make the support payments due hereunder so that the amount unpaid is equal to or greater than the amount payable for one month, the payments required to be made may be collected by the process of continuing garnishment for support.'**
> **(b) Any order of support entered or modified prior to July 1, 1985, shall be construed as a matter of law to contain the provision set forth in subsection (a) of this Code section."**[40]

The second provision is the income deduction order that provides that part of the obligor's wages is to be withheld for the payment of child support.

> "(a)(1) Upon the entry of a judgment or order establishing, enforcing, or modifying a child support obligation through a court or an administrative process, a separate order for income deduction, if one has not been previously entered, shall be entered.
> (a.1)(1) All child support orders which are initially issued in this state on or after January 1, 1994, shall provide for the immediate withholding of such support from the income and earnings of the person required by that order to furnish support unless:
>> (A) The court issuing the order finds there is good cause not to require such immediate withholding; or
>> (B) A written agreement is reached between both parties which provides for an alternative arrangement.
>
> For purposes of this paragraph, any finding that there is good cause not to require withholding must be based on at least a written determination that implementing wage withholding would not be in the best interest of the child and proof of timely payment of previously ordered support in cases involving modification of support orders."[41]

The third provision provides for the deduction of an amount necessary to pay the accident and sickness insurance premiums.

> **"(a) In any case before the court involving child support, the court may inquire into the availability of accident and sickness insurance coverage to any person obligated to support and, if such coverage is reasonably available, may include in the order of support provision for such coverage.**
> **(b) Any order of support of a child entered or modified on or after July 1, 1992, which includes provision for accident and sickness insurance may include a provision for payroll deduction of an amount which is sufficient to provide for the payment of premiums of such accident and sickness insurance."[42]**

MODIFICATION OF CHILD SUPPORT

Child Support May Be Modified Under Certain Circumstances

"The judgment of a court providing permanent alimony for the support of a child or children rendered on or after July 1, 1977, shall be subject to revision upon petition filed by either former spouse showing a change in the income and financial status of either former spouse or in the needs of the child or children. No petition may be filed by either former spouse under this subsection within a period of two years from the date of the final order on a previous petition by the same former spouse. After hearing both parties and the evidence, the jury, or the judge where a jury is not demanded by either party, may modify and revise the previous judgment in accordance with the changed income and financial status of either former spouse or in the needs of the child or children in the case of permanent alimony for the support of a child or children, if such a change in the income and financial status is satisfactorily proved so as to warrant the modification and revision. In the hearing upon a petition filed as provided in this subsection, testimony may be given and evidence introduced relative to the income and financial status of either former spouse."[43]

The Petitioner Has The Burden Of Proof

The petitioner has the burden to prove his or her case by a preponderance of the evidence.

The appellate court has held that **"We think it is implicit in the statute that the petitioner must 'satisfactorily prove' his or her case by a preponderance of the evidence."**[44]

Income And Financial Status Of The Defendant Is Admissible

The petitioner may introduce evidence during the modification trial that proves that the other party's income and financial status have increased.

> **"In the hearing upon a petition filed as provided in this subsection, testimony may be given and evidence introduced relative to the income and financial status of either former spouse."**[45]

Definition Of "Substantial Change"

What constitutes a substantial change in income and financial status to authorize a modification is a fact question.

The appellate court has held that **"It cannot be held as a matter of law that an increase of 10%...in...hourly wages is not a substantial change so as to authorize a change in support payments."**[46]

Child Support Guidelines Do Not Constitute Substantial Change

The appellate court has held that **"The Guidelines do not alter the 'trial court's duty...to allocate resources based upon need and ability to pay.' In an action to modify child support, the 'computational reference' of Section 19-6-15(b) (the guidelines statute) may be applied only after the finder of fact first finds that the requirements of Section 19-6-19(a) (the modification statute) have been satisfied. Accordingly, the trial court in this case erred by determining that the enactment of the guidelines alone was sufficient to justify modifying support obligation without any threshold showing of a substantial change in financial circumstances."**[47]

Child Support Guidelines Apply To Modification Actions

The child support guidelines apply to child support modification actions, even though the divorce decree was entered prior to the effective date of the guidelines statute.

The appellate court has held that the judge was correct in his decision. The court has held that **"We applied the child-support guidelines to a modification action and ruled that the guidelines could be applied retroactively."**[48]

The Judge May Grant A Temporary Modification Of Child Support

> "The court in its discretion may allow, upon motion, the temporary modification of such a judgment, pending the final trial on the petition. In considering an application for temporary modification, the court shall consider evidence of any changed circumstances of the parties and the reasonable probability of the petitioner obtaining revision upon final trial. The order granting temporary modification shall be subject to revision by the court at any time before final trial."[49]

There Is No Absolute Right To A Modification

The appellate court has held that **"OCGA Section 19-6-19 provides that the judge (or jury) 'may modify and revise the previous judgment...if such a change in the income and financial status is satisfactorily proved...' 'A change in the father's income or financial status does not mandate a revision in child support; the statute merely permits such revision.' 'The final decision of whether to modify the award is within the discretion of the trier of fact.'"[50]

The Judge May Not Modify Post-Majority Child Support Unless The Parties Authorize The Judge To Do So

The parties may agree to pay post-majority support. However, the judge has no authority to modify post-majority support unless the parties provide in their settlement agreement that this obligation may be modified by the court.

The appellate court has held that **"A court has no power to modify post-majority child support obligations because the court's power during modification proceedings could not be greater than its power during the original alimony proceedings and that no such power exists in the original proceedings. We hold that parties may alter the effect of the rule against involuntary modification of post-majority child support by their voluntary contract."**[51]

The Obligee May Never Waive The Right To Seek A Modification

The appellate court has held that **"Under our existing case law, the right to bring an original action to recover child support payments, as well as the right to institute a modification action, are rights belonging to the child or children and are not waivable by the custodial parent."**[52]

The Obligor May Waive The Right To Seek A Modification

The obligor may waive his or her right to modify the amount of child support, but the waiver must be expressed in clear and unambiguous language in the agreement.

The appellate court has held that **"An obligor parent may waive his or her right to seek a reduction of periodic child support payments. This court announced that parties to an alimony agreement may obtain modification unless the agreement expressly waives the right of modification by referring specifically to that right in very clear waiver language."**[53]

302 DO YOU REALLY WANT TO BE A STEPPARENT?

Modification Agreement Entered Into By The Parties Is Not Enforceable If It Is Not Approved By The Judge

The parties' agreement to modify the amount of child support must be reviewed and approved by the judge in order to make the agreement enforceable.

The appellate court has held that **"A modification action is the exclusive remedy for obtaining a provision supplementing the child support award contained in a divorce judgment. While parties may enter into an agreement concerning modification of child support, the agreement becomes an enforceable agreement only when made the order of the court. Before a private agreement which includes child support may be incorporated into a court order, the trial court has an obligation to consider whether the agreed-upon support is sufficient based on the child's needs and the parent's ability to pay. In addition, the child-support guidelines are applicable to a modification action. The trial court must review the agreement in light of the child support amounts contained in the child-support guidelines. The trial court did not make a determination that the private agreement incorporated into the court's modification order** was 'in accordance with the changed income and financial status of either former spouse or in the needs of the child...', and did not review the agreement in light of the child-support guidelines. Judgment reversed."[54]

The Obligor May File A Modification Action, Even If The Obligor's Gross Income Has Increased

The obligor whose income has increased may file a modification action to lower the amount of child support.

The appellate court has held that **"There was no holding (in a prior case) that an increase in income would bar a petition for modification or even that such an increase would absolutely preclude a trial court's conclusion that the financial status of the obligor parent had changed in such a way as to warrant reconsideration of the amount of the support obligation. 'In determining a change of the financial condition of a parent, the court should consider every relevant fact.' The proper scope of the trial court's consideration...was whether there had been...such a change in the financial status of each parent as would support a reconsideration of the level of...obligation to provide financial support for the parties' child. Focusing solely on the fact that** (the obligor's) gross income has increased since the initial child support award was error."[55]

Child Support May Not Be Modified Retroactively

The appellate court has held that **"A permanent child support judgment is res judicata and enforceable until modified, vacated or set aside. Until a final decree amending the child support is properly entered in the modification proceeding the permanent judgment stands. A child support judgment can not be modified retroactively."**[56]

The Obligor May Seek A Modification Without Complying With The Divorce Decree

The obligor who has not fully complied with the divorce decree may seek to modify the amount of child support.

The appellate court has held that **"The fact that a parent has not complied with his obligations under a divorce decree does not automatically bar that parent from seeking modification of child support due to changed circumstances."** [57]

Financial Contribution Of A New Spouse May Be Considered In A Modification Action

The fact that you pay some of your significant other's living expenses may be considered by the judge or the jury in an action to increase child support, even though your significant other's income has not significantly increased.

The appellate court has held that **"The question before the jury...was whether there had been a substantial change in (the obligor's) ability to pay. Such a change may be shown by decreased financial obligations or other changed conditions even where there has been no increase in income."**[58]

The story of Abby, Josh, Moe, and Andora

Abby and Josh were divorced eleven years ago. At the time of the divorce, they had one child, Moe, who was two years old. Abby and Josh came to an agreement whereby Josh paid Abby $500.00 per month as child support. Abby worked very hard to support herself and Moe, and she never sought to modify the amount of child support until Josh married Andora.

Andora was an attorney who had a very successful real estate practice. She earned much more money than Josh earned. She really loved Josh. She did not hesitate to financially help Josh as much as she could. She paid for most of Josh's living expenses, including paying for his car.

Abby became furious when she learned of Josh's marriage to Andora. Abby told Josh that she wanted more child support because he had more disposable income than she had. However, Josh's income had never been great and had never really increased all that much. Josh told Abby that he did not believe that Abby should consider Andora's income, and that Andora was not liable for his child support.

Abby went to an attorney who told her that Josh was wrong. Abby filed for an upward modification of child support. At the trial, there was evidence of Josh's income and Andora's payment of Josh's living expenses. The jury modified Abby's child support to $1,200 per month, and the judge ordered Josh to pay Abby's attorney's fees.

Attorney's Fees May Be Awarded

Attorney's fees and expenses of litigation may be awarded to the prevailing party in a modification action. However, the judge has the discretion to award or not award these fees and expenses.

> **"In proceedings for the modification of alimony for the support of a child pursuant to the provisions of this Code section, the court may award attorneys' fees, costs, and expenses of litigation to the prevailing party as the interests of justice may require."[59]**

The Judge May Not Modify Child Support In A Contempt Proceeding

The appellate court has held that **"Trial courts have no authority to modify the amount of child support of a final judgment and decree of divorce in a contempt proceeding."[60]**

Self-Executing Provision In The Agreement Is Permissible

The parties may want to provide in their settlement agreement that in the event the minor child elects to live with the noncustodial parent when the child attains the age of fourteen, custody will be transferred to the noncustodial parent, and he or she will receive a certain amount of child support.

If the noncustodial parent is a fit and proper parent to assume custody of the child, there may be no need for further court intervention. In other words, it may not be necessary to file an action in court to change custody and receive child support.

The appellate court has held that **"There is nothing in the decree indicating that the parties contemplated any further litigation on the issue of custody. The provision was clearly intended to be a self-executing change of legal custody and modification of child support obligations. The trial court which issued the divorce decree participated in the change by adopting the consent agreement. It had an opportunity at that time to review and reject the proposed arrangement for a change of custody at the child's election, but it chose to ratify it instead. The arrangement has the further virtue of comporting with the public policy in favor of the right of a child of appropriate age to select the custodial parent. Finally, since the child's selection is controlling absent a finding of unfitness, a self-executing change serves the interest of judicial economy by affecting the change of custody and the establishment of child support obligations without the necessity of court proceedings in a case...where there are no allegations of parental unfitness."[61]

Obtaining Custody Of One Child May Not Reduce Child Support

The appellate court has held that **"Where the only provision for reduction of a lump sum child support award made for two or more children is when each child reaches the age of eighteen, a change in custody of one of them does not of itself bring about a pro rata reduction in the amount of that support."**[62]

AFTER THE TRIAL ISSUES

Child Support Accrues Interest From The Date The Payment Is Due

Effective July 1, 1996, "All awards of child support expressed in monetary amounts shall accrue interest at the rate of 12 percent per annum commencing 30 days from the day such award or payment is due. This Code section shall apply to all awards, court orders, decrees, and judgments rendered pursuant to Title 19. It shall not be necessary for the party to whom the child support is due to reduce any such award to judgment in order to recover such interest."[63]

Child Support Order Is Enforced In Georgia

"Orders, decrees, or verdicts, permanent or temporary, in favor of the children may be enforced as those in favor of a party."[64]

Child Support Order May Be Enforced By Attachment For Contempt And By Writ Of Fieri Facias

The child support order may be enforced by filing a motion to punish for contempt, and by filing an AFFIDAVIT FOR FI. FA., in which the obligee is requesting that the clerk of the superior court issue an execution (Writ of Fi. Fa.) in favor of the obligee in the amount of child support that is owed, including the costs of the proceeding.

312 DO YOU REALLY WANT TO BE A STEPPARENT?

The appellate court has held that **"Awards of child support are implicit commands of the court and are enforceable by action for contempt...since these are duties which society has a substantial interest. The proper administration of justice demands that courts have the power to enforce their orders and decrees by contempt proceedings. Disobedience to the lawful order of a court is an obstruction of justice, and for such a violation the court, in order to compel respect or compliance, may punish for contempt."**[65]

> **"On application, an order allowing temporary alimony may be enforced either by writ of fieri facias or by attachment for contempt."**[66]

> **"A grant of permanent alimony may be enforced either by writ of fieri facias or by attachment for contempt."**[67]

The Child May Enforce The Payment Of Child Support

Either parent or the child may seek to enforce the child support order in a court of law.

> Child support **"may be enforced by either parent or the child for whose benefit the support is ordered."**[68]

The Obligee Is Regarded As A Creditor

"A child support obligee shall be regarded as a creditor, and a child support obligor shall be regarded as a debtor, for the purposes of attacking as fraudulent a judgment, conveyance, transaction, or other arrangement interfering with the creditor's rights, either at law or in equity."[69]

A License May Be Suspended For Failure To Pay Child Support

"In any proceeding for enforcement of a judgment or order to pay child support, if the court is satisfied by competent proof that the respondent has accumulated support arrears equivalent to or greater than the current support due for 60 days and that the respondent is licensed to conduct a trade, business, profession, or occupation, licensed to hunt or fish, licensed to drive a motor vehicle, owns a motor vehicle which is registered in this state in his or her name, or is applying for the renewal or issuance of any such license or registration, the court may order the appropriate licensing or registering entity to suspend the license or registration or deny the application for such license and to inform the court of the actions it has taken pursuant to such proceedings. Evidence relating to the ability and willingness of the respondent to comply with an order of child support shall be considered by the court prior to the entry of any order under this Code Section."[70]

The Employed Parent May Be Confined For Not Paying Child Support

> "When a person who is gainfully employed violates an order of the court granting temporary or permanent child support and the judge finds the person in contempt of court, the sentencing judge may sentence the respondent to a term of confinement in a diversion center and participation in a diversion program if such a program has been established by a county pursuant to the provisions of Article 8 of Chapter 8 of Title 42."[71]

Reviewing The Child Support Issue
Instructions

Please answer only those questions that are applicable to you.

You do not have to give written answers to these questions. In fact, you should not write your answers until you have consulted with your attorney, if you choose to employ your own attorney, and the attorney who represents your significant other about whether you should or should not write your answers.

If your significant other is already involved in litigation, or if you anticipate that he or she will be, the opposing party, or his or her attorney, *may* have the right to subpoena your written answers. Of course, you do not want to incriminate yourself, or divulge information that you do not have to disclose. Therefore, please consult with the attorney(s) before you write your answers.

Questions

In order to compute the amount of child support that your significant other may have to pay, or that your significant other may receive, please answer the following questions.

What is the range of support according to the Child Support Guidelines for the number of children your significant other has?

What is the yearly gross income of the father?

What is the yearly gross income of the mother?

Does the yearly salary of the obligor include bonuses? If the yearly salary of the obligor does not include yearly bonuses, what percentage of the obligor's yearly bonus should be paid as additional child support?

According to the Guidelines, what are the lowest and the highest amounts of child support that should be paid?

Please explain your answer.

Do you believe that the amount of child support should increase each year as the obligor's income increases?

If the amount of child support increases, should the obligor be obligated to send to the obligee the obligor's tax returns for the previous year?

Please explain your answer.

Are you aware of any special circumstances that would vary the amount of child support from the amount that is suggested by the Child Support Guidelines?

Please explain your answer.

What is your proposal regarding who should pay the expenses for day care, activities, clothes, private school, therapy, summer camps, and allowances?

If the obligor pays these expenses, should that amount be in addition to the amount of child support that is paid directly to the

318 DO YOU REALLY WANT TO BE A STEPPARENT?

obligee?

Should that amount count as a credit toward the total amount of child support that is paid to the obligee?

Please explain your answer.

What is your proposal regarding which parent should pay the medical and dental insurance premiums?

If the obligor pays the premiums, should that cost be deducted from the amount of child support that is paid directly to the obligee?

How long should the child be covered by said insurance?

Should the insurance be maintained through the parent's employment or otherwise in the event the parent loses his or her job? Who should pay those costs that are not covered by the insurance, such as deductibles and uncovered expenses?

If the insurance company furnishes a list of health care providers, which parent should be responsible for those expenses that are not covered where the parent goes outside the approved network for services?

What does the phrase "reasonable and necessary" expenses mean to you, and should the definition be included in the settlement agreement?

Please explain your answer.

What is your proposal regarding which parent should pay the life insurance premiums?

Should the cost of the life insurance premiums be deducted from the amount of child support that is paid directly to the obligee?

Should one parent or both parents maintain life insurance?

What should be the face amount of the policy(s)?

Should the face amount of the policy(s) equal the total amount that would have been paid in child support had the obligor lived, including uncovered medical and dental expenses?

Who should be the owner and beneficiary of the policy(s)?

Should each policy(s) provide for an irrevocable beneficiary?

For what period of time should the policy(s) be kept in full force and effect?

Please explain your answer.

Should the initial amount of child support ever change?

Under what circumstances, if any, should child support be reduced, increased, or suspended?

Should the obligor waive his or her right to modify downward the amount of child support?

Please explain your answer.

When should the child support obligation end? Remember, there is a statute that controls this issue.

Should child support terminate when the child graduates from high school, college (four years or more), reaches a specific age, dies, marries, becomes self-supporting or emancipated, when custody is transferred to the other parent, or when the child elects to live with the other parent?

Should there be a self-executing provision in the settlement agreement that provides for the payment of child support in the event the child elects to live with the other parent?

Please explain your answer.

What is your proposal regarding the payment of the college expenses?

Should your significant other be obligated to pay the college expenses, including room, board, books, and tuition? (A parent is not legally obligated to pay the college expenses, unless a parent voluntarily agrees to be liable for these expenses.)

If so, should the college be a state-supported one, or who should choose the college?

How many years of college should be paid for?

Should trade schools be covered?

Should there be any conditions for paying the college

expenses, such as obtaining a certain grade point average or a partial scholarship?

When should the obligation to pay the college expenses end?

Please explain your answer.

What is your proposal regarding the dependency exemption?

Who should get to claim the child as a dependent? (The custodial parent is granted the right to claim the child as a dependent.)

Should the parents alternate the tax exemption yearly?

Should the parent who does not have real estate claim the child?

Should the parent who benefits from taking the exemption claim the child?

Should the parent have to pay his or her child support on time before being able to claim the child as a dependent?

Please explain your answer.

SUMMARY

Your seventh step toward determining whether or not you really want to be a stepparent includes your review and consideration of some of the child support issues.

This chapter focuses on only a few of the Georgia cases and laws that deal with the child support issues. Please discuss with your attorney, if you choose to employ an attorney, and the attorney who represents your significant other the appellate court cases and statutory laws that relate to your significant other's case.

If you decide to become a stepparent, there are many issues that you need to consider.

If you choose to become a stepparent, you should be aware of the amount of child support that your significant other may be legally ordered to pay if he or she is not the custodial parent. The child support that your significant other pays may leave you and your significant other with very little money to live on as a couple.

You should be aware of the amount of child support that your significant other may receive if he or she is the custodial parent. The child support that your significant other receives may not be sufficient to totally support his or her child.

In either case, you may have to pay some of your significant other's living expenses. That is why it is imperative that you discuss with the attorney(s) all of the pros and cons of becoming a stepparent.

The Georgia statute provides that the child is entitled to be financially supported for a specified period of time, unless the parents voluntarily agree to extend this period.

The parents may agree upon the amount of child support, but the judge has to approve of that amount. The judge may not feel that the amount is sufficient to meet the customary needs of the child. Of course, the judge does consider the financial ability of the obligor.

The judge or the jury must consider the Georgia Child Support Guidelines statute in setting the amount of child support. The initial calculation of child support is based upon the gross income of the obligor. Gross income is income from every source. Even the earning capacity of an asset is counted. However, the judge or the jury may vary the amount of child support according to the evidence presented at trial. The judge or the jury may consider the many factors that are specified in the guideline statute, and may adjust the amount of child support, up or down.

If health insurance for the child is reasonably available at a reasonable cost through the obligor's employment or other group plan, the judge will order the obligor to obtain the insurance, unless the judge directs otherwise.

Either parent or both parents may be ordered to obtain and maintain life insurance.

The judge may not award the tax exemption. However, the custodial parent may agree to give the tax exemption to the noncustodial parent.

The child support order may include a garnishment provision, an income deduction order, and a payroll deduction order for the payment of the health insurance premiums.

The amount of child support may be modified when there has been a change in the income and financial status of either former spouse or in the needs of the child. However, there is no absolute right to a modification.

The obligee may never waive his or her right to seek a modification of the amount of child support.

The obligor may waive his or her right to seek a downward

modification of the amount of child support.

Until the amount of child support is modified, the original amount of child support is due and payable.

All awards of child support accrue interest at the rate of 12% per annum commencing 30 days from the date the payment is due.

Child support may be enforced in Georgia by attachment for contempt and by writ of fieri facias.

In certain cases, the judge may suspend the obligor's license for failure to pay child support, and/or may order the obligor confined in a diversion program.

Your answers to the questions that are included in this chapter may help you decide whether or not you really want to be a stepparent.

KEY TO THE CITATIONS

The terms and abbreviations used in this chapter have been explained in a previous chapter on page 217.

CITATIONS

1. O.C.G.A. Section 39-1-1
2. O.C.G.A. Section 19-6-35(a)(1)
3. O.C.G.A. Section 19-6-35(a)(2)
4. O.C.G.A. Section 19-6-26
5. M v. M, 237 Ga. 57, 226 S.E.2d 591 (1976)
6. O.C.G.A. Section 19-6-26
7. K v. C, 267 Ga. 98, 475 S.E.2d 604 (1996)
8. C v. C, 259 Ga. 68, 377 S.E.2d 663 (1989)
9. O.C.G.A. Section 19-7-2
10. C v. C, 259 Ga. 68, 377 S.E.2d 663 (1989)
11. M v. M, 223 Ga. 246, 154 S.E.2d 209 (1967)
12. H v. H, 233 Ga. 12, 209 S.E.2d 607 (1974)
13. C v. C, 238 Ga. 421, 233 S.E.2d 151 (1977)
14. C v. C, 259 Ga. 68, 377 S.E.2d 663 (1989)
15. O.C.G.A. Section 19-6-15
16. W v. W, 260 Ga. 442, 396 S.E.2d 235 (1990)
17. H v. R, 268 Ga. 10, 485 S.E.2d 750 (1997)

18. O.C.G.A. Section 19-6-15
19. E v. E, 264 Ga. 668, 449 S.E.2d 840 (1994)
20. E v. E, 264 Ga. 668, 449 S.E.2d 840 (1994)
21. M v. G, 225 Ga.App. 752, 484 S.E.2d 789 (1997)
22. H v. C, 261 Ga. 259, 404 S.E.2d 121 (1991)
23. K v. M, 270 Ga. 419, 510 S.E.2d 520 (1999)
24. F v. F, 268 Ga. 465, 490 S.E.2d 377 (1997)
25. O.C.G.A. Section 19-6-15
26. S v. T, 258 Ga. 17, 365 S.E.2d 110 (1988)
27. G v. J, 256 Ga. 635, 352 S.E.2d 386 (1987)
28. M v. M, 238 Ga. 64, 230 S.E.2d 872 (1976)
29. O.C.G.A. Section 19-6-34
30. J v. J, 259 Ga. 560, 385 S.E.2d 279 (1989)
31. M v. M, 190 Ga. 508, 9 S.E.2d 756 (1940)
32. S v. S, 260 Ga. 635, 398 S.E.2d 363 (1990)
33. C v. C, 231 Ga. 683, 203 S.E.2d 524 (1974)
34. H v. S, 126 Ga.App. 5, 189 S.E.2d 882 (1972)
35. H v. H, 251 Ga. 691, 309 S.E.2d 367 (1983)
36. O.C.G.A. Section 19-6-15
37. B v. B, 261 Ga. 11, 401 S.E.2d 714 (1991)
38. O.C.G.A. Section 19-6-15

39. C v. C, 238 Ga. 421, 233 S.E.2d 151 (1977)

40. O.C.G.A. Section 19-6-30

41. O.C.G.A. Section 19-6-32

42. O.C.G.A. Section 19-6-29

43. O.C.G.A. Section 19-6-19

44. S v. S, 236 Ga. 308, 223 S.E.2d 689 (1976)

45. O.C.G.A. Section 19-6-19

46. R v. P, 231 Ga. 16, 200 S.E.2d 108 (1973)

47. W v. W, 261 Ga. 674, 410 S.E.2d 98 (1991)

48. R v. D, 260 Ga. 487, 396 S.E.2d 905 (1990)

49. O.C.G.A. Section 19-6-19

50. M v. M, 252 Ga. 553, 314 S.E.2d 893 (1984)

51. K v. K, 258 Ga. 184, 366 S.E.2d 766 (1988)

52. C v. C, 259 Ga. 68, 377 S.E.2d 663 (1989)

53. N v. M, 265 Ga. 441, 457 S.E.2d 669 (1995)

54. P v. P, 265 Ga. 100, 454 S.E.2d 124 (1995)

55. M v. T, 265 Ga. 147, 454 S.E.2d 498 (1995)

56. A v. GDHR, 264 Ga. 119, 441 S.E.2d 754 (1994)

57. S v. P, 230 Ga. 496, 497 S.E.2d 21 (1998)

58. S v. S, 234 Ga. 687, 217 S.E.2d 251 (1975)

59. O.C.G.A. Section 19-6-19

60. DHR v. G, 222 Ga.App. 489, 474 S.E.2d 682 (1996)

61. W v. J, 260 Ga. 493, 396 S.E.2d 890 (1990)

62. I v. I, 242 Ga. 386, 249 S.E.2d 69 (1978)

63. O.C.G.A. Section 7-4-12.1

64. O.C.G.A. Section 19-6-16

65. G v. B, 239 Ga. 244, 236 S.E.2d 599 (1977)

66. O.C.G.A. Section 19-6-3

67. O.C.G.A. Section 19-6-4

68. O.C.G.A. Section 19-6-15

69. O.C.G.A. Section 19-6-35

70. O.C.G.A. Section 19-6-28.1

71. O.C.G.A. Section 15-1-4

CHAPTER NINE

ALTERNATIVES TO LITIGATION

ALTERNATIVE DISPUTE RESOLUTION (ADR)

You have already reviewed some of the Georgia appellate court cases and statutory laws dealing with child custody, visitation, and child support.

You have also reviewed your answers to the many questions that pertain to you, your stepchild, your attitudes and abilities as they relate to your parenting skills, your relationship with your stepchild, and your motives for wanting to be a stepparent and for not wanting to be a stepparent.

At this time, you may be in a position to make a decision about whether or not you really want to be a stepparent. On the other hand, you may still be undecided.

If you are still considering becoming a stepparent, it may be helpful to review some of the legal procedures that you and your significant other may encounter.

To begin with, the parties should try to settle the disputed issues in their case before they decide to go to court. You may already know that litigation is very costly, emotionally draining, and time-consuming.

The parties may settle their case by themselves, by meeting

with their attorneys, and by engaging in a process that is known as Alternative Dispute Resolution.

First, the parties can meet by themselves. They can discuss all of the issues in the case, and then settle all of the issues or some of the issues. The parties can attempt to resolve the issues that are not agreed upon at mediation, case evaluation, or arbitration. However, before the parties meet, each party should consult with his or her own attorney about his or her legal rights and obligations. Often, the parties want to have one attorney in order to save money. That is not a good idea in my view.

Second, the parties can meet with their attorneys. They can discuss all of the issues in the case, and then settle all of the issues or some of the issues. If the parties come to an agreement, a written memorandum of agreement is signed by both of the parties and their attorneys. After the meeting, the attorneys will prepare a formal settlement agreement that the parties will review and sign. This agreement is then presented to the judge for his or her review and approval. The parties can attempt to resolve the issues that are not agreed upon at mediation, case evaluation, or arbitration.

The story of Alicia, John, Mary, and Sally

Alicia and John had been married for three years when John met Sally, the love of his life. Alicia and John had only one child, Mary, who was two years old.

John told Alicia that he wanted a divorce so that he could marry Sally.

Alicia was angry and heartbroken. However, she reluctantly agreed to an amicable divorce.

Alicia went to her attorney and told him that she wanted to settle the case without going to court.

Alicia, John, and the two attorneys met, and they settled all of the issues in the case.

Everyone agreed that an amicable resolution was best for all of the parties, especially Mary.

Alicia was happy because she was able to get most of what she wanted.

John was happy because he was able to get what he wanted, namely, his beloved Sally.

Third, the parties can participate in a process that is known as Alternative Dispute Resolution, which includes mediation, case evaluation, and arbitration.

Mediation, case evaluation, and arbitration should be attempted before any litigant goes to trial. As you will learn later in this chapter, these methods are extremely effective and efficient for resolving any disputed issue.

In Georgia, the term Alternative Dispute Resolution refers to any method for resolving disputes, other than litigation.

Arbitration, case evaluation, and mediation are methods that are commonly used to resolve disputes.

The following Alternative Dispute Resolution Rules were approved by the Georgia Supreme Court. A portion of the Alternative Dispute Resolution Rules are quoted verbatim.

DEFINITION OF THE TERM- ALTERNATIVE DISPUTE RESOLUTION

"The term Alterative Dispute Resolution (ADR) refers to any method other than litigation for resolution of disputes. A definition of some common ADR terms follows."

DEFINITION OF THE TERM- NEUTRAL

"The term 'neutral' as used in these rules refers to an impartial person who facilitates discussions and dispute resolution between disputants in mediation, case evaluation or early neutral evaluations, and arbitration, or who presides over a summary jury trial or mini trial. Thus, mediators, case evaluators, and arbitrators are all classified as 'neutrals'."

DEFINITION OF THE TERM- MEDIATION

"Mediation is a process in which a neutral facilitates settlement discussions between parties. The neutral has no authority to make a decision or impose a settlement upon the parties. The neutral attempts to focus the attention of the parties upon their needs and interests rather than upon rights and positions. Although in court-annexed or court-referred mediation programs the parties may be ordered to attend a mediation session, any settlement is entirely voluntary. In the absence of settlement the parties lose none of their rights to a jury trial."

DEFINITION OF THE TERM- ARBITRATION

"Arbitration differs from mediation in that an arbitrator or panel of arbitrators renders a decision after hearing an abbreviated version of the evidence. In non-binding arbitration, either party may demand a trial within a specified period. The essential difference between mediation and arbitration is that arbitration is a form of adjudication, whereas mediation is not."

DEFINITION OF THE TERM- CASE EVALUATION OR EARLY NEUTRAL EVALUATION

"Case evaluation or early neutral evaluation is a process in which a lawyer with expertise in the subject matter of the litigation acts as a neutral evaluator of the case. Each side presents a summary of its legal theories and evidence. The evaluator assesses the strength of each side's case and assists the parties in narrowing the legal and factual issues in the case. This conference occurs early in the discovery process and is designed to "streamline" discovery and other pretrial aspects of the case. The early neutral evaluation of the case may also provide a basis for settlement discussions."

DEFINITION OF THE TERM- SUMMARY JURY TRIAL

"The summary jury trial is a non-binding abbreviated trial by mock jurors chosen from the jury pool. A judge or magistrate presides. Principals with authority to settle the case attend. The advisory jury verdict which results is intended to provide the starting point for settlement negotiations."

DEFINITION OF THE TERM- MINI TRIAL

"The mini trial is similar to the summary jury trial in that it is an abbreviated trial usually presided over by a neutral. Attorneys present their best case to party representatives with authority to settle. Generally, no decision is announced by the neutral. After the hearing, the party representatives begin settlement negotiations, perhaps calling on the neutral for an opinion as to how a court might decide the case."

DEFINITION OF THE TERM- CONFIDENTIALITY

"Any statement made during a court-annexed or court-referred mediation or case evaluation or early neutral evaluation conference or as part of intake by program staff in preparation for a mediation, case evaluation or early neutral evaluation is confidential, not subject to disclosure, may not be disclosed by the neutral or program staff, and may not be used as evidence in any subsequent administrative or judicial proceeding. Unless a court's ADR rules provide otherwise, the confidentiality herein applies to non-binding arbitration conferences as well.

Any document or other evidence generated in connection with a court-annexed or court-referred mediation or case evaluation, early neutral evaluation or, unless otherwise provided by court ADR rules, a non-binding arbitration, is not subject to discovery. An agreement resulting from a court-annexed or court-referred mediation, case evaluation or early neutral evaluation conference, or a non-binding arbitration, is not immune from discovery, unless the parties agree in writing. Otherwise discoverable material is not rendered immune from discovery by use in a mediation, case evaluation, or early neutral evaluation, or a non-binding arbitration.

Neither the neutral nor any observer present with permission of the parties in a court-annexed or court-referred ADR process may be subpoenaed or otherwise required to testify concerning a mediation or case evaluation or early neutral evaluation conference or, unless otherwise provided by court ADR rules, a non-binding arbitration, in any subsequent administrative or judicial proceeding. A neutral's notes or records are not subject to discovery. Notes and records of a court ADR program are not subject to discovery to the extent that such notes or records pertain to cases and parties ordered or referred by a court to the program.

Exceptions to confidentiality:

Confidentiality on the part of program staff or the neutral does not extend to the issue of appearance. Confidentiality does not extend to a situation in which a) there are threats of imminent violence to self or others; or b) the mediator believes that a child is abused or that the safety of any party or third person is in danger.

Confidentiality does not extend to documents or communications relevant to legal claims or disciplinary complaints brought against a neutral or an ADR program and arising out of an ADR process. Documents or communications relevant to such claims or complaints may be revealed only to the extent necessary to protect the neutral or ADR program. Nothing in the above rule negates any statutory duty of a neutral to report information. Parties should be informed of limitations on confidentiality at the beginning of the conference. Collection of information necessary to monitor the quality of a program is not considered a breach of confidentiality."

DEFINITION OF THE TERM- IMMUNITY

"No neutral in a court-annexed or court-referred program shall be held liable for civil damages for any statement, action, omission or decision made in the course of any ADR process unless that statement, action, omission or decision is 1) grossly negligent and made with malice or 2) is in wilful disregard of the safety or property of any party to the ADR process."[1]

---

1 The Georgia Supreme Court Alternative Dispute Resolution Rules, Definitions

ARBITRATION- THE PROCESS AND THE BENEFITS

Arbitration is a form of adjudication. One arbitrator, or a panel of arbitrators, hears the evidence presented by the Plaintiff and the Defendant, and then renders a decision. The arbitrator is a neutral person. The term *neutral* implies that the arbitrator has no biases for or against either party or his or her attorney, and has no interest in the outcome of the litigation. The arbitrator may be an attorney who is trained to be an arbitrator, or a person who has extensive experience in a particular area.

In court-ordered arbitration, the panel of arbitrators are chosen by the ADR office.

In private arbitration, the parties choose an arbitrator or a panel of arbitrators. The arbitration hearing is held in the office of the arbitrator. The parties agree to be responsible for the payment of the fees that are charged by the arbitrator(s).

In both court-ordered arbitration and private arbitration, the parties and their attorneys decide whether the arbitration is to be binding or non-binding.

In binding arbitration, the parties agree that the decision of the arbitrator(s) is final, and the parties waive their right to a trial. Regardless of the outcome, the parties are bound by the decision.

In non-binding arbitration, a party who is dissatisfied with the decision and the award may demand a trial within a specified period of time. The failure to file a demand for trial is considered to be a waiver of the right to a trial, and the decision and the award become binding on the parties.

If the parties choose to have a panel of arbitrators, there are usually three panel members. One of the members is the chief arbitrator. At the beginning of the arbitration, the chief arbitrator, in the case of a panel of three arbitrators, introduces the members of the panel and then requests that the parties and their attorneys introduce themselves.

One of the arbitrators explains that the rules of evidence are relaxed. Any questions of admissibility will be discussed and decided by the arbitrator or panel of arbitrators. The attorneys are asked if there are any stipulations as to the facts or issues. For example, the parties can stipulate that the fair market value of the marital domicile is a certain amount.

Another arbitrator explains the following procedures. Arbitration is meant to take less time than a trial. Arbitration usually lasts three (3) hours. The opening and the closing statements are shorter than would be allowed in court. Each side usually has one (1) hour to present his or her case. The witnesses testify under oath. Everyone remains seated. The attorneys are asked if they want each witness, other than the litigants, to wait in another room until the witness testifies and is excused.

Another arbitrator will advise the parties and their attorneys that the panel will begin to deliberate immediately after the closing arguments. After the panel renders a decision, the parties may have the documents that were submitted into evidence.

The parties are also advised that in non-binding arbitration either party who is dissatisfied with the decision of the panel can file a demand for trial within a specified period of time from the date of the decision, or else the panel's decision is binding on the parties.

The procedure begins with the attorneys for the Plaintiff and the Defendant giving brief opening statements. Then, just as it is at trial, the Plaintiff's attorney calls the first witness for direct examination. The Defendant's attorney then has the right to cross-examine the witness. The Plaintiff's attorney is then asked if there is any redirect examination of this witness, i.e., ask the witness follow-up questions. If there are further questions, the Defendant's attorney has the right to recross examination.

After the Plaintiff's witnesses have testified, and the Plaintiff's attorney has presented the Plaintiff's evidence, the Plaintiff rests. The Defendant's attorney then calls the first witness for direct examination, and the process is repeated. After the Defendant's witnesses have testified, and the Defendant's attorney has presented the Defendant's evidence, the Defendant rests.

At this point, each attorney has the opportunity to make a closing argument. At the conclusion of the presentation of the evidence and closing arguments, the arbitrator, or panel of arbitrators, deliberates and renders a decision.

Arbitration affords your significant other the opportunity to have his or her case heard by experienced neutrals before resorting to litigation.

Case Evaluation Or Early Neutral Evaluation-The Process And The Benefits

Case Evaluation or Early Neutral Evaluation is a confidential and non-binding evaluation process. The purpose of this process is to help each side determine the strengths and weaknesses of his or her case. The Early Neutral Evaluation conference should occur early in the litigation process. However, this conference can occur at any time.

The parties and their attorneys usually choose a neutral evaluator from a list of attorneys who are experienced in the particular area of the law that is the subject of the evaluation. Therefore, if the case is a divorce and custody case, the evaluator will be experienced in handling domestic cases.

The parties also agree to be responsible for the fees of the evaluator. Usually, each party pays one-half of the evaluator's fees. The evaluation usually takes place in the private office of the evaluator. However, the parties and their attorneys may agree to another location.

The evaluator makes an opening statement describing the process, and what the parties and their attorneys can expect from the process.

346 DO YOU REALLY WANT TO BE A STEPPARENT?

The evaluator advises everyone that the evaluator has no authority to dictate how the case should be settled, or how each side should present his or her case. The evaluator does not make a ruling as to the merits of the case. This process is unlike arbitration where the arbitrator, or panel of arbitrators, renders a decision.

The evaluator also states that nothing mentioned in the conference will be communicated to the judge.

Each side makes a brief presentation of the facts of the case and the applicable law. This presentation, which usually lasts a half hour per side, may be made by the attorney, the client, or both.

Documents, witness statements, and other evidence, including applicable statutes and appellate court cases, may be introduced. However, there is no live testimony.

Each side can ask the other side questions. The evaluator can also ask each side questions in order to determine the strengths and weaknesses of each side.

The next step is for the evaluator to identify those issues that are not in dispute and those issues that are. That is a very important step because litigants will often argue over issues that can be agreed upon. Therefore, if an issue is not in dispute, that issue should be identified as soon as possible in order that the parties will not have to incur needless litigation expenses.

Following this process, the evaluator leaves the room to prepare his or her evaluation of the case, including the reasons for the evaluation.

The evaluation includes the strengths and weaknesses of each side, which side is likely to win in court, and may include the anticipated cost of litigating the case.

The evaluator then returns to the conference room. The parties may choose to discuss and decide the contested issues in their case. Many issues can be resolved without having to go to trial. There may be some issues that can not be resolved, but that should not prevent the parties from settling those issues that can be.

If either party does not want to talk about settling the case, the evaluator may begin discussing his or her evaluation and the reasons for the evaluation. This can be done in the presence of both sides or with each side individually.

The evaluation remains confidential and is not revealed to the judge and is not introduced in any future arbitration or trial.

If the parties' settlement discussions are not successful, the evaluator can help the parties develop a plan that might position the case for possible future settlement. Both parties must agree to the plan.

The evaluator is also available to discuss a discovery schedule, including when depositions will take place.

MEDIATION-THE PROCESS AND THE BENEFITS

Mediation is an informal and confidential negotiation process.

Everything that is said in mediation is confidential, unless there are threats of violence to self or others, or the mediator thinks that a child is abused, or the safety of any person is in danger. Nothing that is said in mediation may be repeated by a party or his or her attorney in court. No party may subpoena the mediator to testify in court about what was said in mediation.

Unlike arbitration and case evaluation, the mediator does not render a decision, or give an opinion as to the possible outcome of the litigation. The role of the mediator, who is a trained neutral, is to facilitate settlement discussions between the parties. Only the parties have control over whether there will or will not be a settlement in their case.

While the mediator may control how the mediation will be conducted, the mediator may not force the parties to settle their case.

The first step in beginning this process is to select the mediator. The parties may agree on the mediator. If that is not possible, the mediator may be assigned to the parties by the court's ADR office. The appointment is then scheduled for mediation, which usually takes place within thirty days. The cost of each mediation session is usually divided equally between the parties. Each session usually lasts three hours. The parties may request that their attorneys be present at all of the meetings.

The parties should be prepared for the mediation session. In order for mediation to be effective, the parties need to be emotionally ready to make a decision about the issues in the case. Being emotionally ready means that the parties are willing to accept the reality of their situation, including the fact that the marriage is over. The parties should know all of their marital assets and debts, and be prepared to make a division that is fair and reasonable. Moreover, each party should feel that he or she has the right to accept or reject the terms that are proposed by the other party.

At the first meeting, the mediator will instruct the parties as to how the mediation will be conducted, including who speaks first, the rules about not interrupting the other party, not using profanity, and what happens in a caucus, which is a meeting with the mediator and one of the parties and his or her attorney outside the presence of the other party and his or her attorney. The mediator will also explain that mediation is a voluntary process where the parties, not the mediator, make the decisions about any agreement. The parties are advised that mediation is the one process where the parties have absolute control over the results. The mediator also describes the role of the mediator. The mediator will advise the parties that the mediator is a neutral person, is not representing either party, and is not advocating for either side. Neither party may discuss the case with the mediator outside the presence of the other party, except in a caucus.

The mediator and the parties discuss the length and number of the sessions, the role of the attorneys, and the goals of mediation, including the goal of having the parties understand the other party's positions.

The parties are advised that either party may file an action in court to enforce the agreement that is reached in mediation.

It is again stated that even though the parties may be court-ordered to attend the mediation session, the mediator is not there to force them to settle their case. Any full or partial settlement that they reach is entirely voluntary, and they are entirely in control of any resolution that may be obtained. If the parties are unable to settle all of the issues in their case, the mediator merely advises the judge that no agreement was reached. No one is blamed for not arriving at a settlement of their case. If a partial agreement is reached, the judge is advised as to which issues are settled, and which issues remain to be tried.

The parties and their attorneys are then asked to sign a document known as the Domestic Guidelines For Mediation, which is designed to facilitate the process.

These guidelines include an agreement by the parties to do the following:

Focus on the issues, rather than dwelling on who is at fault for the divorce or the custody action;

Make a full and complete disclosure of the parties' assets and liabilities;

Agree not to call the mediator as a witness in any trial, hearing, deposition, or other legal proceeding;

Accept responsibility for their actions;

Accept that the mediator is not acting as the attorney or financial advisor, and, therefore, can not give legal or financial advice; and

Agree not to communicate with the mediator about the issues in their case when the communication is outside the presence of the other party, except in a caucus.

After the parties and their attorneys sign the guidelines, the mediator asks each party to give an opening statement outlining the issues in their case, and how he or she wants to resolve each of these issues. The mediator may then focus on each issue, and ask the parties to discuss these issues. The mediator will usually instruct each party to listen when the other party is speaking, and to not interrupt that party with comments, criticisms, gestures, or statements.

The mediator may want to speak with the attorneys, without their clients, in order to better understand the needs and contentions of the parties.

The mediator may also request that the parties bring to the mediation session all relevant documents necessary for the parties to make a decision. Therefore, the parties may want to bring their completed Domestic Relations Financial Affidavit, bank statements, credit card statements, bills, and all other records, letters, or statements that are relevant to the issues in their case.

During the caucus, each party is free to tell the mediator anything he or she wishes, and may request that anything the party says not be shared with the other party. Unless the party is admitting to acts or threats of bodily harm to self or others, or the mediator thinks that a child is abused, or the safety of any person is in danger, the mediator will not divulge caucus information to anyone without the party's consent.

If there is an agreement as to some or all of the issues, the mediator will prepare a written outline of the issues that are agreed upon. Each page of this document is signed by the parties and their attorneys. The attorneys for the parties prepare the legal document for the judge to review.

The main thing to remember is that the terms contained in the agreement must be clearly stated and not be ambiguous. The judge may not enforce the agreement if the terms are too vague and ambiguous.

Reviewing The Domestic Guidelines For Mediation

The following Domestic Guidelines For Mediation is a sample document. The guidelines contained in this document are very similar to the guidelines used by other mediators and ADR offices.

Please have your significant other review these guidelines so that he or she will be familiar with this document when he or she attends the mediation session.

If your significant other has any questions about the process or the guidelines, he or she should address these questions to the mediator before the mediation session begins.

Domestic Guidelines For Mediation
AGREEMENT TO MEDIATE

This is an agreement between _____ and _____, (hereinafter referred to as "the parties"), their representatives, and _____ (hereinafter referred to as "the mediator").

1. Mediation is a voluntary non-binding process. Either party or the mediator may terminate the mediation at any time. The parties with the assistance of the mediator reach their own agreement. The mediator will not make decisions for the parties. The purpose of the mediation is to attempt to find a mutually acceptable resolution of the issues that they bring to each mediation session. To achieve a mutually acceptable resolution, the mediator, the parties, and their attorneys will work to ensure that each party understands the facts asserted and the contentions of all of the parties.

2. For the mediation to be successful, open and honest communications, negotiations, and statements are essential. Therefore, the parties will make complete and accurate disclosure of all matters relevant to the issues that are the subject of this mediation. This includes providing each

party and the mediator with all relevant information which would be available in the discovery process in litigation. If a party deliberately withholds information or supplies false information relevant to the settlement, then any agreement reached in mediation resulting therefrom may be set aside.

3. Information gathered in the mediation process is confidential and privileged. All communications by the parties shall be treated as strictly confidential by the mediator, by the parties, and by their representatives. The mediator will not disclose any information learned during the mediation without the express permission of the parties. Confidential matters disclosed in a private meeting or caucus with one party will not be disclosed to the other party without the consent of the party making the disclosure.

4. The exception to the confidentiality rules stated in paragraph 3 is that this agreement to mediate and any written agreement made and signed by the parties as a result of the mediation may be used in any relevant proceeding, unless the parties by written agreement mutually decide in writing otherwise.

5. To maintain confidentiality, the parties and their representatives, by this agreement agree not to call the mediator as a witness at any proceeding nor to subpoena or otherwise seek discovery of any written materials in the mediator's possession developed for or in the course of this mediation. To the extent that the law permits discovery from the mediator, the parties hereby waive such rights of discovery.

6. Nothing in this agreement shall be construed to prevent or excuse the mediator from reporting matters such as any threatened crime, imminent threats of bodily injury to a child or a party, or such other matters as to which the law imposes a duty to report.

7. It is expressly understood by the parties and their representatives that the mediator does not offer legal or financial advice in this mediation and is not functioning as an attorney even though the mediator is in fact an attorney. In this mediation, the mediator's role is to aid the parties in reaching an agreement. The construction of a proposed agreement and any question of law or financial and tax matters should be referred by the parties to their own legal

and financial advisors.

8. The mediator is not liable for the results of the mediation. Any agreement written is the agreement of the parties to the mediation. The mediator shall not be held liable for civil damages for any statement, action, omission, or decision made in the course of the mediation process unless that statement, action, omission, or decision is (1) grossly negligent and made with malice, or (2) is in willful disregard of the safety or property of any party to the mediation process.

9. Mediation sessions must be canceled forty-eight (48) hours in advance or the parties may be charged a cancellation fee of $_____.

10. The parties agree to share the fee of the mediator. The fee in this mediation is $_____ per party per hour. Each party shall pay their respective fees at the close of each mediation session.

I have read, understand, and agree to each of the provisions of this agreement.

_____ (Date) _____
Plaintiff

_____ (Date) _____
Plaintiff's Representative

_____ (Date) _____
Defendant

_____ (Date) _____
Defendant's Representative

_____ (Date) _____
Mediator

Reviewing The Domestic Relations Financial Affidavit

The Domestic Relations Financial Affidavit, which is included in this chapter, is quoted verbatim from the Georgia Uniform Superior Court Rule 24.2. Your state may use a different form. This affidavit is one of the first documents that your significant other may need to complete. The affidavit is used in the mediation session, and is usually placed into evidence during any hearing or trial of the case. Therefore, your significant other needs to provide accurate information. If your significant other is not sure of the exact amount of an expense or the value of an item, put an asterisk beside the amount to indicate that this is the approximate sum. If your significant other is not sure about any item, he or she should discuss that with the attorney. *Don't guess.* If your significant other has an expense that does not fit into a category, he or she should list this expense on a separate sheet of paper titled "Miscellaneous."

The following are categories that are in Georgia's affidavit. In addition, I have included other assets and liabilities that are not found in Georgia's affidavit. Your significant other may be able to include these other assets and liabilities in his or her affidavit. He or she should discuss that with the attorney.

GROSS MONTHLY INCOME

All income is based on the monthly average, regardless of when the income was received.

Total the following income to obtain your gross monthly income:
Salary, wages, bonuses, commissions, tips
Pension
Retirement
Military retirement
Annuity payments
Social security benefits
Public assistance (welfare, AFDC payments)
Dividends and interest income
Disability, workers' compensation, unemployment insurance
Child support from previous marriage
Alimony from previous marriage
Rental Income (minus ordinary and necessary expenses)
Business income from self-employment, independent contracts, partnerships, and corporations (from the gross receipts, you subtract the ordinary and necessary expenses needed to generate the business)
Income from royalties, trusts, or estates
All other sources of income

In addition, total the following benefits from employment:
Automobile or automobile allowance
Payment of life, health, disability, or automobile insurance
Club memberships
Reimbursed expenses such as meals, hotels
Employer contribution to a stock plan or retirement program
Any compensation that is deferred

Your net monthly income from employment is obtained by subtracting only your federal and state taxes and FICA. You also indicate whether you get paid monthly or biweekly, and the number of exemptions you claim.

Your assets are divided into non-marital property (generally, property that was acquired by gift, inheritance, or prior to the marriage) and marital property (generally, property acquired during the marriage).

Your marital assets may include, but are not limited to, the following:
Retirement accounts, including 401K, IRA
Pension plan accounts
Stocks and bonds
Certificates of deposit
Money market accounts
Furniture and furnishings
Jewelry
Cash value of life insurance
Collectibles
Bank accounts (checking and savings)
Cash
Equity in real estate
Automobiles
Money owed to you, including a tax refund
Boats
Airplanes

364 DO YOU REALLY WANT TO BE A STEPPARENT?

Your monthly living expenses may include, but are not limited to, the following:

Residence:
Mortgage or rent payment
Property taxes
Property insurance
Electricity
Water
Garbage and sewer
Telephone
Gas for the home
Repairs and maintenance for the home
Lawn care
Pest control
Cable TV
Miscellaneous household items
Burglar alarm
Furniture
Furnishings, linens, towels, sheets

Food:
Grocery items
Meals outside

Pets:
Grooming
Veterinarian
Food

Drugstore Items:
Prescription and non-prescription medicine
Toiletries
Vitamins
Hair products

Personal Expenses:
Postage
Computer supplies
Vacations
Publications
Dues, clubs
Religious contributions
Charitable contributions
Entertainment
Clothing
Medical, dental, vision, therapy
Dry cleaning and laundry
Gifts to others
Safe deposit box fees
Beauty or barber shop expenses
Union dues
Bank charges

Automotive Expenses:
Gasoline and oil
Repairs
Auto tags and license
Insurance
Alternative transportation (bus, taxi)
Tolls and parking

Child's Expenses:
Child care
School tuition, school supplies, and other expenses
Lunch money
Allowance
Clothing
Diapers
Medical, dental, prescription, vision (uncovered)
Grooming/hygiene
Gifts to others
Entertainment
Toys, books, and publications
Summer camps
Sports and extracurricular activities
Tutoring
Therapy

Insurance Premiums:
Health
Life
Disability

Other Payments:
Alimony paid to former spouse(s)
Child support paid for other children

Payment To Creditors:
Name of creditor
Balance due
Monthly payment
Name on account

*Georgia Uniform Superior Court Rule 24.2

DOMESTIC RELATIONS FINANCIAL AFFIDAVIT

1. AFFIANT'S NAME _____ Age _____
   Affiant's Social Security No. _____
   Spouse's Name _____ Age _____
   Date of Marriage _____ Date of Separation _____
   Names and birth dates of children of this marriage:

   Name   Date of Birth   Resides With
   _____
   _____
   _____
   _____

   Names and birth dates of children of prior marriage residing with Affiant:

   Name   Date of Birth
   _____

2. SUMMARY OF AFFIANT'S INCOME AND NEEDS
   (a) Gross monthly income (from Item 3A) $_____
   (b) Net monthly income (from Item 3C) $_____
   (c) Average monthly expenses (Item 5A) $_____
       Monthly payments to creditors (Item 5B)   +   _____
       Total monthly expenses and payments to creditors
       (Item 5C) $_____
   (d) Amount of spousal/child support needed by
       Affiant $_____
   (e) Amount of child support indicated by the Child
       Support Guidelines $_____

368 DO YOU REALLY WANT TO BE A STEPPARENT?

3. A. AFFIANT'S GROSS MONTHLY INCOME
(All income must be entered based on monthly average regardless of date of receipt. Where applicable, income should be annualized.)

- Salary $_____
- Bonuses, commissions, allowances, overtime, tips, and similar payments (based on past 12-month average or time of employment if less than 1 year) ATTACH SHEET ITEMIZING THIS INCOME. _____
- Business income from sources such as self employment, partnership, close corporations and/or independent contracts (gross receipts minus ordinary and necessary expenses required to produce income) ATTACH SHEET ITEMIZING THIS INCOME. _____
- Disability/unemployment/workers' compensation _____
- Pension, retirements or annuity payments _____
- Social security benefits _____
- Other public benefits (specify) _____
- Spousal or child support from prior marriage _____
- Interest and dividends _____
- Rental income (gross receipts minus ordinary and necessary expenses required to produce income) ATTACH SHEET ITEMIZING THIS INCOME. _____
- Income from royalties, trusts or estates _____
- Gains derived from dealing in property (not including non-recurring gains) _____
- Other income of a recurring nature (specify source) _____

GROSS MONTHLY INCOME $_____

B. List and describe all benefits of employment, e.g., automobile and/or auto allowance, insurance (auto, life, disability, etc.), deferred compensation, employer contribution to retirement or stock, club memberships and reimbursed expenses (to the extent they reduce personal living expenses) ATTACH SHEET, IF NECESSARY.

_____
_____
_____
_____
_____
_____

C. Net monthly income from employment (deducting only state and federal taxes and FICA) $ _____
    Affiant's pay period (i.e., weekly, monthly, etc.) _____
    Number of exemptions claimed_____

4. ASSETS

(If you claim or agree that all or part of an asset is non-marital, indicate the non-marital portion under the appropriate spouse's column. The total value of each asset must be listed in the "value" column. "Value" means what you feel the item of property would be worth if it were offered for sale.)

Description	Value	Separate Asset of Husband	Separate Asset of Wife
Cash	$_____	_____	_____
Stocks, bonds	_____	_____	_____
CD's/Money Market accounts	_____	_____	_____
Real estate: home	_____	_____	_____
other	_____	_____	_____
Automobiles	_____	_____	_____

370 DO YOU REALLY WANT TO BE A STEPPARENT?

Money owed you _____ _____ _____
Retirement/IRA _____ _____ _____
Furniture/furnishings _____ _____ _____
Jewelry _____ _____ _____
Life insurance
 (cash value) _____ _____ _____
Collectibles _____ _____ _____
Bank accounts
 (list each account) _____ _____ _____
  _____ _____ _____
  _____ _____ _____

Other assets _____ _____ _____
_____ _____ _____ _____
_____ _____ _____ _____
TOTAL ASSETS $_____ _____ _____

5. A. AVERAGE MONTHLY EXPENSES

HOUSEHOLD
Mortgage or rent payments $_____
Property taxes _____
Insurance _____
Electricity _____
Water _____
Garbage and sewer _____
Telephone _____
Gas _____
Repairs and maintenance _____
Lawn care _____
Pest control _____
Cable TV _____
Miscellaneous household and

grocery items   _____
Meals outside home   _____
Other   _____

AUTOMOBILE
Gasoline and oil   _____
Repairs   _____
Auto tags and license   _____
Insurance   _____

CHILDREN'S EXPENSES
Child care   _____
School tuition   _____
School supplies/expenses   _____
Lunch money   _____
Allowance   _____
Clothing   _____
Diapers   _____
Medical, dental, prescription   _____
Grooming/hygiene   _____
Gifts   _____
Entertainment   _____
Activities   _____

OTHER INSURANCE
Health   _____
Life   _____
Disability   _____
Other (specify)   _____

372 DO YOU REALLY WANT TO BE A STEPPARENT?

AFFIANT'S OTHER EXPENSES
Dry cleaning and laundry _____
Clothing _____
Medical/dental _____
Affiant's gifts(special holidays) _____
Entertainment _____
Vacations _____
Publications _____
Dues, clubs _____
Religious and charities _____
Miscellaneous (attach sheet) _____
Other (attach sheet) _____
Alimony paid to former
   spouse _____
Child support paid to former
   spouse _____
TOTAL ABOVE EXPENSES $_____

B. PAYMENTS TO CREDITORS

To Whom	Balance Due	Monthly Payments
_____	_____	$_____
_____	_____	_____
_____	_____	_____

Total Monthly Payments to Creditors $_____
C. TOTAL MONTHLY EXPENSES $_____

This _____ day of _____, _____ (year).

_____   _____
Notary Public   Affiant
SC-Rule 24.2 Rev. 89
* Georgia Uniform Superior Court Rule 24.2

Summary

If you decide that you really want to be a stepparent, you should be aware that arbitration, case evaluation, and mediation are all methods that are used to resolve contested issues in divorce and custody cases. These methods should be considered before any litigant resorts to expensive and traumatic litigation.

Arbitration is a form of adjudication. Arbitration may be binding or non-binding. The arbitrator, or a panel of arbitrators, hears the evidence presented and then renders a decision. The arbitrator may be a person who is an expert in his or her field, or an experienced attorney who has been trained to be an arbitrator. In non-binding arbitration, a party who is dissatisfied with the decision may have the case decided by the judge or the jury.

Case Evaluation provides an opportunity for the parties to have their case heard by an attorney who has extensive experience in a particular field of law. The case evaluator does not decide the contested issues in the case. However, the case evaluator does point out to the parties the strengths and weaknesses of their case and helps them to define the issues.

Mediation is the one method that allows the parties to control the process. The parties control whether the case will be settled or not and the terms of the settlement. Judges frequently order the parties to attend mediation in order to encourage them to try to settle the contested issues, including the child custody issue.

Mediation has many benefits.

First: The parties maintain control of the process and the resolution of their case. The judge or the jury may never know all of the facts and circumstances that have brought the parties and their child to this impasse.

Second: Everything that is said in the mediation session is confidential, unless there are threats of violence to self or others, or the mediator thinks that a child is abused, or the safety of any person is in danger.

Third: The mediation process is much less expensive than paying two attorneys to wage a litigation war for years.

Fourth: The mediation session usually takes place within thirty days. The parties do not have to wait until the judge has time to hear their case.

Fifth: Mediation is conducted in a private and informal setting. In the courtroom, other people may be listening to all of the intimate details of the private lives of all of the parties involved.

Sixth: The parties can speak freely in mediation about their concerns and what is important to them. The parties are not restricted by the rules of evidence and the time constraints that the judge imposes.

Seventh: Mediation is a learning process that teaches the parties to find alternative ways of dealing with problems that are bound to arise in their relationship with each other.

Eighth: The parties may choose to have their attorneys present at mediation. Often, both parties have legal questions that they want answered before they will agree to certain provisions in their agreement. However, the mediator is not allowed to answer legal questions, even though the mediator may be an attorney. If the attorneys are present, the parties can stop and confer with their attorneys before they make an agreement as to a particular issue.

Ninth: The parties can always agree to have additional mediation sessions in order to address any issues that remain unresolved.

Tenth: The parties can usually choose their mediator, but the parties can not usually choose their judge.

The Domestic Guidelines For Mediation is a document designed to facilitate the process. It is helpful to read and understand the guidelines in order to be able to really benefit from mediation.

The Domestic Relations Financial Affidavit is one of the most important documents that a litigant will complete because it is usually reviewed during the mediation session and submitted into evidence at trial. Please make sure that your significant other includes all of the assets and liabilities.

If the issues in the case are not resolved in the mediation session, please have your significant other consider having the case heard by an arbitrator(s) or a case evaluator before anyone resorts to litigation.

The main thing to remember is that Alternative Dispute Resolution (ADR), which includes mediation, arbitration, and case evaluation, is the *best* way to resolve the parties' differences. Litigation is the *worst*.

CHAPTER TEN

LITIGATION: THE WORST CHOICE

If the parties fail to reach a settlement agreement in their case, or if they do not elect binding arbitration, the parties will have to resort to litigation, which is the last and worst choice. If the parties insist upon litigating their case, they will be forced to participate in an environment that is different from anything they have ever experienced. If you have watched divorce court on television, you will know a little of what actually goes on in court. However, the television version does not accurately reflect what the actual process is like.

As a major participant, your significant other will need to know how to select the right attorney for him or her. Your significant other will need to be aware of the legal issues that are involved in his or her case, including his or her legal rights and obligations. Your significant other will need to be familiar with some of the courtroom procedures.

If you decide that you really want to be a stepparent, you will also be a major participant in this litigation. Therefore, you will want to be familiar with the legal issues and the courtroom procedures.

Please remind your significant other that when the parties elect to go to court, they lose their right to determine the course of their future lives. They are forced to abide by decisions that will affect them as well as their child.

The story of Frank, Lilly, Sam, and Carl

Frank and Lilly had one child, Sam, who was five years old. They were very happy until Lilly met Carl. Carl was an unmarried, handsome executive. Lilly and Carl began meeting almost every day. After a few months, Lilly told Frank that she wanted a divorce, custody of Sam, the house, the car, and child support. She told Frank that he could have the debts. She quickly filed for a divorce. Frank was determined not to give Lilly an easy divorce, regardless of what it cost. Frank and Lilly were tied-up in court for years.

In the meantime, Carl was financially and emotionally supporting Lilly. However, after a year, Carl decided to end their relationship.

The case was finally heard by the judge. The judge awarded each party one-half of the assets and the debts. He also awarded each party joint legal and joint physical custody, and ordered each of them to pay to the other a certain amount of child support.

Frank and Lilly finally realized that they had wasted a lot of time and money on litigating issues that should have been settled years ago.

I.

CHOOSING THE ATTORNEY AND PLANNING THE FIRST MEETING

1) **Find The Family Law Attorney**

There are many ways to find the right attorney. Your significant other can call the state and local bar associations, check with friends and relatives, look in the yellow pages, or obtain a referral from the attorney who handles your significant other's personal matters. However, it is always best to obtain three names so that your significant other can choose the one attorney who is right for your significant other.

Your significant other may find that one attorney's name is given by many sources. He or she would be the first one I would consult before talking with the others.

2) **Determine The Attorney's Expertise, Attitude, And Biases**

I would encourage you to attend the first meeting that your significant other has with the attorney. The attorney should have extensive experience in the field of family law, especially in the area of custody.

You will want to make an appointment with the attorney in order to determine the attorney's expertise, his or her attitude about your significant other and his or her case, and the nature and extent of the attorney's biases.

First, it is important to evaluate the attorney's expertise in family law matters. Does the attorney have a sufficient amount of legal knowledge and trial experience to handle your significant other's case? Your significant other's case may be just another case to the attorney, but your significant other's case is the only case that is important to him or her. Ask the attorney to state the extent of his or her trial experience, including the number of domestic cases handled by him or her in the last five years. Inquire about his or her familiarity with the county court judges. That may be important because each judge may have his or her way of handling custody cases. For example, some judges prefer to appoint a guardian ad litem, and some do not. Some judges refer all of their cases to mediation before any hearing, and some do not.

Second, it is important to consider the attorney's attitude about your significant other, his or her case, and you. Is the attorney focused on your significant other's case when your significant other is explaining the facts and circumstances of the parties and the case? Or, is the attorney busy answering other telephone calls about personal matters? How does the attorney intend to handle your significant other's case? Does your significant other feel that the attorney's aggressive position may hinder any future relationship that your significant other may have with the other parent?

Third, it is important to determine if there are any personal biases that the attorney may have regarding any of the issues in your significant other's case. If your significant other decides not to seek custody, is the attorney going to support him or her in the decision? Is the attorney going to have a negative attitude about your significant other as a parent and as a person if he or she decides not to seek custody? Discuss whether there are any factors or issues in your significant other's case that are of concern to the attorney. Every person has certain biases and, therefore, it is important to determine if the attorney's biases will interfere with his or her handling of your significant other's case. Even though the attorney is paid to be an advocate, personal feelings do surface in the course of litigation.

Fourth, it is important to discuss with the attorney how he or she feels about your significant other as a person. Does your significant other's lifestyle bother the attorney? Does your significant other's membership in certain religious or political groups pose a problem? For example, does the fact that your significant other was divorced conflict with the attorney's religious beliefs?

3) Understand The Law Office Procedures

Your significant other should inquire about the procedures followed in the law office.

Does the office appear to be operating efficiently?

Is it the policy of the law office to promptly mail to your significant other copies of all letters, orders, and other documents that are either received or prepared by the law office? Your significant other will want to maintain a complete file for his or her reference.

Make sure that the office staff always has your significant other's correct address and telephone numbers where he or she can be reached. Your significant other should advise the attorney of any changes in his or her address or telephone numbers.

Let the office staff know whom to call in your significant other's office in the event your significant other is not available. The attorney may have to reach your significant other for a court appearance or conference.

If your significant other wants mail sent to a place other than his or her home, please make sure that the attorney's office has this address in their files.

Insist upon receiving each month a detailed bill, so that there is a record of how much time was billed on your significant other's case, and the type of service that was provided.

Your significant other should be kept advised of all court dates and deposition dates.

4) Avoid Possible Conflicts

Ask the attorney if he or she has any possible conflicts with you, your significant other, or your significant other's case in general.

It is important to know whether the attorney or any member of the law firm has represented the other party in any matter in the past? It is does not matter how long ago in the past. Even though it was twenty years ago, it may be a potential conflict with your significant other's case.

Has anyone in the office checked the law office's records to verify that there is no conflict? You really don't want to learn that there is a conflict when you are on the way to the courthouse.

Has the attorney or any member of the law firm represented any businesses owned by the other party? Has the attorney or any member of the law firm represented any businesses that have had any contractual relations with a business owned by the other party? Has the attorney or any member of the law firm been contacted recently by the other party for a consultation? Please ask the attorney if he or she sees any possible conflict.

5) Review The Contract Of Employment

Your significant other will want to review the contract of employment with the attorney, not the secretary. The employment contract is a binding and enforceable legal document. Therefore, the attorney is the only person who can properly advise your significant other as to the legal consequences of all of the terms contained in the contract.

Another issue is the retainer. Black's Law Dictionary defines retainer as an "act of the client in employing his attorney or counsel, and also denotes the fee which the client pays when he retains the attorney to act for him, and thereby prevents him from acting for his adversary. Term can mean a fee not only for the rendition of professional services when requested, but also for the attorney taking the case, making himself available to handle it, and refusing employment by plaintiff's adversary; or it can mean solely the compensation for services to be performed in a specific case." When does the retainer need to be replenished? Will the retainer be used as a credit toward the bill? Is the retainer merely a sum of money given to the attorney so that he or she can never represent the other party?

What is the hourly rate for each type of service? Usually, the attorney and the staff will bill at different rates. Is there interest charged on the unpaid balance? Is there a flat fee for certain services? Remember, the attorney charges for every minute that is spent on your significant other's case. Therefore, make every call count and avoid nonessential calls. How are the time records kept?

6) Meet The Office Staff

Your significant other should be on friendly terms with the secretary and law clerk who will be working on the case. They usually handle matters that do not require the attorney's time and attention, such as scheduling appointments, conferences, and depositions. How does the staff conduct themselves in the office? Does the secretary or law clerk mention other clients by their names in your presence? Does the secretary or law clerk complain about other clients in your presence? For example, stating that a client is a pest or calls every day. Does the secretary or law clerk discuss other cases in your presence? You do not want your significant other's case discussed in the presence of another client, potential client, or anyone else who is not working in or employed by that law office. Your significant other has the right to expect that all matters pertaining to his or her case will remain confidential and privileged. Therefore, your significant other will want to make sure that nothing will be divulged to any person who is not bound to keep these matters secret. Even though your significant other's attorney will discuss the case with the opposing attorney, the attorney for your significant other will not divulge matters that should remain confidential between him or her and your significant other. Does the secretary or law clerk have other client's privileged correspondence where you can see it? These materials should not be seen by other clients.

Does the secretary or law clerk complain about the attorney? For example, the attorney never knows where the files are, or the attorney is always late for appointments.

Does the secretary or law clerk give legal advice to other clients, either in the office or over the telephone? Please remember that the attorney is the only person who should give your significant other legal advice. Neither the secretary nor the law clerk may give legal advice.

Does the secretary or law clerk treat you and your significant other with the respect that both of you deserve?

You and your significant other need to feel comfortable with the secretary or law clerk since both of you may be spending a lot of time with this person. The case could last longer than a year, and that is a long time to be working with someone who is aggravating.

7) Provide The Attorney With Relevant Documents

It is important to ask the attorney what documents he or she wants to see at the initial meeting.

Many attorneys do not want the client to bring anything to the first meeting. They prefer to talk with the client about the issues in the case, and how the client wants these issues to be resolved.

388 DO YOU REALLY WANT TO BE A STEPPARENT?

If the attorney asks for some information, your significant other may want to bring the following materials:

1) An outline of the issues in your significant other's case, whether they are contested issues or not, and how your significant other wants these issues to be resolved;

2) The Domestic Relations Financial Affidavit;

3) State and Federal Tax returns for the last three years;

4) Bank statements for the last twelve months;

5) Pension and retirement account statements for the last twelve months;

6) Investment account statements from brokerage houses for the last twelve months;

7) Relevant letters, diaries, and pictures;

8) The child's recent school and medical records; and

9) Detective reports.

The Domestic Relations Financial Affidavit answers most of the attorney's questions about your significant other's financial situation, including income, assets, and debts. With this information, the attorney may be able to advise your significant other as to how the assets might be divided, how much child support your significant other could receive or pay, and how the debts could be allocated. This information is extremely important for you to know because you will need to decide whether or not you can live on what your significant other has left after he or she pays his or her child support obligations.

Joint and/or individual tax returns will furnish the attorney with more financial data. Tax returns contain information about investments, income, bank accounts, and deductions.

The bank statements should include checking, savings, and money market accounts.

The pension and retirement account statements should include the money in pension funds, individual retirement accounts, and military retirement accounts.

The investment account statements should include statements from brokerage houses and other evidence of an interest in stocks, bonds, and other securities.

Letters, diaries, and pictures may be relevant if they relate to the issues in the case. For example, a love letter from a friend, a diary containing relevant information that was kept during the marriage, and pictures of you, your significant other, his or her child, and the opposing party.

The child's recent report cards and school records may contain valuable information about the child and both of the parents. The school records may also indicate which parent is involved in the child's academic life. Obviously, the report cards and records will indicate any problem that the child is having in school.

The child's medical records are important if the child has a particular health problem.

A copy of the detective reports may provide further information about you, your significant other, his or her child, the opposing party, and any other issues in the case.

II.

SOME OF THE LEGAL ISSUES

1) Approximate Cost Of The Litigation

The exact cost of the litigation is usually not known at the beginning of your significant other's case. While the exact cost may not be known, the attorney may be able to give the approximate costs associated with the litigation. These costs include the following:

The attorney's fees;

The costs associated with taking depositions and the costs of the transcripts;

The fees charged by the private investigator;

The miscellaneous fees, including subpoena fees and copying charges; and

The fees charged by the expert witness who is involved in the case.

The expert may be asked to do a mental and/or physical examination of you, the parties, and the child. The expert may be asked to testify in court or at a deposition.

Your significant other must decide whether or not he or she can afford to go to court. Needless to say, litigation is very costly, and can quickly deplete most of the family's financial resources.

2) Alternatives To Litigation

Discuss with the attorney whether ADR is available in your state. If so, I would strongly recommend that your significant other try these methods before he or she engages in litigation.

There are several alternatives to litigation, such as mediation, case evaluation, and arbitration.

Many judges require that the parties attend mediation before the judge will have a hearing.

There are many reasons for pursuing mediation before resorting to litigation. Some of these reasons are:

Your significant other can avoid costly litigation;

Your significant other can spare everyone the emotional trauma of a trial; and

Your significant other and the other parent may learn how to work out their differences without relying on the attorneys for expensive legal advice.

3) Types Of Custody That May Be Awarded

It is important that your significant other discuss with the attorney the reasons for seeking a particular type of custody.

Joint legal custody has many pros and cons.

Some of the pros include the following:

> Both parents are actively involved in their child's life, and neither parent is an outsider; and
>
> Both parents have the benefit of the other parent's input in matters regarding the child's health, education, and welfare.

Some of the cons include the following:

> Frequently, the parents disagree about important matters, and that causes more friction between them; and
>
> This type of custody requires constant communication between the parents. If they do not have the ability to discuss matters reasonably, this type of custody will not work.

Joint physical custody has many pros and cons.

Some of the pros include the following:

> Each custodial parent has physical custody of the child approximately half of the time; and
>
> If one parent denies the other parent his or her custodial rights, the parent being denied may seek to enforce his or her rights by applying for a criminal warrant for interference with custody. The parent who has visitation rights can not seek a criminal warrant, but can file a motion to punish for contempt.

Some of the cons include the following:

> If the parents live too far apart, this sort of arrangement is very difficult, if not impossible, for the child and the parents; and
>
> If the parents do not have a good working relationship, this arrangement can be a nightmare. This type of custody requires a lot of contact and communication.

Sole legal and sole physical custody has many pros and cons.

Some of the pros include the following:

> The custodial parent has the right to make all of the decisions regarding the child's health, education, and welfare, and does not have to consult with the other parent; and
>
> In Georgia, the custodial parent has the right to move to another state with the child.

Some of the cons include the following:

> The noncustodial parent may feel that he or she is not a part of the child's life; and
>
> The noncustodial parent may feel that all the custodial parent wants is money. Frequently, the obligor resents paying child support. He or she may avoid paying any support, or pay late, or resist upward modifications of the amount of child support.

4) Chances Of Being Awarded Permanent Custody

Since anything can happen, it is best to inquire about the chances of being awarded permanent custody in the event the other parent is awarded temporary custody.

It is not impossible for the judge to award permanent custody to the parent who was not awarded temporary custody. However, some judges are reluctant to change custody where the child appears to be doing well at home and in school. Therefore, it may be important to hire the attorney who knows the judge's habits.

Discuss with the attorney his or her initial impression about the chances of being awarded the type of custody that your significant other is seeking. If the attorney is not optimistic about your significant other being awarded custody, ask the attorney why he or she feels this way, and how your significant other can increase his or her chances of being awarded the type of custody that he or she is seeking.

5) The Custodial Parent's Rights And Obligations

The custodial parent has many rights and obligations.

The custodial parent has the legal right to make decisions about matters affecting the child's health, including the right to decide which doctor and dentist will treat the child, the right to have the child admitted to a psychiatric hospital, and the right to seek therapy or counseling for the child.

The custodial parent has the legal right to decide which school the child will attend and in which activities the child will participate.

The custodial parent has the legal right to decide who will be the child's babysitters.

The custodial parent has the legal right to decide which day care center the child will attend.

The custodial parent has the legal right to decide who will be the child's friends and associates.

The custodial parent has the legal right to decide what the child will wear.

The custodial parent has the legal right to prohibit the child from going out at night.

The custodial parent may be legally obligated to contribute to the financial support of the child.

The custodial parent may be legally obligated to pay for property that was damaged by the child, under certain circumstances and under certain state laws.

The custodial parent may be legally obligated to provide proper medical and dental care for the child.

The custodial parent is legally obligated to provide the child with proper food, clothing, and shelter.

The custodial parent is legally obligated to maintain a wholesome, safe, and moral environment for the child to live in.

The custodial parent who is denied his or her custodial rights has the right to file a motion to punish the noncustodial parent for being in contempt of the court's order.

The custodial parent may also seek to have the noncustodial parent arrested for interference with custody.

6) Legal Consequences For Failing To Comply With A Court Order

There may be serious legal consequences for failing or refusing to abide by the court order. For example, failing or refusing to communicate with the other parent about important matters concerning the child may be a violation of the judge's order. That may result in being found in contempt and having to pay the other party's attorney's fees.

It is important to know what the legal obligations are under any court order, and the consequences for failing or refusing to abide by the terms of the order.

7) The 14-Year-Old Child's Right To Make An Election

Please discuss with the attorney the law regarding the child's right to decide where the child will live. In Georgia, the child who has reached the age of 14 may elect to live with either parent. Such an election is binding on the judge, unless the judge finds that the selected parent is not a fit and proper parent to assume custody of the child. This right of election only applies to where the child will live, not who has custody of the child. Only the judge decides who has custody of the child.

8) Modification Of Custody

If your significant other believes that he or she has grounds to seek a modification of the custody order, please discuss with the attorney those facts that support your significant other's claim for a modification.

9) Visitation Arrangement In The Event The Custodial Parent Moves

Will the visitation arrangement be changed in the event the custodial parent moves to another state? Is primary physical custody transferred to the parent who does not move? Does the moving parent forfeit primary physical custody during the school year? Since custodial parents move quite often, it is better to plan for this event now.

10) Importance Of A Definite Visitation Schedule

It is important to discuss with the attorney the reasons for seeking a definite visitation schedule.

Obviously, it is important to see the child as much as possible. Therefore, your significant other's work or activities schedule should not conflict with his or her visitation times. There is nothing worse for the child than to wait for the parent who does not come for visitation.

The visitation rights of the noncustodial parent should be defined in any settlement agreement, temporary order, or final order.

The visitation provisions should specify when each parent has the child during the school year, summer, holidays, and all other times during the year. Most judges insist that there be such specificity in any agreement or order of the court.

Your significant other may want to arrange the visitation schedule so that the child will be with a parent or a stepparent rather than with a babysitter.

11) The Noncustodial Parent's Visitation Rights

Discuss with the attorney the noncustodial parent's visitation rights. Remember, visitation is a *right* and not merely a privilege.

The noncustodial parent may enforce his or her visitation rights by filing a motion to punish the custodial parent who is wrongfully withholding visitation rights.

Where the custodial parent has repeatedly denied the noncustodial parent his or her visitation rights, the judge may award the noncustodial parent custody of the child.

12) Modification Of Visitation Rights

Often, parents want to modify the visitation order. There are many reasons why the prior visitation arrangement has to be modified. Please discuss with the attorney the ability to modify the visitation rights in the agreement or final order.

13) Amount Of Child Support That May Be Awarded

If your significant other is the custodial parent, he or she will want to know the amount of child support that he or she may be awarded.

If your significant other is the noncustodial parent, he or she will want to know the amount of child support that he or she may be obligated to pay. This information is especially important for your consideration as well.

The Georgia Child Support Guidelines have already been outlined in a previous chapter. Whether you are a Georgia resident or not, please review the guidelines before meeting with the attorney.

Please discuss with the attorney whether having joint physical custody affects the amount of child support. Some judges may order one custodial parent to pay child support to the other custodial parent who earns less money, or who takes care of the child most of the custodial time. The rationale of these judges is that the child should not be deprived of having a nice lifestyle when the child is living with the parent who earns less.

14) Duration Of The Child Support Obligation

You will find the Georgia statute regarding this issue in a previous chapter. Please note that in any Georgia child support order entered on or after July 1, 1992, either or both parents may be ordered to provide financial assistance to the child who is still in high school when he or she attains the age of 18 if the child has not previously married or has not become emancipated. However, this financial assistance is not required after the child reaches the age of 20. Whether you are from Georgia or from a different state, please discuss this matter with the attorney.

15) The Parent's Obligation To Provide Insurance

In Georgia, the judge or the jury may order a parent to provide health insurance for the child.

The judge or the jury may order one or both parents to pay those expenses that are not covered by the health insurance.

The judge or the jury may order one or both parents to obtain and maintain life insurance for the benefit of the child.

16) The Parent's Obligation To Pay The College Expenses

In Georgia, parents are not legally obligated to pay the child's college expenses. However, the parents can provide in the settlement agreement that one or both of them shall be liable for the payment of these expenses.

Where the agreement is made the order of the court, the judge may enforce this provision. Therefore, please consider whether your significant other will be in a financial position in the future to pay for the college expenses.

If your significant other fails to meet this obligation, the child may request that the judge hold your significant other in willful contempt and jailed for failing to pay the college expenses.

17) The Judge's Power To Award The Tax Exemption

In Georgia, the judge has no power to award the tax exemption to either party. However, the parties can provide in the settlement agreement that one of the parents can claim the child as a dependent on his or her tax returns every year. Or, the parties can agree that one parent can claim the child in odd-numbered years, and the other parent can claim the child in even-numbered years.

18) Tax Consequences Of Paying And Receiving Child Support

Please consult with a tax adviser about the tax consequences of paying and receiving child support. Currently, child support is not deductible by the obligor, and is not taxable as income to the obligee.

19) Documents That May Be Required At A Deposition, Mediation Session, And In Court

The Domestic Relations Financial Affidavit provides the most information about your significant other's income, assets, and liabilities. Usually, the affidavit is used during the mediation session and in court. Therefore, please review each category carefully and answer each with as much accuracy as possible.

The opposing attorney will usually question your significant other about each and every entry that is included in the document.

I have found the best way to include all of the expenses, assets, and liabilities is to review last year's checkbook, income tax returns, statements from creditors, statements from banks, and statements from brokerage houses.

If your significant other does not know the amount that was

spent each month for a certain expense, please average the last twelve months. If the value of an asset is unknown, please try to obtain an appraisal. If an appraisal can not be obtained, put an asterisk beside an amount or value to indicate that it is an approximate figure. If your significant other is unsure about any item, discuss that with the attorney.

If there is an expense that does not fit into a category, please list that expense on a separate sheet of paper titled "Miscellaneous."

If your significant other is anticipating incurring an expense in the very near future, but is not spending that amount now, indicate that on the form, but do not count it as a present expense. Remember, don't inflate the amount that is truly spent.

Your significant other may be requested to bring other written materials, records, and financial documents.

In the case of records and financial documents, the attorney will advise your significant other as to whether the attorney wants copies of only recent documents or documents for a certain period of time.

The following are some of the written materials, records, and documents that your significant other may need:

1) A copy of the bank account statements, checking and savings;

2) A copy of the financial statements prepared by the parties, jointly or individually;

3) A copy of the parties' employment and personnel records;

4) A copy of the statements from all retirement accounts, military retirement accounts, pension fund accounts, individual retirement accounts, investment accounts, money market accounts, certificates of deposit, accounts in which either party has deposited moneys that were acquired by inheritance or gift, trust accounts, and any other accounts in which there is money deposited;

5) A list of the joint and individual debts with an approximate balance of each debt, the name of the creditor, the amount of the monthly payment, and who is responsible for making the payments;

6) A copy of any psychological and/or psychiatric evaluations of the parties and the child;

7) A copy of the child's medical, hospital, and dental records and bills;

8) A copy of the medical and hospital records and bills for either or both of the parties;

9) A copy of the child's report cards and school records;

10) A copy of the court documents that are relevant to the present custody case, including prior court cases involving either or both of the parties;

11) A copy of all relevant photographs, detective reports, video recordings, and tape recordings that your significant other has in his or her possession; and

12) Any other relevant documents, letters, or other written materials that your significant other has in his or her possession.

20) Specific Laws That Relate To The Issues In The Case

Please discuss with the attorney the statutory laws and the appellate court cases that pertain to the issues in your significant other's case. Of course, no one can tell you how the judge will rule in your significant other's case. However, it is very helpful to know how the appellate courts have ruled in cases involving similar issues, and if there are any applicable statutes that govern the issues in your significant other's case.

21) Specific Problems In The Case

Some litigants have said and done something in the past that may affect the outcome of their cases.

If there is something in your significant other's past that may cause a problem in his or her case, now is the time to make this known to the attorney. It is not wise to assume that one's past actions and statements, which are relevant to the case, will not come out in the discovery process or at trial, because they usually do. If it does not, fine. If it does, the attorney will at least be prepared to deal with it.

22) Some Of The Legal Procedures

The attorney can advise you and your significant other about the procedures that must be followed in order to file a complaint for divorce and custody, a petition for change of custody, an answer, or an answer and counterclaim to the complaint or petition that has already been filed.

410 DO YOU REALLY WANT TO BE A STEPPARENT?

The following procedures are based on Georgia practice. Please discuss with the attorney the actual procedures that will be used in your significant other's case. If your significant other is seeking a divorce and custody of his or her child, the first pleading filed in court is the ***Complaint for Divorce.*** If your significant other is seeking a modification of custody, the first pleading filed in court is the ***Petition For Change Of Custody***. These documents are filed in the court having jurisdiction, i.e., the court that is legally empowered to hear these cases.

In a divorce and custody action, your significant other may want to allege in his or her complaint, answer, or answer and counterclaim, who has been the primary caretaker of the child, why it is in the best interest of the child that custody be awarded to your significant other, and why your significant other is a fit and proper person to have custody of his or her child.

In a modification of custody action, your significant other may want to allege in his or her petition that since the prior custody award, the custodial parent is no longer a fit and proper parent to retain custody, or that there is a material change of conditions or circumstances that substantially affects the child and that it is in the best interest of the child to change custody, or that the minor child is now fourteen years old and elects to live with the noncustodial parent.

The person filing the original action is called the ***Plaintiff***.

The person filing the answer or answer and counterclaim is called the ***Defendant***.

At the end of the complaint, petition, answer, or answer and counterclaim is the ***Prayer***. In the Prayer section, the party prays that the judge award the party what he or she is requesting, such as custody, visitation, and child support.

The attorney usually requests that the party sign in the presence of a notary a document called a ***Verification***. In this document, the party verifies the truth and accuracy of what is contained in the complaint, petition, answer, or answer and counterclaim.

Attached to the complaint or petition is the ***Summons***. The Summons tells the Defendant the name of the court, the names of the parties, the date that the action was filed, how many days the Defendant has to file an Answer in order to avoid having a default judgment entered, and the name and address of the attorney for the Plaintiff.

The Defendant is then *served* by having either a sheriff or a duly appointed citizen, not the Plaintiff, deliver the pleading to the Defendant. However, if the Plaintiff chooses, the Defendant does not have to be served in this manner. The Defendant can sign in the presence of a notary an *Acknowledgment of Service*. By signing this document, the Defendant acknowledges that he or she has received the complaint or petition, and that no further service is necessary. However, the Defendant should always seek the advice of an attorney prior to signing anything, including an Acknowledgment of Service.

An *Answer* is the pleading filed by the Defendant. In the Answer, the Defendant responds to each and every allegation contained in the Plaintiff's complaint or petition by either admitting or denying the allegations that are made by the Plaintiff.

Along with the Answer, the Defendant can file a *Counterclaim* in which the Defendant sets forth what the Defendant's position is and what relief the Defendant is seeking.

There is another document that may be attached to the pleading known as the *Order and Rule Nisi*. Most courts in divorce cases now issue a standing mutual restraining order and, if requested, a Rule Nisi Order. The restraining order enjoins and restrains both parties from doing certain acts, including threatening the opposing party or the child, or removing the child from the jurisdiction of the court. Removing the child from the jurisdiction of the court means that the parent cannot remove the child permanently from the court's jurisdiction, not merely taking the child on vacation.

The Rule Nisi is a pleading that informs the other party of the date, time, and place of the temporary or permanent hearing on the issues of custody, visitation, child support, and other related matters.

23) Discovery Process

Please have the attorney explain to your significant other the discovery process and how it affects him or her.

The term discovery means that the party is seeking to discover or obtain information that the party does not already have. This information can be documents, sworn statements of witnesses or parties, and written answers to specific questions. Discovery usually includes a Notice to Produce and Request For Production of Documents, Interrogatories, and Depositions.

414 DO YOU REALLY WANT TO BE A STEPPARENT?

The Notice to Produce and Request for Production of Documents is sent to the opposing party and requests that he or she produce documents in his or her possession or control, including financial records, documents that may be introduced into evidence at the trial, reports, and pictures. The Notice advises when and where these documents are to be produced.

If your significant other receives the Notice to Produce, he or she will have to check to see if he or she has the requested documents. Your significant other will have to advise the attorney about whether or not he or she has these documents so that the attorney can prepare the proper response. There is a certain period of time in which to respond to the Notice. If your significant other fails to respond within the time period, there may be sanctions against him or her, such as having to pay the fees of the other attorney for having to file a Motion To Compel. The opposing attorney files this motion in order to have the judge order your significant other to comply with the Notice to Produce. Therefore, it is important to comply with the Notice to Produce within the time specified.

Interrogatories are written questions, usually no more than fifty (50) questions, including sub-parts, sent by one party to the opposing party. The receiving party is required to make a written response to each question, and then sign a verification in the presence of a notary. The interrogatories may focus on many issues, including the mental and physical health of the party answering the questions, and his or her reasons for seeking custody. The attorney will advise his or her client of the client's right to invoke the privilege against self-incrimination in the event an answer may tend to incriminate the client.

If your significant other receives Interrogatories, he or she will have a certain period of time in which to respond to the Interrogatories. If your significant other fails to respond within the time period, there may be sanctions against him or her, such as having to pay the fees of the other attorney for having to file a Motion To Compel. Therefore, it is important to answer the questions within the time specified.

The purpose of the deposition is to have the deponent, i.e., the person who is answering the questions, testify under oath about matters that are relevant to the case.

The deponent may be your significant other, the other party, you, an expert in the case, or any person having information about the parties or the case. The parties and their attorneys may be present at the deposition. The deponent who is not one of the parties may also have an attorney present. The deposition usually takes place in the office of one of the attorneys. The court reporter is present to take down the questions asked by the attorney and the deponent's answers. The written transcript of the deposition may be used to prepare for trial, as well as for impeachment purposes, i.e., to show that the testimony of the deponent at trial is not the same as it was at the deposition.

24) Importance Of The Psychological Evaluation

Discuss with the attorney whether or not your significant other should request a psychiatric or psychological evaluation in the case. In Georgia, either party may file a motion for an evaluation of the parties and their minor child. The judge may grant or deny this motion.

If the judge deems it necessary, the judge may order an evaluation of the parties, the parties' spouses, and the minor child. The judge will appoint a psychiatrist or psychologist to conduct these evaluations. Usually, this professional will be someone who has previously testified in the judge's court. The judge may also order one or both of the parties to pay for these evaluations.

There are a few reasons not to have these evaluations. First, these psychological evaluations are costly and time-consuming. Second, the judge may reject the results of the psychological or psychiatric evaluation. Third, your significant other may not like the results of these evaluations.

The following comments were made by two Georgia judges. One appellate court judge wrote in a court decision that "Compulsory psychological evaluation of a family's children, coupled with submitting parents to the Minnesota Multiphasic Personality Inventory Psychological evaluation, under the particular facts of this case, appears to be an unacceptable and unreasonable intrusion into family affairs by the State, if not a violation of the Right of Privacy under the First, Fourth and Ninth Amendments to the U.S. Constitution. The preamble to the new State Constitution encourages promoting 'the interest of ...the family' and does not advocate State control over the family except in grave and compelling situations. Were these types of evaluation arbitrarily used on the families of social workers, judges and others who may have unusual and other than normal living habits and situations, harsh psychological and disciplinary guidelines could well become the norm rather than the exception, as there is no assurance that any of us could pass the test. It is presumed that parental discipline and rearing of children is proper and superior to psychological ideas set forth by an employee of the State, who also may never have raised any children. At least until the contrary is shown, care, caution and circumspection should be used prior to authorizing psychological tests of this nature. Parental misconduct, inability, or minor deprivation, not amounting to 'moral unfitness, physical abuse and abandonment' falls short of permitting State control over the family...Otherwise, it could be argued that most parents have some type of psychological, financial, emotional or moral limitation, inability or hang up, which would result in all children becoming subject to psychological study and control in a mythical Brave New World becoming a reality."[1]

---

[1] In re D.H. et al, 178 Ga.App. 119, 342 S.E.2d 367 (1986)

In another case, the judge reviewed the psychologist's evaluation and reasoned that the doctor was "operating on, I think, one level of knowledge and, hopefully, I'm operating on a little higher level of knowledge. I had the benefit of testimony by other people. I had the benefit of seeing the people who did actually testify in this case and applying my own view as to whether or not they were telling the truth, simply by their demeanor and the content of what they said; how they said it."[2]

As you can see, some judges do not consider these evaluations to be particularly valid or beneficial. Other judges, however, do believe that these evaluations provide very valuable information that the judge might not otherwise have. However, when two professionals testify in the same case and reach different conclusions, some judges are outwardly critical about the entire process. Therefore, it is important to determine whether the attorney knows the judge, and knows how the judge regards psychiatric or psychological evaluations. If the judge does not have a high regard for psychiatric and/or psychological evaluations, perhaps it is better not to insist on the evaluation.

[2] In the Interest of B.H., 190 Ga.App. 131, 378 S.E.2d 175 (1989)

25) The Witnesses

Your significant other should begin preparing his or her witness list as soon as possible.

It is important to talk with each potential witness about testifying for your significant other before the attorney does.

Your significant other should ask the potential witness whether or not he or she wants to be involved in the case.

The potential witness should know that he or she may have to take off from work in order to testify in court or may be deposed by the other side.

After all of the potential witnesses have been contacted, make a list of those witnesses who have agreed to testify, and include their names, addresses, telephone numbers, relationship to you or your significant other, and a summary of what each witness knows and can testify about.

It is also important to advise the attorney about anything the witness knows that you or your significant other would not want to be revealed in court.

Witnesses may include the following persons:

1) Character witnesses who know your reputation and the reputation of your significant other in the community and work place;

2) Expert witnesses, including psychiatrists, psychologists, investigators, and any other professionals who have had contact with you, your significant other, the opposing party, or the child;

3) Family members who are familiar with you and your significant other's parenting skills, the opposing party's parenting skills, and any other relevant information;

4) Persons familiar with the child, including teachers, counselors, doctors, therapists, coaches, day care workers, and other persons who know the child;

5) Friends and neighbors who have seen you and/or your significant other interact with the child. These may be mere acquaintances or life-long friends; and

6) Other witnesses who have relevant information about you, your significant other, the opposing party, the child, or the case.

In order to compel the witness to come to court to testify, one must *subpoena* the witness. That means that the witness has to be served with a subpoena, which is a legal document commanding the person to appear in court and testify.

A deputy sheriff, a private investigator, or a party can serve a subpoena.

If your significant other is serving a subpoena, it is important that he or she make a note of the date, time, and place. This information must be included in his or her Affidavit Of Service.

In addition, there is usually a witness fee that must accompany a subpoena in order for a subpoena to be valid.

Even if the witness volunteers to come to court to testify on your significant other's behalf, it is best to hand the witness a subpoena. If the litigant does not subpoena the witness, the litigant may not have a legal excuse in the event the witness fails to appear in court.

Your significant other may or may not want his or her child to talk with the judge in the judge's chambers.

Please discuss in detail with the attorney what the reasons are for not wanting the child to speak with the judge.

Please discuss in detail with the attorney what the reasons are for wanting the child to speak with the judge.

If your significant other wants the child to speak with the judge, please make sure that the child knows what will occur, and that he or she is only expected to tell the truth.

Usually, the judge will not have the child testify in the courtroom. Instead, the judge may request that the child meet with the judge in chambers. Obviously, the judge will not force the child to make a choice about where he or she would like to live.

In Georgia, either party has the right to request that the meeting with the judge be recorded.

Please remember that if the child meets with the judge in chambers, you and your significant other should not make the mistake of interrogating the child about what was said in the meeting.

26) The Guardian Ad Litem

The guardian ad litem is an attorney appointed by the judge to represent the best interest of the child.

The judge may appoint any qualified guardian ad litem, and may order one or both of the parents to pay the guardian's fees.

Either party may file a motion to have a guardian ad litem appointed to represent the child. The judge may or may not grant the motion.

If the judge grants the motion, the judge will appoint the guardian ad litem, and order one or both of the parents to pay the guardian's fees.

III.

COURTROOM PROCEEDINGS

1) A Visit To An Actual Trial

Before your significant other's custody trial, you and your significant other may want to consider observing a custody trial. You and your significant other can observe what takes place in court, and how other litigants conduct themselves. If possible, try to select a case that is being tried before the judge who will be hearing your significant other's case. While this case will not be identical to your significant other's case, your significant other may still get an idea of how the judge views different matters.

2) Transferring The Case To The Juvenile Court

Occasionally, the parties may request that the case be transferred to the juvenile court. However, the superior court judge does not have to transfer the case.

Sometimes, the judge may want to transfer the case to the juvenile court judge for either investigation only, or for investigation and determination.

Where the judge transfers the case for investigation only, the case will be returned to the judge for a ruling on the issues of custody, visitation, and child support.

Where the judge transfers the case for investigation and determination, the juvenile court judge rules on the issues of custody, visitation, and child support.

Some attorneys prefer to have the custody case tried in the juvenile court. They believe that the juvenile court judge will have more time to listen to the case. Moreover, there are usually no spectators permitted in the juvenile courtroom.

3) **Pretrial Conference And Pretrial Order**

Before the actual trial, some judges may want a pretrial conference with the attorneys. The judge may want to know those issues that were settled by the parties and those issues that must be tried in court.

In addition, the judge may require a Pretrial Order. This document, which is prepared by the attorneys, includes, among other things, the names of the attorneys who will try the case, the length of the trial, each party's statement of the issues in the case, the names of the witnesses, what each witness is expected to testify about, a list of the documents to be presented at trial, the applicable law(s), and other related matters. Once the Pretrial Order is signed by the judge and filed with the court, there may be no other matters presented in court, unless the judge permits it.

4) Temporary Hearing

The judge will rule on temporary matters at the temporary hearing. These temporary matters may include the following:

1) Which parent is awarded temporary custody, which parent is awarded temporary visitation, and the visitation that is specifically awarded;

2) Which parent is ordered to pay temporary child support, and the amount of the temporary child support;

3) Which parent(s) is ordered to maintain health and life insurance for the benefit of the child;

4) Which parent(s) is ordered to pay those medical, dental, hospital, and other related expenses that are not covered by insurance;

5) Which parent is awarded the temporary use and possession of the house;

6) Which parent is awarded the temporary use and possession of the cars, furniture, and other property;

7) Which parent is ordered to pay the marital debts; and

8) Which insurances, including life insurance, are to remain in full force and effect.

At the temporary hearing, there may be a limit to the number of witnesses who can testify. In Georgia, the judge usually permits each party to have only one witness who may testify in court, besides the testimony of the party. The other testimony must be in the form of an affidavit or a transcript of the deposition of the witness. A party may have as many affidavits and deposition transcripts as he or she wishes.

An Affidavit is a written statement that is signed in the presence of a notary. The affiant swears that he or she knows the information to be true from his or her own personal knowledge. The information may be about one or both of the parties or about the child.

A deposition has been previously defined and explained.

The temporary hearing is a very important one. The parent who has been awarded temporary custody may argue that he or she should be awarded permanent custody because the child is doing well at home and in school.

5) Final Trial

In Georgia, if there is no demand for a jury trial, the judge will hear and decide all of the issues in the case, including who is awarded permanent custody, the noncustodial parent's visitation rights, who is liable for the payment of child support, how much child support is to be paid and when, who must maintain health insurance for the child, who must pay the uncovered medical and dental expenses for the child, who must maintain life insurance and how much, how the assets and debts are allocated, whether there is an award of attorney's fees, and all other issues that are before the court.

In Georgia, if there is a demand for a jury trial, the jury will decide all of the issues in the case, except the issues of custody, visitation rights, and attorney's fees. These issues are decided by the judge.

6) Courtroom Procedures

It is very important that your significant other's attorney explain what occurs at each stage of the legal proceeding so that you and your significant other can be prepared. The attorney should explain what is heard and decided at each stage of the proceeding.

It is very important to monitor your conduct in the courtroom, and even outside the courtroom. The impression that a person makes is the one that the judge or the jury remembers. If a person loses his or her temper, uses curse words in court, or exhibits inappropriate conduct, the judge may hold that person in contempt. Therefore, you and your significant other must monitor and control your conduct, your verbal expressions, and your body language.

After the judge rules on any preliminary motions, the Plaintiff's attorney gives a brief opening statement outlining what the Plaintiff contends are the issues in the case, the facts as the Plaintiff views them, the law(s) applicable to the case, and what the Plaintiff is seeking. Then, the Defendant's attorney gives a brief opening statement outlining what the Defendant contends are the issues in the case, the facts as the Defendant views them, the law(s) applicable to the case, and what the Defendant is seeking.

At the final trial, the attorneys for the Plaintiff and the Defendant may call as many expert and non-expert witnesses as each side wants, so long as the testimony is not cumulative, i.e., repeats what other witnesses have testified about.

The Plaintiff's attorney calls the first witness to the stand to testify. After the witness testifies under direct examination, i.e., answers questions posed by the attorney who called the witness, the opposing attorney has the opportunity to cross-examine the witness.

The Plaintiff's attorney may then ask follow-up questions, a procedure known as redirect examination.

The Defendant's attorney may then ask follow-up questions, a procedure known as recross examination.

After all of the Plaintiff's witnesses have testified, and the Plaintiff's attorney has submitted into evidence all of the Plaintiff's documents, the Plaintiff rests.

Now, the Defendant's attorney calls the first witness to the stand to testify, and the procedure is repeated as in the Plaintiff's case.

If the attorney asks the witness a question that is objected to by the opposing attorney, the witness should stop testifying, and let the judge rule on the objection. The judge may sustain the objection, i.e., rule that it is not a proper question, or may overrule the objection, i.e., rule that it is a proper question and instruct the witness to answer the question.

Usually, both attorneys have documents that relate to the issues in the case. Documents include a party's bank statement, medical records, and tax returns.

Both attorneys want to have these documents admitted into evidence so that the judge or the jury may consider them. Each document has a number written on the front of the document. After the document is marked, it is called an *Exhibit*. The judge decides whether or not the document is admitted into evidence.

At the end of the Defendant's case, the attorneys make their closing arguments. In the closing argument, each attorney emphasizes those facts and law(s) that support the attorney's position.

After these arguments are concluded, the judge or the jury renders a verdict. Or, if there is no demand for a jury trial, the judge may take the case under advisement, which means that the decision will be made later.

7) Courtroom Tips For Litigants And Other Witnesses

1) Dress conservatively and avoid excessive amounts of jewelry and makeup. A man should come neatly dressed in a suit and a tie. A woman should come neatly dressed in a dress or a suit.

2) Don't chew gum or have anything else in your mouth. Most judges do not allow the parties or the witnesses to chew gum, eat, or drink in the courtroom.

3) Walk, don't run, to the witness stand. It is important that the witness come into the courtroom very quietly.

4) Always be courteous and polite to the judge, the attorneys, and all of the courtroom officials. Do not argue with the opposing attorney. Confine your answers to the questions. Judges do not appreciate any wise cracks from the witnesses, parties, or attorneys.

5) Listen carefully to each question. If you do not hear or understand the question, ask the attorney to repeat or rephrase the question.

6) Look at the judge as much as possible. The judge is trying to assess you and your credibility. Most of the time, the judge is looking at the witness.

7) Speak clearly and loudly so that you are heard by the attorneys, court reporter, and, most importantly, the judge. Since the judge may not strain to hear your testimony, what isn't heard by the judge does not get considered.

8) Answer a question with a "yes" or "no" and then, if necessary, give an explanation. Never answer a question by saying "yeah." Such a response makes it difficult for the court reporter to record, and the judge or the attorneys may not understand what you are saying.

9) If the attorney makes an objection to a question, stop, and wait for the judge's ruling before you continue to testify. Once you hear the phrase, "Objection your Honor," you cease testifying immediately. The judge will tell you whether or not you should answer the question.

10) THE MOST IMPORTANT POINT---Remember, you MUST tell the truth. Perjury is a criminal offense. Moreover, the judge or the jury may disregard all of your testimony if it is proven that you have lied under oath.

SUMMARY

Litigation is complex and unpredictable. Nothing is certain and everything is at risk. Your significant other may think that he or she has a winning case, but he or she may be unpleasantly surprised. Your significant other may think that he or she can be awarded more if there is a trial, but your significant other may not be awarded as much as he or she could have settled for. Therefore, the old saying about the bird in the hand is still valid today.

If your significant other just has to litigate his or her case, at least you and your significant other should be familiar with and knowledgeable about every step of the process.

It is important to choose the right attorney to handle your significant other's case. You may also want to choose the right attorney to advise you about your rights and obligations as a stepparent.

It is important to plan the meeting with the attorney(s) so that no important issue is overlooked.

It is important to be familiar with the legal procedures in order to adequately assist the attorney.

It is important to visit a courtroom and understand how the trial is conducted.

The more you know, the better. Many clients have said that they could have helped prepare their case better if they had known what to expect from the attorneys, the judge, and the litigation process.

Finally, remember four things:

1) It is NEVER too late for your significant other to settle his or her case, even after the trial begins;

2) The terms that your significant other negotiates will usually be more acceptable to him or her than the terms he or she winds up with in the judge's ruling or the jury's verdict;

3) If your significant other has to litigate his or her case, at least be prepared; and

4) Be prepared to accept whatever happens in your significant other's case, including the possibility that your significant other may be awarded physical custody of his or her child.

CHAPTER ELEVEN

LIVING WITH YOUR FINAL DECISION

Hopefully, by now, you have made a final decision about whether or not you really want to be a stepparent. However, if you have not, you may want to consider your answers to the following twenty (20) questions as you continue to weigh the pros and the cons.

1) Do you know how you really feel about becoming a stepparent?

2) Are you in touch with the real you and, therefore, know whether becoming a stepparent is the right decision for you?

3) Are you being honest with yourself in assessing your true feelings?

4) Are you able to admit that becoming a stepparent is not for you?

5) Are you becoming a stepparent without thoroughly examining why you want to be a stepparent?

6) Are you so much in love with your significant other that your judgment is impaired?

7) Have you really had the opportunity to get to know your stepchild?

8) Will you be able to accept the fact that your stepchild and/or his or her friends may accidentally damage your fine furniture?

9) Will you resent having to cancel vacations or other social engagements because your stepchild is ill?

10) Will you be able to tolerate being criticized for what you do and not do for your stepchild?

11) Have you considered that if you make a mistake about becoming a stepparent, your stepchild's life may be adversely affected?

12) Have you thoroughly considered how your lifestyle may be impacted?

13) Will you resent having to devote a large portion of your time and energy to a child who is not your biological child?

14) Will you resent having to put your career on hold because of the time that you will have to devote to your stepchild?

15) Will you resent not being able to devote as much time toward advancing your own education?

16) Will you resent having to share your private time

with your significant other because of the time that he or she must spend with his or her child?

17) Have you considered how your decision may affect your ability to be a full-time parent to your child?

18) Have you considered how your decision may affect the well-being of your child?

19) Have you considered how your child may feel about living with a child who is a total stranger and who is not part of your child's family?

20) Have you considered how your child may feel about having less of your time and attention?

If you decide to become a stepparent, your stepchild will depend on you for love, understanding, and care. Because of what you say or do, you may be the one person who can make a positive difference in this child's life. Therefore, you must pledge to be an active stepparent and a positive role-model for your stepchild for as long as he or she needs you. Moreover, your significant other has the right to expect that you will support him or her as he or she fulfills the role of an active and involved parent.

If you decide that becoming a stepparent is not for you, you need to be honest with your significant other. Moreover, you should not feel guilty about this decision. However, you should let your significant other know how you really feel before his or her child is introduced into the picture. Your stepchild doesn't need to have more negative experiences in his or her life.

The last point I wish to make is that you should always remember that you have the right to do what is in *your* best interest. If becoming a stepparent causes you to feel resentful and angry, it is safe to say that you will not be an effective stepparent or a loving spouse. However, only you know how much you can take before you decide that enough is enough.

You are the only person who knows whether or not it is in your best interest to become a stepparent. Remember, if it is not in your best interest, it will not be in the best interest of your significant other, your stepchild, and your child.

Please review the following pages that contain THE BILL OF RIGHTS FOR STEPPARENTS. This document may help you to reinforce your position that you do have certain rights because you are the stepparent, if you choose to become one.

THE BILL OF RIGHTS FOR STEPPARENTS

1. YOU HAVE THE RIGHT TO BE NUMBER ONE IN YOUR LIFE.

2. YOU HAVE THE RIGHT TO DO WHAT IS IN YOUR BEST INTEREST, EVEN THOUGH YOU ARE THE STEPPARENT.

3. YOU HAVE THE RIGHT TO MAKE YOUR OWN DECISION ABOUT BECOMING A STEPPARENT, REGARDLESS OF WHAT ANYONE MAY SAY OR DO.

4. YOU HAVE THE RIGHT TO BE A LITTLE SELF-CENTERED AT THIS TIME IN YOUR LIFE.

5. YOU HAVE THE RIGHT TO NOT FEEL GUILTY FOR WANTING TO LIVE YOUR LIFE AS YOU CHOOSE.

6. YOU HAVE THE RIGHT TO FEEL THAT YOU ARE NOT A BAD PERSON IF YOU DECIDE NOT TO BECOME A STEPPARENT.

7. YOU HAVE THE RIGHT TO EXPECT YOUR STEPCHILD'S LOVE AND RESPECT.

8. YOU HAVE THE RIGHT TO PARTICIPATE IN ALL ASPECTS OF YOUR STEPCHILD'S LIFE, EVEN THOUGH YOU ARE ONLY THE STEPPARENT.

9. YOU HAVE THE RIGHT TO DEMAND THAT BOTH PARENTS RESPECT YOU AS THE STEPPARENT CARING FOR THEIR CHILD.

10. YOU HAVE THE RIGHT TO BELIEVE THAT YOUR DECISION TO BE OR NOT TO BE A STEPPARENT WILL ALSO BE IN YOUR STEPCHILD'S BEST INTEREST AS WELL AS YOUR OWN.

SUMMARY

You have finally come to the end of this book, and, hopefully, you have made your final decision about whether or not you really want to be a stepparent.

If you are still uncertain about what to do, please reconsider all that you have read in this book, all of your answers to the many questions included in this book, and the professional advice that you have received.

Remember, it is natural to feel torn between wanting to be a stepparent and not wanting the obligation to raise another person's child. Your decision to be or not to be a stepparent must be one that you can live with for a very long time.

All of the pros and cons of becoming a stepparent should be considered, not once but twice. Your significant other should appreciate that you are struggling with a decision that will affect many people's lives, including your life, your significant other's life, your stepchild's life, and your child's life.

Your child should be consulted before you make your final decision. He or she will have to accept the fact that he or she will share you with a child who is not related to your child, except by marriage.

Whatever your decision, I would like to suggest that you remember and apply the following Golden Rules:

GOLDEN RULES

FIRST RULE:

NEVER FORGET THAT YOU DO HAVE CERTAIN RIGHTS BECAUSE YOU ARE THE STEPPARENT.

SECOND RULE:

NEVER ENCOURAGE YOUR STEPCHILD TO SAY OR DO ANYTHING TO HIS OR HER PARENTS THAT YOU WOULD NOT LIKE SAID OR DONE TO YOU.

P.S. I sincerely hope that your decision to be or not to be a stepparent is in your best interest. Please remember that your decision will affect the lives of four very important people, namely, you, your significant other, your stepchild, and your child.

Arline

GLOSSARY

AFFIDAVIT
A written or printed declaration or statement of facts, made voluntarily, and confirmed by the oath or affirmation of the party making it, taken before a person having authority to administer such oath or affirmation.*

AGE OF MAJORITY
The age of legal majority in this state is 18 years; until that age all persons are minors.
O.C.G.A. Section 39-1-1(a).

AGREEMENT
A concord of understanding and intention between two or more parties with respect to the effect upon their relative rights and duties, of certain past or future facts or performances. The consent of two or more persons concurring respecting the transmission of some property, right, or benefits, with the view of contracting an obligation, a mutual obligation.*

ALLEGATION
The assertion, claim, declaration, or statement of a party to an action, made in a pleading, setting out what he expects to prove. A material allegation in a pleading is one essential to the claim or defense.*

ALTERNATIVE DISPUTE RESOLUTION
The term Alternate Dispute Resolution (ADR) refers to any method other than litigation for resolution of disputes.
Georgia Supreme Court Alternative Dispute Resolution Rules.

ANSWER
A pleading by which defendant endeavors to resist the plaintiff's demand by an allegation of facts, either denying allegations of plaintiff's complaint or confessing them and alleging new matter in avoidance, which defendant alleges should prevent recovery on facts alleged by plaintiff.*

APPEAL
Resort to a superior (i.e. appellate) court to review the decision of an inferior (i.e. trial) court or administrative agency.*

ARBITRATION
Arbitration differs from mediation in that an arbitrator or panel of arbitrators renders a decision after hearing an abbreviated version of the evidence. In non-binding arbitration, either party may demand a trial within a specified period. The essential difference between mediation and arbitration is that arbitration is a form of adjudication, whereas mediation is not.
Georgia Supreme Court Alternative Dispute Resolution Rules.

BEST INTEREST OF THE CHILD
The duty of the court shall be to exercise its discretion to look to and determine solely what is for the best interest of the child or children and what will best promote their welfare and happiness and to make its award accordingly.

O.C.G.A. Section 19-9-3(a)(2).

BURDEN OF PROOF
The necessity or duty of affirmatively proving a fact in dispute on an issue raised between the parties in a cause.*

CASE EVALUATION OR EARLY NEUTRAL EVALUATION
A process in which a lawyer with expertise in the subject matter of the litigation acts as a neutral evaluator of the case. Each side presents a summary of its legal theories and evidence. The evaluator assesses the strength of each side's case and assists the parties in narrowing the legal and factual issues in the case. This conference occurs early in the discovery process and is designed to streamline discovery and other pretrial aspects of the case. The early neutral evaluation of the case may also provide a basis for settlement discussions.

Georgia Supreme Court Alternative Dispute Resolution Rules.

CASE LAW
The aggregate of reported cases as forming a body of jurisprudence, or the law of a particular subject as evidenced or formed by the adjudged cases, in distinction to statutes and other sources of law.*

CHILD SUPPORT JURISDICTION
A court of this state may exercise continuing, exclusive jurisdiction for purposes of entering a child support order if the court has subject matter and personal jurisdiction to make such a child support order, and no previous support order has been entered by a court of competent jurisdiction with respect to the child or children named in the support order. A court of this state may exercise continuing, exclusive jurisdiction for purposes of entering a modification of a child support order issued by a court of this state if the child or children named in the child support order or any party to the action resides in this state.
O.C.G.A. Section 19-6-26 (b),(c).

CHILD SUPPORT OBLIGEE

An individual to whom the payment of a child support obligation is owed and includes a custodial parent or caretaker of a child to whom such support obligation is to be paid or a governmental agency entitled by law to enforce a child support obligation on behalf of such parent, caretaker, or child.

O.C.G.A. Section 19-6-35(a)(1).

A child support obligee shall be regarded as a creditor, and a child support obligor shall be regarded as a debtor for the purposes of attacking as fraudulent a judgment, conveyance, transaction, or other arrangement interfering with the creditor's rights, either at law or in equity.

O.C.G.A. Section 19-6-35(b).

CHILD SUPPORT OBLIGOR

An individual owing a duty of support to a child or children, whether or not such duty is evinced by a judgment, order, or decree.

O.C.G.A. Section 19-6-35(a)(2).

CHILD SUPPORT ORDER
A judgment, decree, or order of a court or authorized administrative agency requiring the payment of child support in periodic amounts or in a lump sum and includes (A) a permanent or temporary order and (B) an initial order or a modification of an order.
O.C.G.A. Section 19-6-26(a)(1).

CODE
A systematic collection, compendium or revision of laws, rules, or regulations. A private or official compilation of all permanent laws in force consolidated and classified according to subject matter. Many states have published official codes of all laws in force which have been compiled by code commissions and enacted by the legislatures.*

COMPLAINT
The original or initial pleading by which an action is commenced under codes or Rules of Civil Procedure. The pleading which sets forth a claim for relief.*

CONTEMPT POWER

The powers of the several courts to issue attachments and inflict summary punishment for contempt of court shall extend only to cases of disobedience or resistance of any party to any lawful order, rule, decree, or command of the courts.

O.C.G.A. Section 15-1-4(a)(3).

CONTEMPT PROCEEDING

The judicial hearing or trial conducted to determine whether one has been in contempt of court and to make an appropriate disposition.*

COUNTERCLAIM

A claim presented by a defendant in opposition to or deduction from the claim of the plaintiff.*

CUSTODY DECREE

A custody determination contained in a judicial decree or order made in a custody proceeding and includes, but is not limited to, an initial decree and a modification decree.

O.C.G.A. Section 19-9-42(4).

CUSTODY DETERMINATION

A court decision and court orders and instructions providing for the custody of a child, including, but not limited to, visitation rights.

The term 'custody determination' does not include a decision relating to child support or any other monetary obligation of any person.

O.C.G.A. Section 19-9-42(2).

CUSTODY OF CHILDREN

The care, control and maintenance of a child which may be awarded by a court to one of the parents as in a divorce or separation proceeding. A number of states have adopted the Uniform Child Custody Jurisdiction Act.*

'Custody' includes visitation rights.

O.C.G.A. Section 19-9-22(1).

CUSTODY PROCEEDING

Proceedings in which a custody determination is one of several issues, such as an action for divorce or separation and includes child neglect and dependency proceedings and adoption proceedings.

O.C.G.A. Section 19-9-42(3).

DEFENDANT
The person defending or denying; the party against whom relief or recovery is sought in an action or suit or the accused in a criminal case.*

DEPOSITION
The testimony of a witness taken upon interrogatories, not in open court, and reduced to writing and duly authenticated, and intended to be used upon the trial of a civil action. A discovery device by which one party asks oral questions of the other party or of a witness for the other party. The person who is deposed is called the deponent. The deposition is conducted under oath outside of the courtroom, usually in one of the lawyer's offices. A transcript-word for word account-is made of the deposition.*

DISCOVERY
The pre-trial devices that can be used by one party to obtain facts and information about the case from the other party in order to assist the party's preparation for trial. Tools of discovery include depositions upon oral and written questions, written interrogatories, production of documents or things, permission to enter upon land or other property, physical and mental examinations and requests for admission.*

DOMESTIC RELATIONS FINANCIAL AFFIDAVIT
Every action for temporary or permanent child support shall be accompanied by an affidavit specifying the party's financial circumstances. The opposing party shall make an affidavit regarding his or her financial circumstances.
Uniform Superior Court Rule 24.2.

DUE PROCESS OF LAW
An orderly proceeding wherein a person is served with notice, actual or constructive, and has an opportunity to be heard and to enforce and protect his rights before a court having power to hear and determine the case.*

EVIDENCE
Any species of proof, or probative matter, legally presented at the trial of an issue, by the act of the parties and through the medium of witnesses, records, documents, exhibits, concrete objects, etc., for the purpose of inducing belief in the minds of the court or jury as to their contention.*

FINAL JUDGMENT
One which finally disposes of rights of parties, either upon entire controversy or upon some definite and separate branch thereof. Judgment is considered "final" only if it determines the rights of

the parties and disposes of all of the issues involved so that no future action by the court will be necessary in order to settle and determine the entire controversy.*

FINAL ORDER
One which terminates the litigation between the parties and the merits of the case and leaves nothing to be done but to enforce by execution what has been determined.*

GUARDIAN AD LITEM
When a minor is interested in any litigation pending in any court in this state and he has no guardian or his interest is adverse to that of his guardian, such court may appoint a guardian ad litem for the minor. The guardian ad litem shall be responsible to the minor for his conduct in connection with the litigation in the same manner as if he were a regularly qualified guardian. O.C.G.A. Section 29-4-7.

HEARING
Proceeding of relative formality, (though generally less formal than a trial), generally public, with definite issues of fact or of law to be tried, in which witnesses are heard and parties proceeded against have right to be heard, and is much the same as a trial and may terminate in final order.*

HOME STATE
The state in which the child, immediately preceding the time involved, lived with his parents, a parent, or a person acting as a parent for at least six consecutive months and, in the case of a child less than six months old, the state in which the child lived from birth with any of the persons mentioned.
O.C.G.A. Section 19-9-42(5).

INITIAL DECREE
The first custody decree concerning a particular child.
O.C.G.A. Section 19-9-42(6).

INJUNCTION
A prohibitive, equitable remedy issued or granted by a court at the suit of a party complainant, directed to a party defendant in the action, or to a party made a defendant for that purpose, forbidding the latter to do some act.*

INTERFERENCE WITH CUSTODY
A person commits the offense of interference with custody when without lawful authority to do so the person (A) Knowingly or recklessly takes or entices any child away from the individual who has lawful custody of such child, (B) Knowingly harbors any child who has absconded, or (C) Intentionally and willfully

retains possession within this state of the child upon the expiration of a lawful period of visitation with the child.
O.C.G.A. Section 16-5-45(b)(1).

INTERROGATORIES
A set or series of written questions drawn up for the purpose of being propounded to a party, witness, or other person having information of interest in the case. The answers to the interrogatories are usually given under oath, i.e., the person answering the questions signs a sworn statement that the answers are true.*

JOINT CUSTODY
Joint custody means joint legal custody, joint physical custody, or both joint legal custody and joint physical custody. In making an order for joint custody, the court may order joint legal custody without ordering joint physical custody.
O.C.G.A. Section 19-9-6(1).

JOINT LEGAL CUSTODY
Joint legal custody means both parents have equal rights and responsibilities for major decisions concerning the child, including the child's education, health care, and religious training; provided, however, that the court may designate one

parent to have sole power to make certain decisions while both parents retain equal rights and responsibilities for other decisions. O.C.G.A. Section 19-9-6(2).

JOINT PHYSICAL CUSTODY
Joint physical custody means that physical custody is shared by the parents in such a way as to assure the child of substantially equal time and contact with both parents.
O.C.G.A. Section 19-9-6(3).

JURISDICTION
It is the authority by which courts and judicial officers take cognizance of and decide cases. The legal right by which judges exercise their authority. The right and power of a court to adjudicate concerning the subject matter in a given case.*

JUVENILE COURTS
A court having special jurisdiction, of a paternal nature, over delinquent, dependent, and neglected children.*

LAWFUL CUSTODY
That custody inherent in the natural parents, that custody awarded by proper authority as provided in Code Section 15-11-17, or that custody awarded to a parent, guardian, or other person by a court

of competent jurisdiction.

O.C.G.A. Section 16-5-45.

LEGAL CUSTODIAN

Legal custodian means a person, including, but not limited to, a parent, who has been awarded permanent custody of a child by a court order. A person who has not been awarded custody of a child by court order shall not be considered as the legal custodian while exercising visitation rights. Where custody of a child is shared by two or more persons or where the time of visitation exceeds the time of custody, that person who has the majority of time of custody or visitation shall be the legal custodian.

O.C.G.A. Section 19-9-22(2).

MEDIATION

Mediation is a process in which a neutral facilitates settlement discussions between parties. The neutral has no authority to make a decision or impose a settlement upon the parties. The neutral attempts to focus the attention of the parties upon their needs and interests rather than upon rights and positions. Although in court-annexed or court-referred mediation programs the parties may be ordered to attend a mediation session, any settlement is entirely voluntary. In the absence of settlement the parties lose

none of their rights to a jury trial.
Georgia Supreme Court Alternative Dispute Resolution Rules.

NEUTRAL
An impartial person who facilitates discussions and dispute resolution between disputants in mediation, case evaluation or early neutral evaluations, and arbitration, or who presides over a summary jury trial or mini trial. Thus mediators, case evaluators, and arbitrators are all classified as 'neutrals'.
Georgia Supreme Court Alternative Dispute Resolution Rules.

O.C.G.A.
Official Code of Georgia Annotated.

PARTIES
The persons who take part in the performance of any act, or who are directly interested in any affair, contract, or conveyance, or who are actively concerned in the prosecution and defense of any legal proceeding.*

PETITION
A formal, written application to a court requesting judicial action on a certain matter.*

PHYSICAL CUSTODIAN

Physical custodian means a person, including, but not limited to, a parent, who is not the 'legal custodian' of a child but who has physical custody of the child.

O.C.G.A. Section 19-9-22(3).

PHYSICAL CUSTODY

Physical custody means actual possession and control of a child.

O.C.G.A. Section 19-9-42(9).

PLAINTIFF

A person who brings an action; the party who complains or sues in a civil action, and is so named on the record. A person who seeks remedial relief for an injury to rights.*

PREPONDERANCE OF EVIDENCE

Evidence which is of greater weight or more convincing than the evidence which is offered in opposition to it; that is, evidence which as a whole shows that the fact sought to be proved is more probable than not.*

PRIMA FACIE

A fact presumed to be true unless disproved by some evidence to the contrary.*

In all cases in which custody of any minor child or children is at issue between the parents, there shall be no prima-facie right to the custody of the child or children in the father or mother. O.C.G.A. Section 19-9-3(a).

REBUTTABLE PRESUMPTION
In the law of evidence, a presumption which may be rebutted by evidence. A species of legal presumption which holds good until evidence contrary to it is introduced.*

RES JUDICATA
A matter adjudged; a thing judicially acted upon or decided; a thing or matter settled by judgment. Rule that a final judgment rendered by a court of competent jurisdiction on the merits is conclusive as to the rights of the parties and their privies, and, as to them, constitutes an absolute bar to a subsequent action involving the same claim, demand or cause of action.*

RESTRAINING ORDER
An order in the nature of an injunction. An order which may issue upon filing of an application for an injunction forbidding the defendant to do the threatened act until a hearing on the application can be had, and it is distinguishable from an injunction, in that the former is intended only as a restraint until

the propriety of granting an injunction can be determined and it does no more than restrain the proceeding until such determination.*

RULE NISI
A rule which will become imperative and final unless cause be shown against it. This rule commands the party to show cause why he should not be compelled to do the act required, or why the object of the rule should not be enforced.*

SERVICE OF PROCESS
The service of writs, summonses, etc., signifies the delivering to or leaving them with the party to whom or with whom they ought to be delivered or left; and, when they are so delivered, they are then said to have been served. Usually a copy only is served and the original is shown. The service must furnish reasonable notice to defendant of proceedings to afford him opportunity to appear and be heard.*

SOLE CUSTODY
Sole custody means a person, including, but not limited to, a parent, has been awarded permanent custody of a child by a court order. Unless otherwise provided by court order, the person awarded sole custody of a child shall have the rights and

responsibilities for major decisions concerning the child, including the child's education, health care, and religious training, and the noncustodial parent shall have the right to visitation. A person who has not been awarded custody of a child by court order shall not be considered as the sole legal custodian while exercising visitation rights.
O.C.G.A. Section 19-9-6(4).

STANDING ORDERS
Rules adopted by particular courts for governing practice before them. They may include rules as to the time at which court commences each day, a procedure for requesting continuances of cases and a method by which cases are placed on the trial list of that particular court.*

STATUTE
An act of the legislature declaring, commanding, or prohibiting something; a particular law enacted and established by the will of the legislative department of government.*

SUBPOENA
A subpoena is a command to appear at a certain time and place to give testimony upon a certain matter.*

SUMMONS

Instrument used to commence a civil action or special proceeding and is a means of acquiring jurisdiction over a party. The summons shall be signed by the clerk, be under the seal of the court and contain the name of the court and the names of the parties, be directed to the defendant, state the name and address of the plaintiff's attorney, if any, otherwise the plaintiff's address, and the time within which these rules require the defendant to appear and defend, and shall notify him that in case of his failure to do so judgment by default will be rendered against him for the relief demanded in the complaint.*

SUPERIOR COURT

Courts of general or extensive jurisdiction, as distinguished from the inferior courts. As the official style of a tribunal, the term "superior court" bears a different meaning in different states. In some it is a court of intermediate jurisdiction between the trial courts and the chief appellate court; elsewhere it is the designation of the trial courts.*

TRIAL COURT

The court of original jurisdiction; the first court to consider litigation.*

TRIER OF FACT

Term includes (a) the jury and (b) the court when the court is trying an issue of fact other than one relating to the admissibility of evidence.*

* Black's Law Dictionary, Fifth Edition
   The definitions are quoted verbatim from the source.

INDEX

Affidavit, 445
Age of majority, 261, 445
Agreement, 445
Allegation, 445
Alternative Dispute Resolution (ADR), 331, 335, 445
Answer, 445
Appeal, 446
Arbitration, 336, 341, 446
Attorney, choosing, 379

Best Interest Of The Child, 446
Best Interest Of The Stepparent, 1
Bill Of Rights For Stepparents, 441
Burden of proof, 446

Case Evaluation/Early Neutral Evaluation, 336, 345, 446
Case law, 447
Child custody issues, 141
    After the trial issues, 193
    Attorney's fees, 192
    Before the trial issues, 147
    Child age 11, 154
    Child age 14, 152
    Custody decree, 449
    Custody determination, 449
    Custody of children, 450
    Custody proceeding, 450
    Custody to a third party, 176
    During the trial issues, 159
    Enforcing the order, 194
    Evaluation, 160
    Factors to consider, 164
    Georgia cases/statues, 141
    Grandparents' rights, 196
    Judge's decision, 159
    Modification, 177, 178
        Changed condition, 180
        Examples, insufficient, 181
        Examples, sufficient,183
    Self-executing clause, 192
    State's policy, 147
    Temporary custody, 168
    Types of custody, 171
Child Support Guidelines, 269
Child support issues, 255
    After the trial issues, 311
    Before the trial issues, 261
    Child support obligee, 261, 447
    Child support obligor, 261, 448
    Child support order, 261, 448
    Definition, terms, 261
    Duration, 292
    During the trial issues, 269

Emancipation, 262
Enforcing the order, 311
Georgia cases/statutes, 255
Guidelines statute, 269
Modification, 262, 296
    Attorney's fees, 307
    Definition of change, 297
    Parents' obligations, 262
    State's policy, 262
Code, 448
Complaint, 448
Confidentiality, 337
Contempt power, 449
Counterclaim, 449
Courtroom proceedings, 425, 429

Deposition, 450
Discovery process, 413, 451
Domestic Mediation Guidelines, 355, 356
Domestic Relations Financial Affidavit, 361, 367, 451
Due process of law, 451

Election of child age 14, 152
Evidence, 451
Examining your motives, 51
Experts' opinions, 14

Final judgment, 451
Final order, 452
Final trial, 429

Glossary, 445
Golden Rules, 444
Grandparents' custody, 196
Guardian ad litem, 162, 424, 452

Hearing, 452
Home state, 452

Immunity, 340
Initial decree, 453
Injunction, 453
Interference with custody, 453
Interrogatories, 453

Joint custody, 170, 171, 454
Joint legal, 171, 175, 176, 454
Joint physical, 171, 454
Jurisdiction, 454
Juvenile courts, 454

Kerman Stepparent Questionnaire, 79, 82

Lawful custody, 455
Legal custodian, 172, 455
Litigation, 377
    Choosing attorney, 379
    Courtroom tips, 433
    Legal issues, 391
    Proceedings in court, 425
Living with final decision, 437

Mediation, 150, 335, 349, 455
    Domestic Guidelines, 355
Mini trial, 337
Modification of child support, 296
Modification of custody, 177
Modification of visitation, 239
Motivation, definition, 52
Motives, 51
    Why some people do not want to be stepparents, 61
    Why some people want to be stepparents, 54

Neutral, 335, 456

O.C.G.A., 456

Physical custodian, 456
Physical custody, 456
Psychological evaluation, 160, 416

Restraining order, 458
Rule Nisi, 458

Sole custody, 172, 458
Stepparent Data Record, 107, 121
Stepparent, definition, 4
Subpoena, 459
Summary jury trial, 337

Temporary custody, 168
Temporary hearing, 427

Visitation issues, 221
    After the trial issues, 243
        Attorney's fees, 246
        Contempt of order, 245
        Enforcing the order, 243
    Basic principles, 225
    Before the trial issues, 225
    Bond, 235
    Child age 14, 240
    During the trial issues, 227
    Georgia cases/statutes, 221
    Judge's decision, 227
    Modification, 239
    Right to visitation, 230
    Standard provisions, 227
    State's policy, 226

Witnesses, 420

QUESTIONS YOU WANT TO REMEMBER TO ASK

CHAPTER ONE

CHAPTER TWO

CHAPTER THREE

CHAPTER FOUR

CHAPTER FIVE

CHAPTER SIX

CHAPTER SEVEN

CHAPTER EIGHT

CHAPTER NINE

CHAPTER TEN

CHAPTER ELEVEN